WHEREWARLIVES

WHERE WAR LIVES

A JOURNEY INTO THE HEART OF WAR

PAUL WATSON

RODALE

Rodale books may be purchased for business or promotional use or for special sales.
For information, please write to:
Special Sales Department, Rodale Inc,
733 Third Avenue, New York, NY 10017

Printed in the United States of America

Rodale Inc. makes every effort to use acid-free ∞, recycled paper ♻

Photo on pages ii–iii © Andrew Stawicki: Paul Watson preparing to take a photo.
Photo on page vi © Paul Watson: His Pulitzer Prize-winning photo of a Somali mob
dragging Staff Sergeant David Cleveland through the streets of Mogadishu.

A previous edition of *Where War Lives* was published by McClelland & Stewart (Canada),
2007, hardcover, ISBN 978–0–7710–8822–3

Library of Congress Cataloging-in-Publication Data

CIP data is on file with the publisher

ISBN 13 978–1–59486–957–0   hardcover

ISBN 10 1–59486–957–X   hardcover

Distributed to the trade by Macmillan

2   4   6   8   10   9   7   5   3   1   hardcover

We inspire and enable people to improve their lives and the world around them
For more of our products visit **rodalestore.com** or call 800-848-4735

For the silenced,
and the suffering

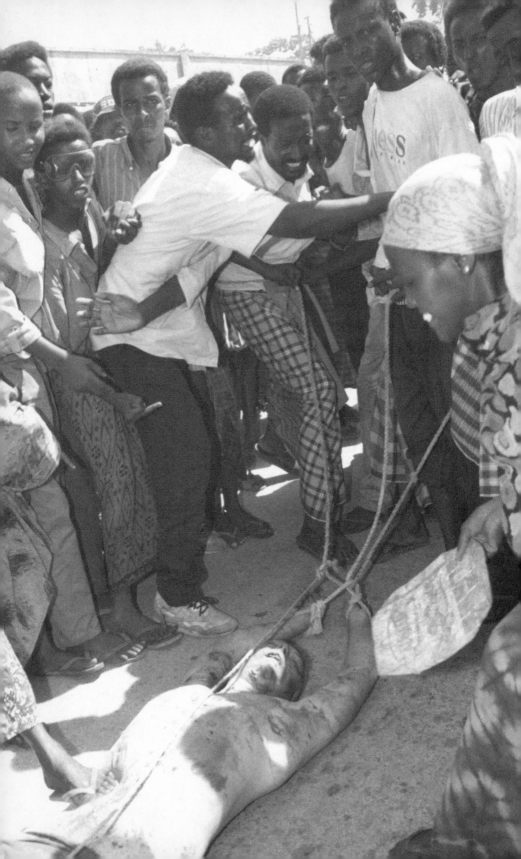

CONTENTS

PROLOGUE

*The dissenter is every human being at those moments of his life
when he resigns momentarily from the herd and thinks for himself.*
ARCHIBALD MACLEISH

I was born a rebel with one hand. I grew up thinking it took two to fire an assault rifle, or play jazz piano, so I became a journalist instead. I was aching to go to war. It's shameful to admit now, but at first I got off on the killing. Surviving when so many others died was a rush like what a chronic gambler feels when a slot machine pays off big and a room full of losers stare daggers. If someone had to die to satisfy my hunger to feel big, so be it—I wasn't pulling the trigger. After covering more than a dozen conflicts on several continents over the past two decades, the thrill of adventure is long gone. I am left looking into the lifeless eyes of bodies that have piled up in my mind, ruefully wondering why I'm still alive.

Years ago, during one of many moves, I gathered the scraps of memories from my desk drawer, crammed them into a small, pink plastic bag, and placed the lot into a cardboard box. The marriage commissioner's certificate is near the top of the pile, issued on the first day of October 1997 in the city of Vancouver. It is tucked into a cream-colored envelope with a receipt for seventy-five dollars, plus tax, along with a greeting card from friends who witnessed the civil ceremony in the commissioner's living room. I can feel the wet wind again, and hear green chestnuts falling like little bombs on the roofs of parked cars lining the street.

Next, there are two letters from readers who wanted to help a penniless Afghan zookeeper feed a one-eyed lion languishing in Kabul's zoo that I wrote about soon after the Taliban seized power in the fall of 1996. Marjarlion had made the mistake of killing a Panjshiri soldier who climbed into his pen on a bet and tried to pet him. The soldier's brother tried to settle the blood score by tossing in a hand grenade, which blew up in the lion's face as he tried to eat it. One Samaritan reader sent money, which was passed on to the zookeeper, who was murdered soon thereafter.

A large invitation card, embossed with the golden crest of a dying empire, requests the pleasure of my company at a farewell reception for the Governor of Hong Kong and Mrs. Patten, on June 16, 1997—two weeks before British rule ended. Dress: Lounge Suit.

There are receipts and warranties for things I don't even own any more. An Angolan press card from 1992, and a journalist's pass to Mother Teresa's state funeral five years later, are thrown in with an old passport filled with stamps from Afghanistan, China, India, Nepal, Pakistan, Vietnam. My handwritten confession to the Indonesian police, who arrested me in 1998 for photographing rioters looting a Chinese shop in Sumatra while undercover cops supervised, is stapled to their deportation order. There is the business card of an old girlfriend, and a pleading letter from a psychotic woman who almost killed me because her threats to kill herself didn't get sufficient sympathy from me; a doctor's assessment of the endless ringing in my ears; and a psychiatrist's diagnosis of a much different malady: chronic post-traumatic stress disorder and depression. It is dated November 25, 1994, the year I witnessed the Rwandan genocide. It is addressed: To Whom It May Concern.

Over recent months, the world has tried to process images of soldiers on several continents, urged by politicians, clerics, and zealous murderers to fight the good fight, only to lose their grip on humanity. In England, at an army training base where four privates committed suicide, local police accuse non-commissioned army officers of raping female recruits, urinating on them, and forcing them to swim in cesspools. Insurgents in the northern Iraqi city of Mosul go on a killing spree, shooting more than fifty members of the security forces and civilians in the head, chopping up some of their bodies, and dumping the pieces at the roadside. Israeli newspapers publish pictures of ultra-orthodox soldiers sticking a dead Palestinian's head on a pole and putting a cigarette in its mouth. Nightmares of the Holocaust are revived when Israeli soldiers at a checkpoint are videotaped forcing an Arab music student to play his violin in the lineup of people waiting for permission to cross. "Play something sad," an officer orders, and the soldiers laugh at the humiliation. In Fallujah, a U.S. Marine executes a wounded prisoner in a mosque, eight months after Fallujans burned and dismembered four Americans, and hung two of the corpses from a bridge. And Navy documents show that eleven Marines were punished for abusing detainees by, among other things, torturing them with electric shocks or putting an unloaded pistol to the heads of four Iraqi juvenile looters and pulling the trigger in mock executions.

Three-star Marine Corps Lieutenant General James Mattis happily tells an audience that war is "a hell of a hoot. It's fun to shoot some people . . . You go into Afghanistan, you got guys who slapped women around for five years because they didn't wear a veil. You know, guys like that ain't got no manhood left anyway. So it's a hell of a lot of fun to shoot them." Nine months later, after a roadside bomb kills one of their own, Marines in the Iraqi city of Haditha are accused of shooting twenty-four civilians, several of them women and children, at close range in their homes. Only after the massacre is reported in a U.S. newsmagazine are the alleged murders investigated. In another crime, five American soldiers plotted the gang rape of a fourteen-year-old Iraqi. They got drunk, hit some golf balls, and raped the girl. They murdered the victim, her six-year-old sister, and their parents, and then grilled some chicken wings.

Far from the front lines, anguished people ask: Why? When the question comes my way, I think of the fear that haunts me every day: there is a murderer hiding within each of us. Pushed far enough, or given the right training, even the best of us are capable of taking human life, and justifying the wrong any way we must.

For as long as humans have honored organized killing with the name war, storytellers and writers have tried to give it meaning. On September 7, 1939, five days after my father left a small, centuries-old coal mining village in the Canadian Maritimes to join the war in Europe, Albert Camus was in Algeria, ready to fight on a different front in the French Resistance. He wrote in his notebook that he had solved the mystery of where war lives. It lives in all of us. He described the internal conflict that consumes us, whether it's in the hearts of soldiers on the battlefield, or those of folks safe back home, wondering, and regretting "that they can't share the way the others are going to die."

Camus continued: "It's there, that's where it really is, and we were looking for it in the blue sky and the world's indifference. It is in this terrible loneliness both of the combatants and of the noncombatants, in this humiliated despair that we all feel, in the baseness that we feel growing in our faces as the days go by. The reign of the beasts has begun."

Loneliness and humiliation: I think they explain a lot about war and terrorism. When the questions echoing in my mind speak with a voice other than my own, it is usually that of a ghost I fear, a man with whom I desperately want to make peace. For too long, I have known him only the way a camera lens, and my anger and guilt, allowed me to see him: the battered corpse of an American soldier, bound by thick ropes, lying at the feet of Somalis celebrating their victory over the world's most powerful military. Now I long to restore some of the honor that I stole in that second when I pressed a button, and a thin metal shutter opened and closed in a blink of history's eye.

Paul Watson

Kabul

December 2006

1

THE BEGINNING OF THE END

War would end if the dead could return.
STANLEY BALDWIN

L ittle Birds and Black Hawks crisscrossed the sky like dragonflies
darting over a pond at dusk. The helicopters were a few miles
away, far enough to be a faint hum against a warm, salty breeze blowing in from the Indian Ocean. The sky was slowly shifting from
indigo to gold as the sun set. I was on the roof of Mogadishu's low-rise
Sahafi Hotel. Arabic for journalist, the Sahafi was the retreat where I
went each evening to get above it all, to hear the wind and to toast
another day of surviving Somalia's anarchy. With each tilt of my beer
can, I tried to flush my mind, but the alcohol only shifted the fear a
little, sending it slithering down to the void where it coiled up like a
snake, tensed to strike.

It was a Sunday evening: October 3, 1993, and I was on assignment in Somalia for the *Toronto Star*. The day's news seemed far away:
in Moscow, Boris Yeltsin was amassing tanks to capture Parliament.
Next to the drama of war on the streets of a nuclear-armed former
superpower, yet another skirmish in the swirling grit of Mogadishu
was easily missed by the world. Murders and kidnapping threats had

cleared the city of all but a few reporters, and the main wire service offices had been evacuated. I didn't have my own satellite phone, so there was no worry about being on the foreign editor's speed-dial. I could file when I felt like it. And on this beautiful evening in Mogadishu, after weeks of chasing a story that had dropped off the map, I felt like getting drunk.

The charcoal black U.S. Army helicopters flying low over the city, banking hard this way or that, were a pleasant diversion, like a country-fair air show for the tailgaters far below in the parking lot. The soldiers sitting on the Black Hawks' door sills, their legs dangling in mid-air, had tried and failed so many times to arrest fugitive Somali warlord Mohammed Farah Aideed that a sky buzzing with combat helicopters wasn't much to get excited over any longer.

I'd never heard of Operation Gothic Serpent. I had no idea that the code-named raid for this October day, one that would weaken the U.S. for years to come, was unraveling before my eyes. And I never would have guessed that more than a decade later I'd still be struggling to escape its vortex.

The afternoon had been as ordinary as one could be in the anarchy of Mogadishu, capital of a looted country where warring clans ruled the land and blood in the water lured shivers of man-eating sharks to blinding white beaches. My driver and gunman got me safely through the ten-minute hurtle from the Sahafi to the Pakistani army checkpoint, and then on to the heavily fortified U.S. embassy compound for the afternoon briefing. I pushed past the begging kids, who pawed at me with grimy fingers, calling me by my street name, Gamay, or "The Man with One Hand," in Somali. "Give me money! Gamay, give me money!" they shrieked.

After shaking them off, I entered through the sandbagged gate and into the safe cocoon of the JIB, or Joint Information Bureau, where military flacks dispensed each day's ration of spin, half-truths, and outright lies. They often passed around a plate of candies or cookies, as if we were hyperactive kids easily soothed with a sugary snack and a good nap. When that game was over, and I had little more in my notebook than the day's troop number update and numerous assertions that the world was unfolding as it should, I walked to the Israeli PX, military shorthand for Post Exchange, a makeshift duty-free shop in a circle of rusty shipping containers on the embassy grounds. True to habit, I bought a twelve-pack of Amstel and drinking snacks. After almost two years covering Somalia, I needed the better part of a case of beer just to get through each day, order the disorder into some kind of story, and put myself to sleep. Around the same time that the Israeli duty-free man was ringing up my purchases, a U.S. Army Special Forces crew was approaching its target area in a Black Hawk code-named Super Six-Four.

Not long after 4:30, when my gunman, Mohomud Hersi Ali, had loaded the beer and groceries into the trunk, my driver wheeled the car around for the race back to the relative safety of the Sahafi. Less than three miles away, Staff Sergeant William David Cleveland had his finger on the trigger of a machine gun pointing out the chopper's side door, near the Olympic Hotel in Aideed's Bakara Market stronghold. He was trying to cover the crew of another Black Hawk brought down by a rocket-propelled grenade (RPG). Below, he could see swarms of Somali fighters running along a warren of streets and back alleys, sprinting from behind one tin shack only to disappear behind another. Gray smoke trails snaked up into the sky around him as the guerrillas tried for another aerial takedown. Attackers fired a barrage of more than one hundred airburst RPG rounds at the choppers.

Cleveland was a fifteen-year military veteran, the son of a Navy chief petty officer, and the latest to serve in a family that has had a soldier in every generation since the Civil War. Now Cleveland was a Night Stalker, a member of the U.S. Army's 160th Special Operations Aviation Regiment. They are an elite corps of warriors who live and die by the creed that theirs "is a calling only a few will answer, for the mission is constantly demanding and hard. And when the impossible has been accomplished the only reward is another mission that no one else will try." Cleveland and the rest of the five-man crew on Super Six-Four had each sworn a solemn pledge to "guard my unit's mission with secrecy, for my only true ally is the night and the elements of surprise."

And here they were, hovering in the harsh afternoon light, a chopper full of soldiers sent in to arrest some of Aideed's top lieutenants. The operation was in the middle of the warlord's turf, and hundreds of guerrillas in his Somali National Army faction were fighting back hard. They'd shot down one Black Hawk, and were taking aim at Super Six-Four as it flew some seventy-five feet above the street, in a blitz of bullets and rocket-propelled grenades, trying to save fallen comrades. Cleveland, one of two crew chiefs on board, was manning an M134, a six-barrel, air-cooled Gatling gun that could spew four thousand bullets per minute. The chopper's pilot, Chief Warrant Officer Michael Durant, wouldn't throw the cockpit switch to arm Cleveland's electric weapon until the last minute. He didn't want any friendly fire coming from his bird. The troops would fast-rope down to the target, the chopper would pull out, and Cleveland would be back to base with the rest of Super Six-Four's crew in a matter of minutes. He was just weeks away from going on leave to his hometown, Peoria, Arizona, with a plan he had rehearsed over and over in his

4

mind. He would walk up to the door of his mom's trailer home and surprise her for Christmas—and then . . .

BANG

An RPG exploded near Super Six-Four's tail rotor, blasting the blades and gearbox, and sending the Black Hawk into a fatal spin as the pilots fought to keep control.

"We're going in hard," Durant radioed.

Just over a mile from the crash site, I was still alone in my rooftop world, oblivious to the quickening battle, which would inflict the worst combat losses on U.S. troops since Vietnam. The day's tension was starting to melt from my shoulders. I felt a warm touch of nostalgia for the person I was before I came to this place. I remembered how much I used to love helicopters. When I was a child, watching Hueys sweeping over the jungles of Southeast Asia on the news, I thought for the first time: *War is cool.*

To a suburban kid like me, a sponge for sterilized media images flickering across the TV screen, a Huey was just another 1960s mod icon, like Twiggy or the peace sign. Hueys shared their rounded lines. Front on, their noses were blunt, not hard-edged and sinister-looking like the generations of attack helicopters that followed. I was thrilled by the thump of rotors and the sheer magic of their hover, as brave men with a rifle in one hand and the other holding down a helmet jumped into rice paddies swirling in the downdraft. Hueys often flew low and slow into combat drop zones, daring the enemy to take his best shot. They came to save lives as much as take them. Huey medevac crews who did the ambulance runs were airborne white knights.

Somalia made me hate helicopters and the men who looked down from them. I vividly remember the first time that I saw helicopters as most Somalis did, with a mixture of awe at the choppers' power and anger at the military arrogance they came to symbolize. I was in a weapons collection point where militias stored their aging artillery guns and tanks to meet the U.N.'s demand for disarmament. To make sure militia fighters didn't suddenly reclaim the weapons, the U.S. military decided to put them permanently out of commission with hovering Cobra attack helicopters. The three-barrel 20-mm cannon mounted under a Cobra's nose is wired to nimbly swivel wherever the pilot looks. One of the two-man crew wouldn't take his eyes off me. He hovered overhead, just to one side, and as I held my arms and notebook above my head in mock surrender, the Cobra's nose cannon scanned me up and down, focusing in on my head, doing a tight circle as it traced the perimeter of my face, like some nightmare of a giant mosquito sniffing around for the softest spot to stab its proboscis. Every day after that, I wondered while driving through Mogadishu whether someone was staring from above through a gun sight trained on my rented white Toyota Cressida.

The mission to save Somalia from itself was a tragicomedy from the moment, ten months earlier, when the white TV lights fired up just after midnight on December 9, 1992, at the start of Operation Restore Hope, the U.S.-led invasion to help feed starving Somalis. There was a party atmosphere on the beach as a few dozen journalists awaited the nighttime landing of U.S. troops dispatched to stop marauding militias from stealing relief food. In the town of Baidoa, the famine's epicenter, gunmen went on a final spree of looting and killing and, like cockroaches skittering from the light, fled into the desert as foreign troops approached.

Many Somalis welcomed the U.S.-led invasion as their salvation. The warlords all promised their men would not fire on foreign troops. They even vowed finally to make peace with each other. In the time since the Cold War had ended, and U.S.-backed dictator Mohammed Siad Barre's regime collapsed in anarchy in 1991, this cursed country on the Horn of Africa had never seemed so connected to the rest of humanity. Suddenly Somalia mattered. If it was only to be a backdrop in a morality play to showcase the military's new humanitarian face, well, that was better than shouting to the wilderness about war and famine, as I'd been doing with other journalists for almost two years.

The big three U.S. network anchors were all in place, seated in front of banks of studio lights, powered by rumbling generators deployed outside the derelict airport terminal. We were clowns in a media circus, ridiculous pawns of a Pentagon information strategy that was supposed to bring the military fully out from under the shadow of Vietnam. The politicians wanted heroic pictures of U.S. soldiers coming to the rescue to replace the embarrassing horrors of defenseless, starving children, so U.S. military officials gave advance details of the landing place and time to make sure the networks were ready for live coverage. They ended up making brave soldiers trained to fight and kill look like bit players in a comical propaganda newsreel.

There were so many reporters and cameras waiting in Mogadishu to watch the Americans invade Somalia that back in Washington, Pentagon spokesman Pete Williams had to make a bizarre appeal for the media to stay off the beach so they didn't get in the way of the Marine assault. He even offered to meet with the networks to suggest the safest camera positions. This was a made-for-TV drama.

I found a quiet spot on the beach and fell asleep, only to be rudely awakened by the ruckus of journalists stumbling over cables and each other in the dark as they chased the first Navy SEAL frogmen who waded ashore a little after 12:30 a.m. The commandos squinted in the glare of the TV lights, like some rare aquatic species just dredged from the bottom of the sea. These were among the best-trained stealth warriors and all they could do was shout at us to go away. The photographers' strobes kept flashing into the SEALs' grease-painted faces. Less than an hour later, the assault's second wave hit Mogadishu beach: three Marines seized a rocky dune near the airport's main runway, only to be surrounded by a phalanx of journalists and TV crews. "Can you smile for the cameras, please," one French reporter asked, pushing her microphone closer as the soldiers stared stone-faced into the white light.

During a lull around 2 a.m., Lieutenant Kirk Coker of the 15th Marine Expeditionary Unit walked alone out of the darkness, and like a field producer, asked the twenty-five journalists lounging in the sand if they'd mind making way for amphibious landing vehicles heading toward shore. "You guys here really spoiled our nice little raid that we came in with," Coker said, and disappeared back into the night.

The famine that the troops had come to end was already long past its peak. In early 1992, when aid agencies were warning that drought and civil war threatened to set off mass starvation in Somalia, hunger was killing thirty people a day in Bur-Acaba, a bush town in what would become the heart of the famine hot zone, about one hundred miles northwest of Mogadishu. By September, the death toll climbed to 350 a day in nearby Baidoa, where relief workers were feeding some twenty thousand people a day, and then in the next month, it began a steady decline. Famine deaths had fallen sharply to around fifty a day by the time U.S. troops landed in December 1992. The declining death toll had more to do with the stamina of aid workers, and the cold laws of Malthusian mathematics, than the belated military intervention. Starvation killed the young and sick first, and then it slowed, like a brush fire running out of fuel.

President George H.W. Bush knew there was no reason to stay long in Somalia. Things went so well in the early days of the famine relief mission that Bush said U.S. troops could start withdrawing within weeks, by the time Bill Clinton was sworn in as his successor in January. Aideed, whose militia was the biggest potential threat to U.S. forces, was still cooperating. His own son, Hussein, had briefly served with the U.S. Marines in Somalia before returning home to Los Angeles. By the spring of 1993, the U.S. military's withdrawal was well underway. But as the humanitarian emergency eased, and a new administration took over, the American force soon fell victim to mission creep, the very Vietnam syndrome that the Pentagon was trying to cure. An operation that Bush had strictly limited to protecting food relief was transformed under Clinton to include an effort to disarm Somalia's myriad militias and rebuild the state that had collapsed with Siad Barre's fall.

By June 1993, the U.S. force had dropped to around four thousand soldiers, among some eighteen thousand foreign troops, who were part of an ill-conceived U.N. attempt at peacemaking. Aideed saw his moment to strike. The United Nations didn't like what it heard from Aideed's radio station, which was accused of broadcasting anti-U.N. propaganda. When the United Nations sent in some Pakistani peacekeepers to inspect arms dumps in the area, Aideed's guerrillas took it as a long-anticipated assault to seize the station and attacked. They killed twenty-five Pakistani soldiers, some of whom were tortured to death.

Right and wrong always seemed to be in the eye of the beholder in Somalia. The United Nations' military police unit said it received at least one allegation a day that warranted investigation from Somalis reporting rape, theft, or murder by U.N. troops. In the final weeks of the street war, the Canadian air force major in charge of the U.N. peacekeepers' MPs told me that he still didn't have any trained investigators on his staff. He also complained that various commanders blocked efforts to probe the charges that were piling up. I've kept my own evidence for a long time on a microcassette tape, stored in the plastic bag that retains many of my most important memories. It would never prove anything to the outside world. But it's enough to remind me of how my own innocence died.

The tape is preserved in the case that I bought it in. Through the clear plastic, I can see my handwriting, which summarizes in smudged black ink one of the most terrifying minutes of my life: Somalia massacre '93. I punched out the cassette's top corner tabs soon after the shooting stopped, to make sure I would never record over those sounds. This was a memory that had to last forever: my awakening, the day I learned how easily the military lies after it kills, and that in war, all crimes are relative. It was June 13, 1993, eight days after the twenty-five Pakistani soldiers were massacred. Foreign forces still held the moral high ground. But Aideed's strategists kept turning the screws, especially on the Pakistani forces, which Al Qaeda loyalists in Pakistan saw as a weak link in the U.N. military operation. Aideed's militia fighters offered up women and children for sacrifice to win a propaganda victory for their cause. I'd been there long enough to take that for granted. I just didn't expect U.N. troops to bite so greedily at the bait.

American soldiers called the city they couldn't conquer The Mog. It was a hostile urban jungle into which U.N. and U.S. troops sometimes ventured on patrol, but had largely abandoned to the Somali militia fighters. Some parts of the city were completely off limits to any foreign ground troops. The Pakistani troops' bunker at the K-4 traffic circle was a strategic outpost, surrounded by the enemy. The Pakistanis were the last line of defense on the main road to Mogadishu's airport, the busy hub for U.S. and U.N. military and civilian air operations. Pakistani soldiers were holed up behind low walls of sandbags stacked where the windows used to be in a four-story building that was badly damaged and looted in the civil war. The soldiers peered down nervously from their machine-gun nests at the bustling circle of hawkers, donkey carts, and pedestrians below, trying to spot the next threat. Across the street was our hotel. Together, we marked the gateway to the airport, and attackers could come from any direction. Five two-lane roads converged on the K-4 traffic circle, like the spokes of a huge wheel.

A large, empty pedestal stood in the middle of the traffic circle. It used to hold up a statue of Imam Ahmad ibn Ibrahim, but looters carted him off for export, along with most of the capital's telephone cables, power wires, pipes, fixtures—even the bathroom tiles and toilet bowls—in the anarchy that followed the overthrow of Siad Barre's regime. The sixteenth-century imam was a national hero who led a Muslim conquest of the Somalis' Christian neighbors in Abyssinia, now called Ethiopia. With Portuguese help, the Abyssinians killed Ahmad, but he left a lasting legacy in his homeland by bringing Somalia's fractious clans together in the first semblance of a Somali nation. When twentieth-century looters knocked him off his pedestal, Somalia was sliding back into the centuries-old inter-clan warfare that Ibrahim had stopped. Perhaps it was better that his statue was gone. The great imam would have looked a little foolish standing there as the nation he helped create was ruthlessly torn apart. Any Somalis old enough to miss the national icon knew their hero by his nickname, Ahmad "Gurey," the Left-Handed. It reminded me of my own nickname.

At around 10:30 a.m., we were driving back to the Sahafi, and as usual, my bodyguard was in the front passenger seat with the window cracked just enough for the barrel of his assault rifle to poke out at a forty-five-degree angle. Whenever we entered the traffic circle, his finger came off the trigger and he rolled up the window. This was normally the moment when the stress eased. When we drove into the traffic circle that morning, I figured I'd beaten the odds again and made it back to the relative safety of the Sahafi. But this time I noticed everyone on the street was either staring up a slight hill that faced the Pakistani building, or scattering for cover. I told the driver to stop and I got out to see what was going on. In the distance, there were at least three thousand protesters, led by women and children waving tree branches as symbols of peace and the blue-and-white Somali flag as a sign of their nationalist defiance. They were marching toward the Pakistani position, still so far away that I could barely hear them chanting Aideed's name.

They were fired up by the aerial assault on Aideed's radio station, and four weapons storage sites, during the night. U.S. Cobra attack helicopters and Specter gunships, essentially flying 105-mm artillery guns, had finally succeeded in blasting Aideed's station off the air. Now the warlord's supporters were really riled. Aideed's strategists wanted dead civilians to mobilize opposition. And the Pakistanis wanted revenge. It was a recipe for disaster, but I'd only thought far enough ahead to imagine troops scattering the demonstrators by firing over their heads from the top floors of a building. So I stood at the corner of a short row of shops, looking away from the Pakistani position with a clear view of the demonstrators. I figured that if anyone was going to shoot close to the ground, it would be the Somalis, and the wall would give me protection. Any return Pakistani fire, I thought, would be aimed high and straight up the road—not at me.

The protesters were about two blocks away from the traffic circle when I heard the sharp crack of the first rifle shots. The sound was loud and close and came from the building about fifty yards behind me, not from the marchers approaching from the opposite direction, much farther up the road. The United Nations said later that the Pakistanis had been fired on at least six times before they returned fire in self-defense. That isn't what I heard, or saw. When the peace-keepers' heavy machine guns opened up, I hugged a corner wall first, and then, about halfway through the barrage, I had the presence of mind to lift a hand up and start my pocket cassette recorder. The tape captured thirty seconds of horror, and it was barely half of it. I kept my eyes closed—tried to melt into the brick—and waited to die. I could hear people getting shot all around me.

My stomach tightens every time I listen to the tape now.

Too many guns are firing to count, but one stands out amid the crackle of assault rifles. It pounds like a drill hammer, firing a rapid succession of at least twenty rounds, and then another machine gun opens up with several, shorter bursts. There is a second-long pause, just enough to hear a child moaning, and then several more guns fire off bursts, and a child screams out. The shooting stops for four more seconds, and a panicky, man's voice pleads to God for his life. "Allah!" he shouts. Others cry out, "Stop! Stop!" in Somali.

Their cries are answered by the heavy crack of an assault rifle shot, and another, and after a final burst, a woman screams at the U.N. soldiers who had come to bring Somalia peace to please spare her now.

When the shooting was over, I slowly stood up, and in a dazed reflex, turned to the sound of the moaning and wailing about twenty yards behind me. I walked toward a boy who looked about eight years old, and who was lying on the ground with his back to the Pakistani soldiers. It looked like he had been riding in the bed of a pickup truck that had stopped, at roughly a forty-five-degree angle to the Pakistanis' building, as it was about to leave the traffic circle. Everyone had scrambled out and tried to hide behind the truck from what they also must have thought was the greater of two dangers: the advancing crowd. As I looked down at the boy, I realized I was standing in chunks of rippled, gray mush.

But I looked more closely at the child and there wasn't any blood on his body. Then I stepped to one side and almost threw up. The top of his head was sliced clean off, as if a kitchen knife had cut open an eggshell. The skull was white and empty. The bone looked dry and almost spotless, as if someone had swished it with a damp cloth. A spray of bullets had blown the boy's brains out, and I was standing in them. A woman, probably his mother, was sitting stunned on the street nearby, rocking slowly back and forth, and moaning, "Allah, Allah." A man in the group of about seven people lay face down on the road, his arm lying flat across his back. A fusillade of machine-gun fire had almost cut him in half at the waist, eviscerating his hips and stomach into burgundy red, bullet-riddled flesh.

Minutes after the shooting, peacekeepers in three armored personnel carriers, painted white with the large, black letters UN on the side, drove slowly past the wounded on the road and looked down. They did not stop. It was one of several U.N. vehicles that passed wounded and dying Somali civilians in the traffic circle, and several blocks up the road, but did nothing to rescue them.

Staff at two local hospitals, which had no blood for transfusions and very little medicine, told me at least twenty people were killed, and many more wounded, in shooting that had lasted just over a minute. A two-year-old boy, naked except for a dirty brown shirt, was killed by a stray bullet while he walked with his mother, half a mile away from the protest march. Three women who were in the crowd of

14

protesters lay dying with head and leg wounds that bled into the white sand at the roadside.

At Benadir hospital, where I went to do my own body count, I saw four corpses laid out on cardboard just inside the front door. Two men, two children. The faces of the children were covered with cardboard shrouds, pieces torn from old cartons that once carried Italian photocopying equipment. The word *Fragile* was printed on one piece in bold red letters. When someone lifted it up, I saw the face and shattered skull of the boy who was killed in the traffic circle, just behind me.

Like the United Nations, Pakistan's government insisted its troops had done nothing wrong. They were under orders not to fire at civilians and they didn't, a foreign ministry spokesman insisted. Only gunmen who shot first at the peacekeepers got killed. Reports to the contrary were "inaccurate and misleading." It wasn't the first time that official statements flatly contradicted the reality of what I'd seen and heard on the spot. It wouldn't be the last. But it was infuriating just the same. Killing innocent people was one thing. Lying about it exposed such cowardice and hypocrisy that it stripped away whatever moral force the United Nations had left in its arguments for waging war in Somalia. If it had been white soldiers shooting at anti-apartheid protesters in South Africa, there would have been an international outcry. The dead and wounded Somali protesters were enemies of the United Nations, so the massacre passed largely unnoticed by the world.

Efforts to stop the senseless killing and talk peace in Somalia were not silenced by foreign guns alone. Somali warlords and Al Qaeda also played their role.

At the time a fringe terror group, Osama bin Laden's Al Qaeda network was probing for weaknesses, waiting for opportunities to prove to skeptics that a global jihad could be fought and won. They soon saw Mogadishu as an ideal battleground on which to fight U.S. troops in a new war where incendiary news images would prove to be weapons as powerful as improvised explosive devices.

Aideed was an opportunist, not an Islamic extremist, but he made a convenient Al Qaeda ally. A former general in Siad Barre's army, Aideed had led one of the strongest factions in the uprising against the dictator. He thought that made him the legitimate heir. When the United Nations tried to neutralize him, claiming it favored none of the warlords, Aideed saw it as a conspiracy to deny him power. Bin Laden, who was based in nearby Sudan at the time, was looking for a war with the Americans. Aideed needed help getting rid of them. Al Qaeda was happy to oblige.

A special force of elite U.S. Army Rangers and ultra-secret Delta Force commandos, called Task Force Ranger, arrived in late August to try to capture Aideed and put him on trial for war crimes. In the first arrest attempt on August 30, a dozen helicopters arrived over their target, a Mogadishu house, just before 3 a.m. That was when, by military psychologists' calculations, Somali gunmen were most likely to be dozing as the buzz of the qat plants that they incessantly chewed was wearing off. The military said it had arrested a few suspects, but not Aideed, in what it called a command and control center. After the sun came up, people living in what was actually just a house told a much different story. They were foreign U.N. staff members, in a residence clearly marked with a blue-and-white U.N. flag flying from the roof.

In the most bizarre arrest attempt, U.S. forces dropped into their closest allies' territory in north Mogadishu and grabbed a man who, like Aideed, was balding and gray-haired, but a lot taller than the fugitive warlord. Ahmed Jilow, a former mayor of Mogadishu, was also head of the U.N.'s police committee. When an American soldier accused Jilow of being Aideed, he denied it. But when the soldier smacked his head with a rifle butt, Jilow said he was indeed Aideed. The main military spokesman for the United Nations' military operation, U.S. Army Major David Stockwell, refused to talk about the bungled raid. He insisted it was classified and called it a "routine operation."

"Not catching Aideed has become routine," an exasperated U.N. official wisecracked.

Farce descended into horror on September 9, less than a month before the mission to capture Aideed imploded. On a major street running across the north of the city, Aideed's guerrillas attacked Pakistani troops holed up in several armored vehicles, who were protecting American soldiers manning a bulldozer. An RPG set one of the Pakistani tanks on fire. The others opened up on the surrounding neighborhood. When Somalis tried to steal the bulldozer, U.S. Cobra attack helicopters fired anti-tank missiles and destroyed it.

Just as they'd been doing throughout a long and vicious civil war, Somali women and children crowded into the combat zone. Many protested in the middle of the road. The military alleged that other women and children threw grenades and fired assault rifles from behind a wall. Two Cobras strafed them all with 20-mm nose cannons. The weapons, designed to knock out tanks and other heavy artillery, can fire at least 750 armor-piercing rounds per minute. The guerrilla ambush that started the three-hour battle wounded two American soldiers, who recovered, but the U.S. military estimated the counter-attack killed sixty Somali women, children, and guerrillas. Somali doctors who treated the casualties said at least 125 were killed and 300 injured.

At one hospital, fifty severely wounded patients were women or children. At another, eleven children were among forty-four victims lying on bloodstained foam mattresses or reed mats on the floor. The youngest was a one-year-old boy whose lower lip had been blown off by shrapnel from a Pakistani tank shell. His mother's body was beside him.

It was a massacre by any definition I knew. Surprisingly, Stockwell didn't deny that attack helicopters had strafed unarmed civilians. The major, whose parting words after each briefing were always a sincere "Be safe out there," had given us a walkie-talkie to keep at the Sahafi Hotel in case gunmen stormed the compound walls and we needed to call for help. The battle, one of the most intense the war-ravaged city had seen, lasted into the night, so Stockwell radioed us at the hotel and we gathered around the walkie-talkie to hear what was so urgent—half expecting it was news that Aideed had been captured. Stockwell admitted straight out that civilians had been killed. But he insisted that Somali women and children "became combatants, armed or not" because Aideed's fighters routinely used them as "human shields."

"There are no sidelines or spectator seats," Stockwell stressed later. "The people on the ground are considered combatants."

In a matter of weeks, Aideed had succeeded in bringing foreign troops down to his level. And they still couldn't find him. Somali spies were jerking the Americans' chain, giving them bad leads, or more often, playing both sides so that whenever the Americans got close, Aideed was always a few steps ahead of them.

There was a condescending air to the foreign military operation that rubbed the Somalis, a fiercely nationalistic people, the wrong way. To Aideed's supporters, who dominated the capital, the Americans were leading an occupation force. The Black Hawks, which pounded the air as they flew low over the city and often blew roofs off tin shacks in the middle of the night with their powerful rotor wash, symbolized the insult in high-tech. The human embodiment was officials such as retired Admiral Jonathan Howe, the civilian head of the U.N. mission in Somalia. The humorless, pallid-faced American pressed hardest for Aideed's arrest despite warnings, in Somalia and from abroad, that he was only digging a deeper hole.

A slightly more entertaining version of him was Major Mike Collier, a silver-haired Marine veteran of Vietnam who strutted down the street with a pistol-grip shotgun slung across his back; an Israeli-made Galil assault rifle, with nine magazines; two bandoliers of 240 bullets draped across his chest; a 9-mm Beretta pistol, with five magazines; an M79 grenade launcher, with thirty-six grenades; three light disposable anti-tank bazookas; and two nine-inch Randall knives—and a well-chewed cigar in his mouth. "If you have to carry a gun for a living, it'd be foolish to carry just one," Collier once told me in a soft-spoken Tennessee drawl. "Anything mechanical can fail."

"When I point my shotgun at a driver's head, the only sound you hear is knuckles hitting the ceiling," he added.

Somalis had a nickname for pretty well anyone who stood out, which Collier did in a big way. They called him "Tobaako Weyne"— Big Tobacco. The military put him in charge of liaison and security for non-governmental aid groups, which was like throwing a shark into a goldfish pond. The Somalis put a twenty-five-thousand-dollar bounty on Collier's head, and he regularly walked alone in the street, literally armed to the teeth, daring anyone to take a shot at collecting the reward. Some tried, but Collier always outgunned them. In mid-September, when the hunt for Aideed was just days away from disaster, the Marine major was as confident of his invulnerability as ever. "I'll be swift and deadly. And Somalis respect that," the Marine said.

"These guys aren't fighting for their flag. They're fighting for money. And very few people are willing to risk their lives for a few bags of grain or a little cash."

It might have been easy to dismiss Collier as an irrelevant oddball, except to a lot of people, he symbolized all that was going wrong with the U.S. military's mission in Somalia. Like Collier, subtlety was not its strong point. Both operated on the belief that Somalis understood threat and intimidation, which in fact backfired and made more Somalis willing to die to drive the Americans out. Collier and commanders who thought like him were not the American military's strength, but its Achilles heel, which Al Qaeda and other extremists would become very deft at exploiting as their broader war against the West spread like a virus around the world.

The arrest mission peaked on September 21, when the airborne posse captured Aideed's arms supplier and bagman, Osman Hassan Ali, better known as "Ato"—The Thin One—to Somalis. That night, Ato's defenders fired at least a dozen rocket-propelled grenades into the air in another failed attempt to blow one of the choppers out of the sky. U.S. helicopter gunships shot back at Ato's guards with heavy machine guns, and several of his men were killed.

The next morning, I went to the house where Ato was captured to see if he'd left anything interesting behind. When I went in the front gate, the place was empty. But after about ten minutes, several Somalis warned me to get out fast. As I hurried back onto the street, a battered old car pulled up in front of the gate, and I glanced at the back seat for a split second. Several women were crammed in shoulder-to-shoulder, all of them taller than the balding, portly man who was squeezed in between them. Aideed. The moment his face registered I was already turning away to save my life. Several of Aideed's gunmen surrounded the car, and they screamed at me to go. As they wildly

20

waved assault rifles, I walked down the street counting each breath, waiting for them to shoot me in the back.

Four days later, the Somalis' new battle tactics paid off. For weeks, we'd been seeing RPGs streaking up toward Black Hawks, but they always missed. The grenades are designed to explode on impact against ground targets, but hitting a Black Hawk in flight, in just the right spot to bring it down, takes training and considerable skill—or very good luck. On the street, Somalis said Aideed's guerrillas had learned how to modify the grenades' fuses so that the rounds exploded at a certain height. The optimum height was easy to calculate because the choppers approached and hovered at around the same level each time they delivered troops, who slid down ropes to their targets. A blast close enough to the tail rotor could knock a chopper out of the sky without a direct hit. Just who was doing the teaching, no one said. Years later, in a dusty police file in Indian Kashmir, I would find the confession of a Pakistani militant leader, with close links to Al Qaeda, that showed bin Laden's network had spent months aiding the Somalis' war against American forces.

On September 25, the training showed stunning results—and the world barely noticed. For the first time, Somali gunmen in flip-flops and sarongs snatched a mighty Black Hawk down from the sky. The chopper was searching for a mortar firing position around 2 a.m., after six mortar bombs landed at the Americans' airport base. An RPG hit the Black Hawk in the belly, and it crashed in a narrow alley near the Green Line, the front line of crumbling war ruins that separated Aideed's faction from its main Somali rival in north Mogadishu.

Stockwell called it "a lucky strike" and said he believed that the bodies of three crewmen who died in the fiery crash had been retrieved by a recovery crew. Not all of them had. When I arrived at the crash site, the charred engine and long rotor blades were still burning. Embers glowed orange-red in the gray ash of the fuselage's smoldering wreckage. A small group of Somalis were dancing nearby, chanting Aideed's name in celebration. A woman with a fiendish smile swung a piece of stringy, scorched flesh from a stick in front of my face. Another woman rushed up to show me a human tooth wrapped in a small piece of dirt-smeared paper.

"America! America!" they shouted gleefully. They claimed their best trophy, the headless torso of one of the soldiers killed in the crash, had been dragged off for display in Bakara Market. It would be suicide for a foreigner to go there, so my Somali friend and interpreter, Harun Macruf Hassan, went for me. Harun, a journalist I'd worked with many times over the previous year, and a man I trusted with my life, returned to say he'd seen the torso in a burlap sack. Somalis were charging people money for a peek. Unfortunately, I hadn't sent Harun with a camera. But I didn't doubt a word of his description, and I filed a story that Somalis were parading American body parts in the streets. I had pictures of scorched flesh on a stick. But that didn't register as an atrocity against Americans in the public mind.

I was a reporter who happened to carry a camera, a 35-mm Nikon that I bought myself because my editors wouldn't give me one. They didn't want a problem with the unions. I had been taking pictures for newspapers since journalism school, but the pressure on me was usually to find the truth and write, not photograph, it. Taking pictures had always been a sideline, a matter of choice—until a Somali mob murdered four journalists in retaliation for a massacre by American Cobra attack helicopters a couple of months earlier, on July 12, eventually leaving me as the only foreign photographer to record the unraveling over the coming weeks. A Somali spy had alerted the Americans that Aideed was attending a meeting of clan elders and Muslim clerics at one of his lieutenant's villas. They were discussing a possible offer to make peace. Aideed had his own spies among the hundreds of Somalis who cleaned out the trash or did other menial labor on the U.S. airbase. Children playing on the hillsides overlooking the base were also said to be spotters who informed Aideed's gunmen when the helicopter engines started to warm with a piercing whine. Minutes after Aideed slipped out of the villa, Cobras hovering at a distance opened fire with TOW missiles. The blasts collapsed the building before those Aideed left behind could escape. More than seventy Somalis died in the attack that, the U.S. military admitted, was not provoked by any Somali fire from the ground.

Several foreign journalists waited for guarantees of protection from Aideed's militia before going to the demolished villa, where dozens of corpses lay in the rubble. But a mob turned on them anyway, and like a pack of rabid dogs pursuing their prey, they chased the journalists who were the only hope that an accurate account of the massacre would reach the outside world. The mob shot, stoned, and stabbed to death Hansi Krauss, a German Associated Press photographer; Hosea Maina, a Kenyan shooting for Reuters; Dan Eldon, a Reuters photographer with American and British citizenship; and Anthony Macharia, a Kenyan TV soundman with Reuters. A Black Hawk pilot reported to base that he had seen a white man running from a mob. He waited for confirmation that all U.S. troops were safe and accounted for, and then flew away, leaving Eldon to die a horrific death.

By the time I found myself at the crash site in late September, the small corps of committed journalists who had been such a thorn in the side of the U.N. and U.S. operations had withered away. Soon after the July massacre, Reuters closed its Mogadishu bureau, but left behind its satellite phone and TV set. They said I could use the sat-fone for free as long as I called them in Nairobi when there was news, so I phoned and told them about the shooting down of the Black Hawk and the ghoulish displays Harun and I had seen. Minutes after Reuters moved the story as an urgent bulletin, I heard the electronic trill of the satfone's ring. It was CNN. A producer in Atlanta said he wanted to put me on the air right away to describe what I'd seen. Then another voice broke in: "This is Tom Johnson, president of CNN. Do you know the implications of what you're saying?"

I had to laugh. "I fully understand the implications of what I'm saying, sir," I told him. "But if you want to know the truth, I'll be happy to tell it."

At the top of the hour, I was on the air, saying the same thing I'd told Reuters. Within hours, the Pentagon was effectively calling me a liar. "The story has no basis in fact," an unidentified Pentagon spokes-man told Reuters. "We have recovered all the remains. We don't know what they were allegedly parading."

Without pictures, there was no proof, and little impact in the United States. If there had been photographic evidence of the Black Hawk downed on that September day, the October 3 fiasco might never have happened. And Al Qaeda would have been denied a crucial propaganda victory in its new war against America.

The Mogadishu press corps shrank dramatically again in late Sep-tember after the U.S. embassy warned that Aideed supporters were plot-ting to kidnap Americans. The U.N. force sent three military officers in an armored personnel carrier to the Sahafi to evacuate the AP corre-spondent. Now the AP and Reuters, the world's two leading wire ser-vices, had shut down operations in Somalia. Few reporters were eager to be the last ones left to turn out the lights in Mogadishu, so most of those remaining called a meeting and tried to impose a group exodus, couched as some kind of protest action. In fact, it was to provide professional cover for anyone who was losing his nerve. If we all left, no one had to worry about getting beaten on the story. I told them to do what they must, but I was staying. I hadn't stuck with the story this long only to give it up just when it was getting really interesting. I'd lived with the fear of "what if" for so long that I had stopped caring.

By the time the Black Hawks powered up their rotors on the afternoon of October 3, it took only one hand to count the number of foreign journalists left in Mogadishu. One of the holdouts, an Australian radio reporter, had joined me on the roof of the Sahafi that evening with a Somali interpreter who worked for another reporter, and a U.N. contract worker. We were making small talk, a little bored with what looked like another training exercise, or another botched attempt to get Aideed. But then a pulse of adrenalin. I focused on the horizon to the east. I thought I saw a small flash of fiery yellow light behind a chopper's tail rotor. It might have been the setting sun glinting off a car window, and I was almost through the first beer, so I could just as easily have been seeing things. I did a double take and looked again at the spot where I thought I'd seen a Black Hawk flying low.

I'm sure of it.

"Did you see that?" I said to the Australian radio reporter.

"What?"

"I thought I saw a flash behind one of those choppers. I think it went behind that hill over there, but I don't see it now."

I took another swig of beer. You had to be careful not to make too much out of things. Nobody wanted to be the guy who ducked when a car backfired. It meant you were either in over your head, or burnt out. Maybe I was both.

Within minutes, as dusk fell, a convoy of about twelve U.S. Army trucks and Humvees with probably one hundred soldiers in them inched through the traffic circle across from the hotel. The soldiers were in five-ton trucks, facing each other on benches, with their backs pressed against wooden slats, rifles between their knees. "That's a pretty stupid way to drive through Mogadishu," I thought, and as the lead vehicle moved slowly into the K-4 traffic circle, heading north from the airport to Aideed's main stronghold, I saw dozens of Somalis running down back alleys in front of the hotel, ready to ambush with rifles and grenade launchers. They blasted the front vehicle, which exploded in flames. The rest of the convoy opened up on any building they could see, laying down a circle of fire. Their .50-caliber guns pounded like pneumatic drills. Grenade launchers pumped out 40-mm rounds.

We hit the roof. I pressed myself into the concrete as fiery orange tracer bullets hissed barely an inch above the three-foot parapet just beside us. A grenade blast blew a rectangular hole a yard across in the flimsy wall, leaving only sharp-edged hunks of concrete. Jagged fragments of wall and bits of grenade shrapnel showered down on us. Suddenly I was praying for intervention from a Heaven I didn't believe existed.

Please God, don't let it hit my head.

Another grenade exploded next to where the first hit, and then another, as the grenade launcher blasted a line along the wall that was the only thing between us and death. My ears buzzed and chunks of concrete sprayed everywhere. I froze, trying to guess whether it was safer to stay or move.

What would the Army training manual say? "When assaulting a building, lay down your ordnance in a line, return to the starting point, and repeat?" Or would it instruct soldiers to spread the grenades around more? They're firing right to left. Should I go right or will they redirect, which means I should . . .

"Fucking get out of here!" the Australian screamed. I crawled behind him, following the soles of his shoes, staying as flat as I could. He was talking into his microphone as he squatted for a moment at the doorway and then disappeared down the stairwell. I couldn't help but think that he was about to record my death on a cassette tape.

We regrouped in the hallway, the wrong place to stop and think. The hotel backed onto the street where the American convoy was still trying to fight its way out of a ferocious ambush. Eight more grenade blasts shook the hotel over the next hour. Machine-gun rounds pierced the walls. It felt like they were trying to level the place. The Somali interpreter was bleeding from a head wound, and it looked like he was going to pass out. All we had was a small first aid kit. My stomach went queasy when everyone turned to me to decide what to do next. If I'm the best we've got, I thought, we're doomed. Someone handed me the walkie-talkie that Stockwell had left us for emergencies. I had nothing more than memories of war movies for instruction on how to radio the U.S. military for backup. And a few weeks earlier, I'd watched a CNN producer talk to the Pentagon on his satellite phone to call in a Black Hawk airstrike after two of the network's vehicles got trapped in clan crossfire on the airport road.

My voice shifted to faux military. I paused, trying to keep it together, and then keyed the radio. "Mayday! Mayday! Be advised that your forces are firing at a civilian hotel at K-4 traffic circle. Repeat. We are unarmed civilians and we are under fire."

The walkie-talkie crackled, and after a few seconds of dead air, an American voice replied. "Repeat your location."

"We are taking cover in the third-floor hallway. Please be advised your forces are hitting the building with grenade and machine-gun fire. And we have one wounded."

"Copy. We'll see what we can do."

No rescue squad ever came. The military had its hands full saving its own. During a lull in the fighting, we took shelter in our rooms, crawling along the hallways and stairwells to avoid any sniper fire or stray bullets. I wrote the little that I knew about what was going on outside, and wondered whether the hotel would be overrun in the night by Somali gunmen looking for revenge. To deaden that unpleasant thought, I pulled another can of beer from the fridge and settled in to watch fuzzy live coverage on CNN of Russians fighting in the streets of Moscow. I drifted into sleep just a few hours before the sun rose on a new day that would change my life forever.

2

DEAD MAN'S DANCE

If any question why we died, tell them, because our fathers lied.
RUDYARD KIPLING, AFTER THE DEATH
OF HIS SON IN WORLD WAR I

I woke up hungover and still dressed, lying in front of the fuzzy TV as the first rays of sunlight struck Mogadishu through a drifting, post-apocalyptic haze from hundreds of burning-tire barricades. It was eerily quiet, and the streets were almost empty of cars. The few moving vehicles were mostly battered pickup trucks collecting bullet-riddled Somali corpses. The battle through the night had left eighteen American soldiers dead and seventy-five wounded. To get the rest of their force back alive, American helicopters and troops had killed more than six hundred Somalis, many of them women and children huddling in the darkness when bullets or shrapnel pierced the tin walls of their shacks. It was the bloodbath I had stayed to see, and I paced the hallways, anxious to get out on the streets but wishing I could find someplace to hide.

I had to wait for my crew, and with the seconds ticking off, I ran through all the worst possible reasons why Harun, my armed guard, and the driver were late. My head buzzing on adrenaline and last night's beer, I tried to keep things together by stumbling through a mental checklist of what I'd need once we were mobile and past the gates. There wouldn't be time for second chances. Pen. Notepad. Tape recorder. Film. I rifled through the pockets of my camera bag, digging deep into the bits of paper, shoelaces, and stale crumbs. No film. Of course . . . I'd run out of the very thing I needed to justify staying in this hellhole. Panicked, I ran down the stairs and found the hotel owner, a coolheaded businessman and consummate problem solver named Mohammed Jirdeh Hussein. I persuaded him to open up the abandoned AP bureau office. This *was* Somalia, in the middle of a news emergency, so I looted a few rolls from the supply cabinet.

"I'm sure they won't mind," I assured Hussein, as I ripped open the cellophane on packs of film and stuffed the black plastic containers into my pockets and bag. "Nationalized in the interests of the people!" Hussein smiled, and locked up as I rushed out to the parking lot to look again for Harun and our car.

It wasn't like him to be late. Everything Harun did, his polite tone, the refined way he dressed and carried himself, defied the chaos all around him. The son of an abusive, philandering man who owned several hundred cattle, Harun took his strength from his mother, a kind, illiterate woman who wed at fifteen and taught her six children there was nothing more important than education and respect. Above all, she told him, be truthful. "If one person in this world knows you're a liar, you really have a big problem," she would say. In 1992, when his father was dying of malaria in the neighboring country of Djibouti, he sent word that it would be an answer to his prayers if he could see Harun once more before he died. The reunion never happened, and Harun was tormented knowing that he would never reconcile with his father.

I liked and respected Harun so deeply that I wanted nothing more than for him to live long enough to get out of Somalia. He had stayed to take care of his mother, and I dreaded the thought of having to sit in front of her one day and tell her he had died working for me. That's always been the hardest part of the job for me: convincing good people, who get none of a newspaper byline's ego gratification, to put their lives on the line. In Somalia, my crew was long past doing it for the money. The translator got thirty dollars a day, the driver and bodyguard split one hundred dollars a day. It was a very good income in a ruined nation, but not exactly wealth worth dying for. We'd been through so much in the past year that we were like a family now, even though I'd taken so many risks I'd developed an air of impending disaster. A lot of people were surprised I'd stayed alive this long.

Standing in the parking lot, I tried to talk myself out of thinking that if Harun weren't dead, he had finally abandoned me. And then his close friend and colleague Abdulkdir Abdi Gutale came through the hotel's heavy gate after running the gauntlet of militiamen still looking for a fight. Harun was fine, Gutale assured me, but he couldn't make it and had asked Gutale to come help me. The two of them almost hadn't survived the night.

"They're shooting at anything that moves now," Gutale said, his voice rising. "*Even donkeys.*"

"Near our compound, they were shooting people on sight," he said. "They didn't care if there were gunmen or not. Even I was almost killed."

Gutale wasn't one to exaggerate. If anything, I realized, he was understating the battle raging in a neighborhood he knew well. He and Harun risked their lives every day writing for a respected Somali-language newspaper printed on a mimeograph machine in a small office in a three-story building on one of Mogadishu's main streets. It was just half a mile north of the Olympic Hotel, the target of the U.S. forces' October 3 raid. The newsroom was on the ground floor, and

Harun and Gutale lived on the first floor. While I was watching the battle unfold from the Sahafi's roof the previous night, Gutale was moving along the streets of Bakara Market for a closer look. He was with the cousin of my bodyguard when, rounding a corner, they stumbled unarmed into a free-fire zone.

Four American soldiers were trapped in a five-ton truck, much like the ones I'd seen in the K-4 ambush. This one had several wheels shot out. The soldiers were back-to-back, like frontiersmen in a stockade under siege, pumping out a wall of fire from heavy machine guns to keep Somali gunmen at bay. They were trying to head south back to the K-4 traffic circle and the American airbase, unloading magazines as they went. To Gutale, they looked lost and scared.

As the truck crawled along on a couple of wheels, Gutale and his friend ducked back behind a building, but when they came around the other side, the soldiers spotted them and opened fire. The first round was aimed at Gutale, but just missed when he dived into the door of the newspaper office. The second round hit one of his neighbors, a grocer in his twenties named Ali "Dhere"—Tall Ali—as he stood watching from an alleyway. "He was more or less cut in half," Gutale said.

Gutale had clearly been through enough. But I kept working on him in the hotel parking lot, gently tried to coax him into taking me into the middle of a street war, as American choppers crisscrossed the sky searching for fresh targets, knowing that our car could easily draw fire from either side. It was a very hard sell. Rumors of a desecrated American had reached the hotel long before Gutale, but they didn't strike him as a big story. Like most who had survived Somalia's descent into lawlessness, a switch had shut off in his mind, and the most gruesome possibilities were just another day of life.

Mogadishu was once a beautiful city with white-painted Italianate villas, the capital of the most stable state in Africa. It had been considered one of the safest places on the continent. Now women drained of fear carried on with their grocery shopping as clan militias fired heavy weapons at each other along broad avenues. Children played at the front lines, running water and ammunition alongside their mothers to keep the gunmen well supplied. One day, Gutale was sitting in front of the newspaper office when he saw an Aideed supporter returning from a demonstration, cheerfully waving what looked like meat hanging from a stick, as if it were a pennant from a college football game. "This is an American!" the young man shouted to onlookers. Gutale dismissed it as cheap propaganda. He figured the flesh was really goat's meat or dog or something other than human. When the story of a dead American dragged in the streets did the rounds early on October 4, Gutale didn't think it was worth getting killed running down what he expected to be just another Aideed ploy.

I told Gutale that we had no choice. We had to at least look to see if people were telling the truth about the American being dragged through the streets, or maybe even see if we could find a live prisoner, so that the Pentagon couldn't brush off the story with denials again.

Gutale finally gave in. He walked over to the hotel guard house next to the front gate and looked through the guard's rifles for one to borrow. It was the first time I'd seen him with a weapon, suddenly looking like an expert as he checked the chamber and his aim. I wondered whether he would have to kill for me this day. Or whether he would die himself because of me. He told one of the guards, who looked even less dangerous, to come with us. My regular armed guard, Mohomud Hersi Ali, took the front passenger seat with his AK-47 and we headed out to see the damage from sixteen hours of all-out street war. They put me in the middle of the back seat, hoping I'd be harder to see from the street, and less likely to trigger an attack.

Within a few minutes, we passed corpse collectors, men carrying limp bodies by their hands and feet, who glared into the car as if they wanted my blood. Our car crawled tentatively from one block to the next, and we pulled over to ask people whether they knew anything about a captured American soldier. Some said they'd seen him alive, tied up in a wheelbarrow, others said he was dead. Near the smoldering wreckage of a downed Black Hawk, a cheerful crowd let me take pictures of children bouncing on the rotor blades. Had anyone seen the American corpse? we asked. The crowd pointed the way, and we followed, stopping every minute or so to ask passersby for information. Whenever a Black Hawk thundered past overhead, people would wave fists and shout at it.

We stopped first at the crash site northeast of the Olympic Hotel, where Black Hawk Super Six-One went down, and Cleveland's crew came in to provide cover from Super Six-Four. A Black Hawk's long tail section was sitting at a forty-five-degree angle, with its rear wheel resting on the dirt. The other end was torn metal and wires pointing to the sky, as if a giant hand had snapped it like a toy. We found children clambering on the chopper's remains, like kids on a jungle gym, where it crashed and burned between two corrugated tin shacks in a squatter area. Somalis called the warren of shanties where they lived "Tokyo," an ironic comment on its ugly squalor. Several hundred yards south, Super Six-Four had crashed, just off National Street, while desperately trying to make it back to the airport a couple of miles away. We never made it to that site because people at the first said they knew where the body was headed. Some were going to join the grisly procession as it dragged the soldier through the city. They pointed the way for us.

Our driver, Mohamed Mohomud Ahmed, a man of few words in his forties who I always thought was incredibly brave, was pissed off

34

and even more scared than the rest of us. Gutale thought he was a coward and decided not to translate his complaints to make things easier for me. Mohamed was most worried about the car, a fine one with air conditioning and power windows in a city with few functioning motorized vehicles amid the rickety donkey carts. It was also his only source of income, which a large extended family depended on. Driving around with a white journalist in this frenzy was just inviting someone to destroy it. He'd be lucky if they let him escape alive to join the donkey cart drivers.

We'd done a good circuit of the most likely places to find a body being dragged in Mogadishu and come up blank. After driving around for an hour and a half, we were almost ready to give up and go back to the Sahafi. We had already pushed our luck way past the limit. If the Somalis didn't kill us, and we managed to find the American corpse, then we risked getting cut down by attack helicopters that were trying to retrieve several Americans still missing in action. Suddenly Mohamed spotted a mob moving slowly down a steep side street, and he made a U-turn. Our Cressida, which was well known in Aideed's territory, pulled up behind the seething crowd of two hundred Somalis.

Gutale told me to stay in the car while he and the two guards went with him to gauge the scene. It's Gamay in the car, he told them. Would it be okay if he took some pictures? Gutale came back and stuck his head in the car, and with a nervous smile said I had permission from the mob leaders. My heart raced and my head felt light, terrified of death and full of life all at once.

I walked, hyper-alert, shielded only by a triangle of protectors who stood no chance if the mob turned on us. And then the crowd parted, forming a manic horseshoe around the corpse. My eyes panned the frenzy. I looked to the ground. And that is how I came to know Staff Sergeant William David Cleveland.

In less than the time it took to breathe, I had to decide whether to take the picture. The moment of choice, in the swirl of dust and sweat, hatred and fear, is still trapped in my mind, denying me peace: just as I was about to press the shutter on my camera, the world went quiet, everything around me melted into a slow-motion blur, and I heard the voice:

If you do this, I will own you forever.

"I'm sorry," I thought. I wanted him to understand. To forgive. I'd photographed many corpses before, several more gruesome than this soldier's, but there was something different about Cleveland, a connection that it would take me years to understand. In that split second when I still had a choice, I knew what I had to do. My nerves were taut, every sense ultra-sharp and alert to whoever might be moving in to attack. I was bent slightly forward, trying to get the best angle, shoulders down, stiffened for the blows. A blur of new questions whirled in my mind. Like a coroner performing an autopsy, I tried to be the cold observer. I didn't want to freeze. Any pause, any flinch of uncertainty, could invite the first rock and then I would go down in a flurry of rocks, feet, and fists, just as four colleagues had in July.

The mob danced and cheered and beat Cleveland's corpse with such gusto it seemed that in their blood-addled minds they weren't simply desecrating the body of one fallen soldier, but stomping in victory on a whole, defeated army. Some spat on him. Others kicked and stoned him. A young man wearing a chopper crewman's goggles shoved his way into the picture, his face contorted with glee as he gave the dead crew chief the finger. An old man raised his cane like a club and brought it down fast with a sharp *thwack!* against lifeless flesh. Then he wound up for another. *Thwack!* The giddy younger men in the crowd thought it was hilarious.

I winced with each blow. I had no idea who the corpse was, and after weeks of looking at dead and maimed Somali women and children, I despised men like him who killed from the sky. Until now. Here we were on the same ground, in the blowing dirt and sour stench of fetid trash, on this nameless Somali side street where neither of us belonged, and for the first time, it felt like it was us against them. And there was nothing I could do to help him. Each new disgrace sent a ripple of celebration through the crowd, which undulated like a wave, feeding on its own frenzy. The men controlling the heavy ropes that bound the airman's wrists, stretching his arms high above his head, rolled the body back and forth in the hammering white light of a Mogadishu morning. The dead man danced with his tormentors like a broken marionette.

I felt like I was floating above it all, watching someone else do the insane: snapping pictures of humans become beasts. I tried to focus on reality one step removed—the image in the frame—struggling to make sure that in the seconds I had, I got proof that the military couldn't deny. No room for error. So in the chaos, when a normal person would be thinking about how to save himself, which way to run, I was worried that maybe I'd loaded the film wrong, or the shutter speed was too slow, or whether I should risk using a flash to brighten the shadows cast by the pounding sun.

Did I put those fresh batteries in?

Click

The corpse is limp: Could he have been dead long?

Click

Those bullet wounds on his legs: Did they shoot him in the street or at the crash site?

Click

Maybe he's only unconscious: Could he still be alive?

Click

You poor man: Who are you?

Click

I'd only managed to squeeze off those few frames when Gutale and my main gunman heard the crowd that had tolerated me at first now starting to turn. "What is *he* doing here?" someone shouted in Somali.

Gutale quickly pulled me into the car. The rear doors slammed shut and suddenly the world was silent, except for the soft idling of the engine and the muffled noise of the mob. My pulse pounded like a timpani in my temples. I felt like I'd stepped out from in front of a tornado and into a cool temple. I was trembling. Rivulets of sweat ran down my back. The crowd closed around the corpse, like a malevolent cell consuming a foreign organism, and slowly turned left at the end of the street. I sat next to the right rear door, rewinding the last few minutes through my mind, itemizing the images that I had taken, as the driver waited for the crowd to move off, dragging the corpse with it.

And another voice spoke.

It was Andrew Stawicki, a Polish émigré photographer with an eye that found beauty in places that seemed anything but. I'd worked with him two years earlier in rebel-held southern Sudan. We were drifting in a canoe on the Sobat River at dusk, when Andrew saw several boys, running naked and single file along the river bank, silhouetted against the sunset. He raised his camera with a telephoto lens, and I could tell he had made a wonderful image. "That's going to be a great picture," I said.

Andrew put his camera back in the bottom of the canoe and shrugged off my compliment. He knew newspaper editors too well. "They'll never print it," he said. "The kids' dicks are showing."

And in a lightning-quick zoom, my mind's eye focused on the

38

dead soldier's army-issue green underwear, the only bit of clothing left on the corpse. The underwear was slightly askew, exposing a sliver of his scrotum. I at least had a chance of getting a dead body into the paper. A glimpse of a sexual organ? Far too risqué.

"I've got to go back out," I told Gutale. He said it was too dangerous. "I have to get more pictures," I insisted. "They won't print this one."

Without wasting time to explain—or to give anyone a chance to hold me back—I pulled the door handle and jumped out. Gutale reluctantly followed, but our main bodyguard stayed back with the car, expecting the mob to attack. This time, my focus was tighter, showing just half of the soldier's body. A woman beat him with a flattened tin can. The mob was in a real rage now, and I could tell by the killer stares from several men with bloodshot eyes that I was on the very edge. They had been fighting for more than sixteen hours, no doubt chewing on *qat* to sharpen their fighting edge, and it would mean as much as crushing a cockroach for them to kill an infidel who couldn't take a hint. I turned and ran back to the car, this time with an image that just might get into print.

The driver hit the gas and headed for the Sahafi, and in a matter of minutes the hotel guards were opening the steel gates. The slip of the rusty latch and the squeak of the opening door always made me breathe a little easier, as if the couple of sleepy gunmen there were enough to defend the fortress and keep the killers at bay. I took the steps two at a time up to my room, locked the door behind me, slipped the roll of film under my mattress, switched on the air conditioner, and collapsed on the bed, my eyes tightly closed against the world. And I wept. It was in the half-light of my hotel room, where the only sounds were the air conditioner's hiss and my throbbing heart, that the reality of what I'd done struck like a crushing wave.

I didn't have long to cry, or hide. Getting the pictures, and surviving, was only half the battle. Now I had to get the film out. I had no way to develop the pictures. The fleeing AP staff hadn't left behind a developing kit, and even if they had, I didn't have the equipment to scan the negatives and transmit the images by satellite phone. Photo scanners are practically toys that kids play with on desktop computers today, but in 1993, a negative scanner was a big and very expensive machine, and was one of the first things a photographer was supposed to grab when the evacuation order came down.

So I had to go back out onto the streets, where U.S. forces on the ground, and in attack helicopters buzzing above, were hunting for soldiers missing in action. It was a short run to the airport, just down the street behind the Sahafi. But it was the same street where I'd watched gunmen ambush American soldiers the previous afternoon, hardly the first time that Somalis had put the maze of alleyways and shanties to lethal use. As I got ready to use the road, the images of an attack on two CNN vehicles just over three weeks earlier were also fresh in my mind. Five of CNN's Somali drivers and armed guards had died, and another four were injured, in an ambush sprung when they entered a rival clan's turf to cover the aftermath of a battle with U.N. forces. That skirmish left 126 Somalis and one Pakistani peace-keeper dead.

That day, I had spent several hours peering over the parapet on the Sahafi's roof as the battle unfolded half a block behind the hotel. The attackers unleashed a barrage of machine-gun and grenade fire, and as members of CNN's crew lay dying in their bullet-riddled SUVs, the network's foreign staff watched helplessly from the rooftop. When it became obvious that there was no chance of getting clan elders to negotiate a truce in time to get the wounded Somalis to a hospital, a CNN producer placed a satellite call to network headquarters in

Atlanta, which then contacted the Pentagon, which sent orders to American commanders in Mogadishu. In minutes, a Black Hawk helicopter was circling over the road to the airport, and it fired at least two machine-gun bursts into the alleyways as cover for the trapped CNN crew. In the history of combat journalism, it has to be recorded as the first air assault called in by a cable news network. But to little effect. As usual, the ambushers simply regrouped and resumed firing.

My best hope now was that after a long night of intense street warfare, the militiamen were either too tired or too busy to bother with a Toyota Cressida driving to the airport. I put the single roll of film in a manila envelope, sealed it with several layers of duct tape, marked it NEWS FILM: FOR URGENT DELIVERY, and headed back out through the steel gates. We made it to the airport perimeter without a hitch, but the American soldiers on guard weren't in a welcoming mood. Once I'd convinced them to open up the fort, I had to beg the woman behind the desk at the U.N. flight office to take my package, persuade a pilot to take it on his plane, and then hope that I could find someone to meet the flight at the other end in Nairobi—the closest civilization—and move the pictures to Toronto.

The U.N. flight ops people were anxious to hear about the battle that raged outside, so I had some leverage. They promised to ask the pilot of the afternoon flight, the only one out to Nairobi that day, to take the film. But it was his call, the woman said. And if he took it, there was no guarantee that someone could get to him at the other end before the film was locked away in some drawer for the night—or worse, simply lost forever. At this point, my mind was prone to nightmare scenarios, so I told the woman too many times that nothing was more important than getting my film to Nairobi.

I made it back to the Sahafi and, taking advantage of my deal for free use of Reuters' phone again, called their Nairobi bureau to see if they would collect the film and move the pictures. The only condition for their use of the shots: that all of my paper's Canadian competitors be blacked out. Reuters' photo desk refused, so I called Reid Miller, the AP bureau chief in Nairobi and a good friend. He sounded stunned to hear the AP could provide any of the pictures to subscribers around the world, free of charge, for the simple guarantee that only my paper could use them in Canada. We immediately had a deal. I warned him the pictures were graphic, and begged him to make sure the *Toronto Star* got everything so that I could try to persuade editors there to print at least one. I didn't think anyone else would publish them.

After I'd got the film to the airport, we heard new rumors that an American soldier had been captured alive and was being held prisoner by Aideed's militia. Adrenaline was coursing through me, and I was looking for a distraction from worrying about whether my pictures would ever be published. So I took another tour with Gutale and our bodyguards, asking every so often if anyone had seen the American prisoner. It was getting close to sunset when we gave up and headed for the Sahafi again. At the corner of Via Lenin, the driver stopped as a small group of children walked up, dragging the corpse of another dead soldier. One of the boys, still holding onto a rope, glared at me through the closed window with a killer's cold eyes.

"Do you want to take their picture?" Gutale asked. "They want you to."

"No," I said. "This is too much. And the plane has left for Nairobi by now anyway. Let's get out of here."

That night, after Miller told me that he'd walked onto the airport tarmac in Nairobi to make sure he got the film as soon as the pilot got off the plane, I knew the rest was up to the fickle minds of editors. So I retired to the Reuters office, just a few doors down from my room. A TV set with a coat hanger antenna was part of the equipment left behind. Wiggled just right, it would pick up snowy video, but no sound, from the CNN signal that rebroadcast from the U.S. embassy compound. I switched on to non-stop Breaking News, which is my version of a housewife's soap operas. I felt grounded and safe, watching another night of someone else's civil strife, far away.

Moscow was fast descending into the worst fighting since the 1917 Bolshevik Revolution. Rioters overturned cars and set them on fire. Communists and reformists killed each other in the streets. Yeltsin had ordered camouflaged T-72 tanks to take up position in front of Parliament, where pro-Communist rebels were holed up, braced for the final showdown. As I waited for sunrise in Somalia, and a chance to see what I assumed would be a major offensive against Aideed's forces, I could only stay locked to the screen, like millions of others around the world, waiting to see what would happen when the tanks opened up in Moscow. I sat alone in the ghostly glow of a fuzzy TV screen, listening to the rattle and blast of the battle for Mogadishu outside, slowly getting drunk on cans of Amstel, wondering whether the world would care about the corpse of a dead American airman when nuclear-armed Russia was on the brink of civil war. I figured not.

It wasn't until late the following night, October 5, that I had the slightest sense of the fallout the pictures would have. The satellite phone rang. It was a reporter from *Newsday* who wanted to ask about the pictures for a story he was writing. I told him I was surprised that the AP had moved any of them. The reporter sounded like he thought I was kidding, and then said: "You don't know what impact these pictures are having, do you?"

It was as if he'd throttled me. I had to struggle to breathe. I hoped the sound of my crying would be lost in the synthesized whine of the signal bouncing off a satellite somewhere in space. I hung up, and the satfone rang with an electronic chirp, chirp, chirp for hours, while I slouched in the gloom. At first, I was relieved by the simple effect of a voice from the outside. Then I was consumed by anger, fear, and shame, and just wanted to disappear. I felt like I'd stolen a man's soul to make a point.

The AP wire photo desk in New York decided to distribute only the second set of pictures to avoid offending subscribers and their readers with any hint of inappropriate nudity. As always, obscene violence was okay. Showing newspaper readers a flash of a sexual organ over breakfast, even just a bit of a dead man's scrotum, would be in bad taste. Months later, a senior AP photo editor confirmed to me that there was no way he would have sent the full-body pictures out to subscribers because of the slightly exposed scrotum. AP had a strict rule against altering photos. *Time* magazine bought the full-body picture, and ran it full-page color. The magazine digitally altered the underwear to make sure standards of modesty were upheld.

The photo caused an uproar in the United States. President Bill Clinton called an immediate halt to the hunt for Aideed's operation. Safe to resurface, Aideed quickly sent a trusted envoy to invite me to dinner, Mohammed Noor Gutale, the son of a businessman from Aideed's clan who had grown rich renting out vehicles to journalists and aid workers, even the U.N. mission that Aideed and his supporters so viciously opposed.

"He wants to thank you for what you've done," Gutale smiled in the doorway of my hotel room. He insisted that I come alone, without an interpreter. Despite Clinton's assurances, Aideed was suspicious of a double-cross and was still in hiding.

After convincing myself that I was after an exclusive interview, and not Aideed's gratitude, I went with Gutale to dine with the warlord in a safe house. The curtains were drawn, and the light was dim, but Aideed's smile was bright and as confident as ever. His weeks on the run hadn't diminished the politician's sheen. He reached to shake my hand, and embraced me with the other, and I felt like a kid shrinking away from his dodgy uncle, trying not to seem disrespectful.

Sitting across from Aideed at a small dining table, listening to him gloat and knowing that I had helped lift him off the hook, I wanted to melt into the floor in shame. I didn't listen much to what he said, and only picked at the food. I had one question I was aching to ask. "Sir, did I see you in the back of a car in front of Osman Ato's house?"

Aideed smiled, in his grandfatherly way, and nodded. "Yes, that was me," he said. "I wanted to speak to the people, to calm them down."

Even in victory over a military giant, he was trying to play selfless peacemaker.

Weeks later, after Somalia dropped from the headlines one last time, I took a vacation with my brother to Cape Town, hoping to blot out what had happened with lots of South African wine, seafood, and lazy hours on the beach. On a daytrip to the Cape of Good Hope, we found a secluded spot with magnificent waves pounding in a relentless rhythm into jagged rocks and white sand. I put my camera down, covered it with a neat pile of our clothes, and walked into the surf.

When I turned to make sure no one had sneaked down and stolen everything, I saw a large male baboon sitting on its haunches, grinning with glistening canines as big as a junkyard dog's. It rolled the camera back and forth in its huge paws. I ran toward it, expecting the animal to drop something that wasn't edible and retreat. But it clamped its jaws down on the camera strap and ran up a path. It stopped, turned, and stared, a long, angry glare that dared me to try to take the camera back. I hollered and waved my arms. The baboon only retreated a little farther. He sat there, challenging me to take another step, and I was sure he was bracing to strike. I backed off and tried to pelt him with rocks as he bolted up a cliff and disappeared at the top. Just when I thought he'd given up and run, I saw the camera arc through the blue sky, high over the cliff's edge, and fall some thirty feet to land on a flat rock below.

It exploded on impact, spilling out the electronic guts of the machine that captured the image of Cleveland's corpse.

3

SON OF A SOLDIER

Only those are fit to live who are not afraid to die.
GENERAL DOUGLAS MACARTHUR

For as long as I've understood that I had a father, I've known him only in two dimensions. He is a grainy figure in black and white, trapped in time in a silver photograph frame that sits on a side table in my mother's dining room. A strolling photographer snapped the picture at a summer fair, posing our family in two lines of descending order, from a giant of a father preparing to die to a baby in a stroller just starting to live. Raymond J. Watson suffered from a genetic disease that gradually choked off his kidneys with clusters of cysts, a decade before the transplant operation that would have saved his life became routine. He died fifty days short of my second birthday, so I never knew him. As a boy, lying at the foot of our housekeeper Louie's bed one night, watching a movie on her portable black-and-white TV, I decided my father must have been very much like Mr. Atticus Finch.

As soon as I saw Scout in Atticus's lap, on the rocking chair under the porch light, I knew that my father also must have been a man of simple words and great wisdom. There was no question that my dad

47

was a loving, learned man of peace who, when left no other choice, could take up a gun and be a crack shot. I knew that he was a person of infinite patience, a man who would always have known what to say to make me feel safe in a scary world. When I cried alone, I thought of my father and saw Atticus, felt his arm around my shoulders, and heard the calm voice of reason reassure me that sometimes the only way is to stand on your own. For years, the man I concocted in my mind was enough of a father for me. But eventually, I came to understand the kinship with war that I had inherited from him and his father before him.

Like me, Ray was the son of a soldier, a veteran of World War I who took a French war bride who lived less than one hundred miles from the village, where, by a quirk of wartime fate, my maternal grandmother also married a Canadian soldier following the war. Oscar Guy Watson, just O.G. or Jack to most folks, was a gadabout drunk and a gambler with a bad temper who divided his age by four because he was born on February 29 in a leap year. He drifted from one job to the next, blasting rock in the mines of New Brunswick, selling lobsters door-to-door, losing what little money he had on a farm-and-grocery venture in Saskatchewan, always shifting and dodging to stay ahead of the creditors. He had to outrun his partner on the farm, too. It seems the man's wife had attracted O.G.'s wandering eyes. Once he'd made it off the Prairie alive, O.G. had another great idea. He decided he'd like to be a soldier in the war to end all wars.

Just two months after World War I broke out, O.G. enlisted in the Overseas battalion of the Canadian Expeditionary Force's 3rd Field Ambulance. His enlistment forms say he was thirty years and seven months old, a farmer of five feet, eleven inches, with gray eyes, a dark complexion, and a thirty-seven-inch girth, when fully expanded. He spent six months in boot camp and landed in France in the middle of

April 1915 to join a unit that was based in the northern town of Steen-voorde, near the Belgian border. O.G. was a private trained as a cyclist soldier, one of a new breed of Canadian army troopers who rode bicy-cles on the battlefront. They were later amalgamated into the Cana-dian Corps Cyclist Battalion, which quickly developed a reputation as a suicide unit. Oddjobbers who served as dispatch riders, intelligence scouts, stretcher-bearers, and even mobile infantry, the bicycle soldiers suffered a casualty rate of 22 percent.

When O.G. arrived in France to join the 3rd Field Ambulance, its medics had just moved into a local school, close to the trenches along the Western front. On April 22, a surprise German gas attack sent hundreds of choking soldiers running in a desperate scramble for medical care. The shocked, collapsing men didn't know what had hit them. It was the Germans' first chlorine gas attack. As soldiers and refugees fled the spreading cloud of deadly gas, O.G.'s unit was ordered to move toward the front line at night on their bicycles as artillery shells whined overhead, and snipers tried to pick them off. German troops had broken through as panicked French soldiers retreated, shouting, "The war is finished!" The Canadian cyclists pushed past them, noses covered with wet socks because they didn't have gas masks.

The day had broken with an unusual calm, and the men could suddenly hear the birds again over the shelling. Medical staff were just finishing dinner when a rush of footsteps drew their attention to the window, where they saw the "disorderly bodies of Algerian troops hurrying past, devoid of rifles and without equipment." "Then the milder gas cases started to come in," the unit's official war diary recorded, "and soon we had about 200 patients in our Hospital who brought with them an indescribably acrid odor that clung to their clothes and filled the air with fumes which caused intense smarting of

the eyes, running of the nose, dry throat and irritative cough to everyone who came in contact with them."

They staggered, exhausted, through the ward. Many vomited
without warning. The first death came soon after a gassed soldier was
admitted for treatment. The victims were British, French, Algerian,
Indian, and Canadian—one never-ending stream that lasted day and
night for seven days without cease, in all some 5,200 cases. "Wounds
here, wounds there, wounds everywhere," the journal noted. "Legs,
feet, hands missing, bleeding stumps controlled by rough field tour-
niquets; large portions of abdominal walls shot away; faces horribly
mutilated; bones shattered to pieces; holes that you could put your
clenched fist into, filled with dirt, mud, bits of equipment, and clothing until it all became like a hideous nightmare—as if they were living in the seventh hell of the damned, and the thousand guns seemed
to be laughing in fiendish glee at their work as they spurted forth
their messengers of hate and destruction."

O.G. made it through two more years of the war, carrying the
wounded, running water to the lines, and his only physical injury was
a groin ailment. He was promoted to corporal, awarded the Good
Conduct Badge and the Military Medal, and granted the army's permission to marry his French girlfriend, Anna Marie LeFait, before he
was discharged in 1919. His army file and his unit's diaries don't reveal
how much harm was inflicted on my grandfather's mind. And it's
hard to measure from the way he lived after the war. He was trouble
before he took up the gun and he was trouble after.

But from the few stories I have heard of his restless life, and from
a cracked photograph of O.G. in uniform, I can guess that war never
completely let go of him. In the picture, he is posed next to a tall
white stool, against a backdrop of what looks like warplanes in a dog-
fight above the countryside. A touch of the rascal's smirk has survived,

but his sunken eyes look tired and sad. He looks defiant and defeated all at once. My father was delivered on Christmas Eve 1921 into the arms of this conflicted man to inherit a legacy that he would then bequeath to me.

Ray grew up in the village of Minto, New Brunswick, whose men had been mining coal from an open pit at nearby Grand Lake since 1639, when North America's oldest working mine started shipping coal to Boston. His family's house was on Main Street, next to Doc Gardner's and DiCarlo's General Store. In a bleak, sepia-toned photograph from the early 1940s, Main Street is a broad dirt road full of potholes and a long puddle as big as a pond.

Minto was a magnet for immigrants from Belgium, France, Germany, Romania, Poland, and other parts of Europe, who came to the village with one thing in mind: they wanted to dig coal. They worked when they could—or if the urge moved them. In the months before the Great Depression gave way to war, Minto's miners were lucky if they earned money three or four days a week. It was common for fathers to take sons as young as fourteen some ninety feet down into the mines. Boys worked with picks and shovels alongside men, pushing cartloads of mud along narrow tracks or digging and chipping away at coal faces, bent over in spaces just eighteen inches high where the temperature was a steady forty-seven degrees, and it was so wet that the rock was like clouds pouring rain.

It was a grim, often depressing life, and more than one miner ended it with suicide by dynamite. A lot of the men kept sticks of it, and blasting caps, at home for different DIY jobs. Doc Gardner told of searching half an hour for one man's heart and still not finding it. He'd wired a stick of dynamite to a battery and blown himself up. Another miner stuck some dynamite under the kitchen table, lay on top of it, and said goodbye.

Minto had a hard-nosed reputation and O.G. helped spread it far and wide. He could snap and do something crazy at any moment. Ray was walking home from school for lunch one day when he saw the house on fire, which his father admitted starting. Folks suspected O.G. needed the insurance money for his next big idea. While he watched the house burn, neighbors braved the flames to at least save the fridge.

Ray was fast running out of reasons to stay in Minto. After he got hit in the right eye with a pickax while working in the mines with his father, Ray insisted he wasn't going back down to work the coal faces ever again. When Germany invaded Poland and World War II began in the fall of 1939, he finally saw the door open to a bigger world that promised room and board and a steady paycheck.

This is the story about my father that I cherish most: He badly wanted to join the fight in World War II, but he was just seventeen. So he got O.G. to swear in an affidavit that the boy was really a man of eighteen, and enlisted with four schoolmates on Labor Day 1939. It was just one day after Britain declared war on Nazi Germany, and just one day before he was supposed to go back to high school. Because of the pickax injury, Ray's eyesight was weak enough to keep him out of the army, which was his only ticket out of a life in the coal mines. So he needed a good trick—and fast.

On enlistment day, the doctor noted on Ray's Certificate of Medical Examination that he stood six feet, four inches tall, weighed 145 pounds, had a light complexion, blue eyes, "good development," and a strawberry birthmark inside his shoulder blade. "Are you now receiving, or have you in the past received, disability pension or compensation?" the doctor asked.

Ray copped to the pickax injury, which the doctor duly noted on his certificate. When it was time for the eye test, Ray took a spot in line behind his friends. Each one memorized a row from the eye chart, and whispered it to him on their way out. When his turn came, the doctor wrote on the certificate: Vision, right 20/25; left 20/30. His hearing, lungs, urine, and reflexes all checked out, he was clean of any sexual or other diseases, he didn't have flat feet, nasal trouble, or varicose veins. He was officially fit to fight.

Ray was one of several Minto men who went off to war against the fascists while others stayed behind and guarded European Jews who had fled them. Just south of Minto, where the Richibucto Road passed through the village of Ripples, the Canadian government built No. 70 Internment Camp in a forest swarming with bloodthirsty blackflies and mosquitoes. For the first year, it held 711 Jews, among them physicians, scientists, artists, and children who had fled to England to escape Hitler's advancing Holocaust. Claiming there might be spies among them, British prime minister Winston Churchill asked Canada to take them. They were promptly locked up as a security threat.

Across the Atlantic, it was taking Ray much longer to get into combat than he had bargained for. He spent the war's first few years in England, training in battle drill and assault tactics, working his way up the ranks from corporal to lieutenant, trying to beat a bout of scabies in hospital, waiting to be called into action. His time finally came in 1944, when the D-Day invasion of Normandy loomed. He was one of 673 Canadian army lieutenants and captains who volunteered to fill the decimated ranks of British army officers and lead a platoon against the Nazi forces. Most were frustrated men eager to get into the fight.

"Tall. Splendid physique, soldierly," wrote Brigadier R.D. Sutherland, chairman of the Officers Survey and Classification Board about Ray. "Frank. Pleasant manner. Clear, decisive expression of thought. Determined and confident. Creates good impression. Previous overseas service."

Ray was posted as a platoon commander in the 1st/7th Battalion of the Royal Warwickshire Regiment, which was part of an Allied force sent in to take Caen, a medieval city of winding narrow streets, stone houses, and ancient abbeys, convents, and churches. It was also the burial place of William the Conqueror, who led the Norman invasion of England in 1066. At a briefing at 3 p.m. on July 7, Allied commanders laid out the assault plan using sand models and aerial photographs. Ray's orders were to lead his platoon into Villons-les-Buissons, a small farming village of limestone homes four miles north of Caen. It was defended by some of Hitler's most fanatical fighters, including seventeen- and eighteen-year-old members of Hitler Youth in the 25th Panzergrenadiers, diehard Nazis who fought from reinforced basements under relentless bombardment and the terrifying blaze of flame throwers that howled like dragons.

Their commander was SS-Brigadeführer Kurt Meyer, who led a ruthless battle against attacking forces through June from the Abbey d'Ardennes, near Villons-les-Buissons. When his soldiers brought him eleven POWs, who surrendered during a heavy battle on June 8, he ordered them executed. They shot some in the head, and apparently clubbed others to death, in the garden of an adjacent château. The following day, seven more captured men were murdered. Meyer was later indicted for war crimes and the counts against him included the charge that he ordered his teenaged soldiers that they must not surrender, or take any prisoners. He was imprisoned in New Brunswick and later transferred to West Germany, only to be released in 1954, after serving just nine years for his crimes.

Meyer's forces had fought back so hard through June that the brigade called Villons-les-Buissons Hell's Corner. In less than a day, Ray's platoon helped take the village. During the fierce fighting, a bullet tore into his right thigh. But in those rare moments when he spoke of the war later, the true terror was reborn in memories of his men. A machine gunner hit one of them as Ray lay in tall grass. Unable to move closer, he could only watch the wounded young soldier writhe in pain. Each time he stirred, the German gunner hit him again.

Ray wasn't admitted to hospital until July 10, a day after the smoking ruins of Caen's northern districts fell to the Allies. While the rest of Ray's unit scavenged guns and ammunition from the battlefield, he was moved back across the Channel to Meanwood Park Emergency Hospital in Leeds. But the stalemate in northern France was broken. On August 24, Paris was liberated and the following week, Ray returned to duty. He volunteered to return to the front in early 1945, when the Allies were massing forces to cross the Rhine in Operation Plunder.

This time he was assigned to the 1st Battalion of the 51st Highland Division, named The Black Watch after the color of the regimental tartan on the Scottish soldiers' kilts. On March 23, 1945, Ray was preparing his platoon to join a massive assault by British and American forces that would capture thirty thousand of Hitler's soldiers, kill thousands more, and drive the holdouts deeper in retreat. The Allies' 5,500 artillery guns opened up along a twenty-two-mile front at 5 p.m., and four hours later the first assault battalions entered the water in amtrak landing vehicles under bright moonlight, with almost no return fire from the Germans.

Ray's platoon was tasked to help take the village of Speldrop, which consisted of around a dozen large farms and outbuildings. The assault went quickly and by 6 a.m. on March 24, C Company reported that it had cleared the village and taken more than sixty prisoners. But half an hour later a runner came into the battalion headquarters to report that the situation was fast falling apart. The Germans had launched a heavy counterattack from the northeast, down the main road into Speldrop. They fired from Spandau machine guns, three tanks, and two smaller, more agile, self-propelled guns. The Germans not only took back the village and freed their captured comrades, but also cut off one Black Watch platoon and half of another, and threatened to surround a whole company.

Another member of the unit had his revolver shot out of his hand, so he grabbed a shovel, charged the German, and beat him to death. Sometime during the assault against Speldrop, as the Germans fought back with flame-throwers and heavy machine-gun fire, Ray was walking down a village street, taking cover by a wall. Just as he was about to round a corner, he heard the sharp metallic click of a weapon cocked to fire. Thinking it was one of his own men, he shouted: "Don't shoot! It's only me."

The German pulled the trigger. The bullet struck the third finger of Ray's left hand, fracturing it in several places. He was among fifty-two men wounded in the Black Watch's 1st Battalion by the time reinforcements had moved in to take Speldrop late that night. The battalion lost at least twelve more men in the battle, including two officers. Another twelve were missing.

Ray survived his two wounds, and after the war he followed his father out west to Vancouver, where O.G. was living in a boarding house, still drunk, broke, and a fighter. Ray failed the entrance exam for engineering school, but the registrar told him to come back after finishing high school physics and apply to the new pharmacy school. He got in and worked part-time as an apprentice at While's Drug Store, and lived upstairs with my mother in a flat with a fold-up Murphy bed. Whenever the manager, Mr. Jones, needed help at the counter, he beat the pipes with a wrench to call Ray down. One night, O.G. phoned my father with his own emergency. He told him to hurry over with a bag of plaster.

"What happened to the other fellow?" Ray asked when he got a look at O.G.'s broken hand.

"What other fellow?" he asked.

"The fellow you hit with your hand."

"He called me a son of a bitch, and nobody's gonna call my mother a bitch," he replied. "I knocked him down the stairs."

O.G. outlived his son by six days shy of two years. Ray's kidneys eventually gave out and he bled to death in a Toronto hospital bed on May 24, 1961. He'd known for months that he was dying, but still found it too painful to talk about the war that had consumed the prime of his life. Warriors of his generation thought the horrors were to be suffered in silence. Those who did admit to fear, even just to get a few weeks' break, were usually humiliated. Airmen had only a fifty-fifty chance of coming back alive through clouds of flak that peppered Allied planes during air raids over Europe. But if one showed the good sense of being afraid, and said he wanted a little time off to get his head back together, he was declared LMF—Lacks Moral Fiber—and permanently grounded. To the men in uniform who send others off to die, a healthy sense of self-preservation was a career-ending disability.

After making it through the war, Ray had to do battle with his own body. He was diagnosed with polycystic kidney disease. The symptoms of what seemed to be eating away at his soul had not yet been categorized as a mental ailment. But they strongly suggest what we now know as post-traumatic stress disorder.

My mother, Mae, was a single child who grew up in Nanaimo, B.C., during the Great Depression, when the family name took a bit of a battering. Her grandfather, Senator Albert E. Planta, ran a financial insurance business, and in 1934, he was charged with fraudulently using a client's seven-hundred-dollar mortgage for his own use. He paid the money back, but a judge found him guilty and sentenced him to two years in the penitentiary. My great-grandfather's lawyer protested, "It was a case of a man of honor and high standing in the community being sacrificed to satisfy somebody's ill will." Conservative prime minister Robert Borden had appointed him to the Senate in 1917, during the First World War. As Planta was led off to prison, his supporters claimed it was a Liberal plot to get his Senate seat.

Later, my mother's father climbed out a window one night and ran off with an American woman. Every year, he sent flowers on my mother's birthday, but I didn't meet him until he was bedridden and unable to speak, after a series of strokes in Minnesota. When he died, my mom used the opportunity to bring her mother and stepmother together to reconcile, and to spread her father's ashes in the sea off the coast of Vancouver Island. They did it from the deck of a ferry, on a windy day. Much of the remains blew back in their faces, and they laughed together. My mother had learned at a young age that no matter how powerful the men of the family might seem, they could be gone before you knew it. When her turn came to raise a family alone, she was ready, and stronger than any person I knew.

She met Ray in Vancouver after the war, and when she started dating him in 1946, he was constantly tense and withdrawn. When anyone tried to help, he would shut down. Once, he was sitting next to my mother on the streetcar and then suddenly was gone out the door. My mother sat and watched him from the window until the streetcar reached the end of the line. Then she walked behind him to his boarding house and waited on the steps for him to come out and talk.

Darkness always came over him without warning; some unseen mental trigger drew him back, and he was in the tall grass again, the smell of cordite, cold earth, and fear washing over him.

4

LOOKING FOR TROUBLE

The childhood shows the man, as morning shows the day.
JOHN MILTON

Somewhere in the twisted strands of my DNA, I must be wired to crave risk. Before I was even old enough to talk, I began pushing my luck. Not long after I'd taken my first steps, I set out to test the limits of gravity—and my mother's sanity. I toddled over to the head of the stairs where, with my back turned to the bottom, I happily teetered at the top. No matter how many times she pulled me to safety, I'd be back to try it again. I was just strong enough to stand on my own, and already it was time to look for trouble. Walking the razor's edge soon became a habit, a game that I could win, and get attention on my own terms. I guess that just felt better than the troubled, misty-eyed stares, the nosy questions from complete strangers who stopped my mother to say how sorry they were, and to ask, "How did it happen?"

It was the age of thalidomide. The morning-sickness pills had caused birth defects in twelve thousand children in forty-six countries. Many were born with short arms and hands that looked like flippers. Compared to that, my birth defect was somewhere between cross-eyes and a cleft lip. To others, it appeared much more grave.

Sometimes it seemed every passing woman wanted to know what had deformed me, as if they were tracking the advance of some horrible plague down their street. I wasn't a thalidomide baby. Maybe God, or blind fate, was to blame. Maybe bad genes, or atmospheric nuclear testing. What did it matter? As far as I knew, I was just a normal kid, like any other. But even when the conversation is several feet above your head, and you just want to be somewhere else playing, you hear the stranger speak the pained words *How did it happen?*

And each repetition fixes in your mind that you are different. That sometimes you *scare* people. My mother taught me how to deal with it, on the surface. She drilled into me that when other children crowded around, I would wait for the bravest to reach out and touch the stump. She taught me to understand their curiosity and that I should try to teach children and adults alike not to be afraid or pitiful about what, after all, was pretty minor in a universe of troubles. I actually have a left hand, attached to a short arm, with a wrist that bends and a palm about the size of an infant's. For some inexplicable reason, my left side didn't develop along with my right, and my fingers didn't grow at all in the womb. As a baby, I had little nubbins the size of peas on my left hand, but the only thing between them and my palm were thin bits of skin. So a doctor surgically removed them rather than risk my tearing them off in the playground.

As I grew, I learned to turn an oddity into an asset. I entered Treasure Trail Nursery School wearing a prosthetic arm with a heavy, shiny metal hook that looked to other kids like the jaws of some robot arm, or a stainless steel beast. When I extended my left arm a few inches, a cable pulled a lever made stiff by a thick elastic band, and the hook slowly opened. It was guaranteed to get a shriek. Every time. So when the game called for a scary bad guy, I was it. When they needed a Captain Hook, I was a natural. I looked at the bright side.

Playing the dark character, with a smile, was an easy way to be needed.

Normally, having one hand means very little to me. I don't really notice unless someone else points it out—or I have to tie my shoes or pull the cork from a bottle of wine. You don't miss what you don't know. When I was a child, the doctors and therapists conditioned me with this stock lesson: No one is perfect. Everyone is different. You are not a freak, just special. Yet whenever strangers looked my way, I could tell from their piercing stares that the deformity was what they saw. It took longer for them to see me. Some never did. I always thought it was harder on my mother, who had to listen to all the unwanted sympathy, and wonder how I would overcome the stupidity of people like that.

I started out life in the Toronto suburb of Etobicoke, where my family had resettled from Vancouver before I was born. A developer had planted a maple tree in the center of each front lawn. My street was Princess Margaret Boulevard. My first school was Princess Margaret Public School. We had a milkman, a mailman, a paperboy, a plaza with a grocery store and a pharmacy a short walk across a field, and a bus stop outside our front door. As a kid, I knew only what I saw on the walk to school or in its classrooms, from the back of my mother's Chevrolet convertible, or in those most magic of moments, on trips to see my grandmother out on the Pacific Coast, where the air was a mix of brine, seaweed, and pulp mill sulphur. Most of the time, the world was no bigger than our split-level house, or more threatening than nighttime shadows on the bedroom wall, and whatever monsters lurked in the closet.

When my father died, my mother was left to raise five kids on her own. Following a plan worked out with my father in his dying months, she sold our upmarket bungalow near the exclusive St. George's Golf and Country Club. Then she moved us down the hill, from luxury to lower-middle-class. With the money from the house, a few modest investments, and a new job as a secretary in Air Canada's freight office, my mother had a fighting chance to keep us off welfare and in good schools, climbing back up toward where our father had left us.

Our neighbor on the left was the son of Italian immigrants. He worked on the loading dock of Brewers Retail, a government-owned beer store monopoly. His wife was a disembodied, megaphonic voice, shouting through the screen door: "Al! Hit that kid!" On the right lived the Wallaces, a retired couple. Every morning, through my bedroom window, I saw Mrs. Wallace washing dishes at the kitchen sink, and if I lingered long enough, she usually looked up and smiled. Mr. Wallace gave me a bat kite. He attached it to one of his old fishing rods so I could fly it as high as it would go, and be able to reel it in one-handed. A metal burr on one of the rod's eyelets soon cut through the line, the kite escaped on the wind, and the fishing rod joined the rest of the junk in the garage.

Our street was all white save for one Asian man, who shared a house with a white man. People whispered that they were homosexuals, which sounded to me like another exotic nationality. All I cared was that they had a power lawn mower. I cut their grass every two weeks for pocket money. But I heeded all the warnings and never went inside when they offered lemonade. Payment was always in cash, on the front doorstep. The real danger, I was convinced, was several doors down, around the corner, a forbidden place where a middle-aged man we knew only as The Child Molester lived alone. When I thought to look, I wondered who lived behind the overgrown shrubs and tightly closed blinds. Whoever he was, he was our Boo Radley.

Growing up in Toronto, my older brother and I used to sneak behind the orange Formica bar in our basement to fool around with a whiskey decanter that played tinkling Chopin. One day my brother took me there and made me swear not to tell anyone what I was about to see. He rummaged through some boxes and piles of paper and pulled out a black leather holster, unsnapped the cover, and carefully drew a black military pistol. "It's a German Lugar," he whispered. "Dad brought it back from the war."

The clip was empty and removed from the weapon's grip, but my brother still wouldn't let me hold the gun. I could only look, and wonder at the power of such a thing, and the man who once had his finger on the trigger. The look didn't last long. My brother quickly slid the gun back into the holster, closed the cover, and returned the weapon to its hiding place. It remained there, out of sight but clear in my mind, until years later, when the Canadian government announced a firearms amnesty to get unlicensed handguns off the streets. My mother, who always wanted to do the right thing, went down to the local police station and surrendered my late father's war trophy to the cops. I was sorry to see it go.

The closest friend I ever had, the person who guided my childhood, was a lost soul named Richard who homed in on me early on. He liked to stage epic battles with molded plastic soldiers in the imaginary jungle of his front lawn. Where I saw pebbles and anthills, he saw pillboxes and anti-tank berms. He knew all the names of the big land battles of World War I, so each encounter in the grass had a historically accurate title. To make the combat more realistic, he stuck ladyfinger firecrackers between the toy soldiers' legs and lit the fuses.

Richard also liked to eat anything you shouldn't: road salt, the powder sucked from a broken firecracker, pencil leads, and Mucilage glue that they handed out in little bottles with rubber-nipple tops at school. In time, he graduated to drugs and turned me on to them, too.

I'm sure my mom had more constructive endeavors in mind when she put a purple Panasonic Take-N-Tape under the Christmas tree one year. I was crestfallen at first. I thought it looked like a geeky lunch box. But when the weather warmed up, school let out, civic workers went on strike, and the grass grew tall in the field of electrical towers behind my house, the Take-N-Tape became very cool. Richard burned a small, circular patch in the field, close to the plaza that was our main source of hallucinogens. On muggy afternoons we would hide in the grass, drop acid, smoke pot to speed the LSD's effect, and listen to Pink Floyd's *Meddle* and *Dark Side of the Moon* in mono. That summer, it seemed all questions had perfectly clear answers.

I started high school at Martingrove Collegiate Institute, a windowless education factory, where I got stoned a lot, and played the class clown. By mutual agreement, I was transferred after the first year, which brought me back to the neighborhood where I thought I belonged. Richview Collegiate was just down the block from the clubhouse of St. George's Golf and Country Club, at the top end of Princess Margaret Boulevard. The architects of modern mass education hadn't intruded here yet. The classrooms had windows and the student body was small enough for the principal known as "Truckin' Tom" to greet each of us by name as he patrolled the hallways, making sure he knew who was there and what they were up to. But a better school, with richer kids, meant more powerful drugs. I quickly graduated from smoking pot at lunch to dropping hallucinogens like LSD and peyote just before gym class to get off on the colorful trails from kids doing somersaults over the vaulting horse.

One day, a friend introduced me to a visitor who managed to duck "Truckin' Tom" and walk through the school corridors. He towered above everyone, and everything about him said "dangerous criminal." He was a drug dealer in black leather pants, jacket, and boots, who said I could score something special if I followed him from the school to a woodlot across the road. He had a craggy face, talked about Vietnam a lot, and was at least twenty years older than me, which sent everyone else in the other direction. But I wanted to be stronger, cooler than I was, so I went with him. We talked in the trees for a while, and the conversation drifted to girls, and how I couldn't get any. The dealer had drawn a long hunting knife from his belt and he was digging the lethal tip into a dry log, his mind doing a slow burn as he spoke. "That's the trouble with chicks," he said, driving the blade deeper. "They always want perfection."

I was relieved when he sheathed the knife and said it was time to score. He took me north on the Islington Avenue bus to a motel at the city's edge, where he pulled out a bottle of rye and a baggie full of different-colored pills, a pocket-sized pharmacy of tablets and capsules of tantalizing shades, which he promised would send me up or down. My choice. He got a couple of glasses from the bathroom, poured us each a healthy shot of rye, and popped a tape in the cassette player on a bedside table. Then he rolled back the top of the baggie with both hands and told me to pick one, like a friendly neighbor offering candy to a trick-or-treater. I took two.

I washed them down with a belt of rye. I expected something sweet, and instead it burned the back of my throat, and I felt a pounding headache coming on. I drained the bathroom glass and let the dealer pour me another drink. He looked worried. He told me I'd taken heavy downers, and one was more than enough. The next thing I remember is him shaking me awake on the bed, hauling my right arm around his shoulder, like a soldier lifting a wounded comrade, and then dumping me into a taxi idling in the motel parking lot. Everything was spinning. My muscles were rubber. I threw up in the back seat of the cab. The dealer was starting to freak. "It's my little brother," he told the cabbie. "Can't hold his drink. Pull over here."

The taxi stopped in the middle of a road construction project, where noisy dump trucks, graders, and compactors pushing huge, knobby rollers were churning up clouds of dust. I was on all fours in the dirt when the cab door slammed shut and the taxi disappeared. It took all the mental strength I had left to try and thumb a ride. Someone picked me up and got me as far as the subway station, where I stumbled onto a bus, right next to a girl who lived around the corner from my house. I asked her to wake me up at our stop and passed out. I managed to get home and into bed before my mom got back from work. When I came to hours later, and realized it wasn't just a nightmare, I could only imagine what the dealer might have done to me in that hotel room during those lost hours, which should have shaken me to my senses. But I only reveled in the risk, and the escape, and took it as more proof that I was invincible.

Delusions of immortality are part of being a teenager. But mine were a little different. I didn't think I would live forever, just long enough to enjoy my teens. Even when I was a lot younger, I'd always shocked relatives by insisting that I didn't plan to survive much past eighteen. I was certain that's when the fun would end. Richard steered me toward books that sharpened my view that life can only be lived in the moment. He was a voracious reader, and he got me into Nietzsche, Hesse, and Camus, leading me on deep philosophical discussions under the stars while we were high on LSD. We talked about life and death, why we were here and was there a God. For a time, we elucidated a logical proof that, if carefully considered by a clear-thinking mind, suicide can be a perfectly rational and justified act.

It sounded good on whatever strain of LSD was on sale in the Glen Agar Plaza parking lot that week: Purple Microdot, Windowpane, or California Sunshine.

Richard thought it would be radical if I started driving to school. So

66

I borrowed my mother's yellow Chevy Malibu convertible, with an electric top and eight-track stereo, after she boarded a bus to work. Problem was I was only fifteen, too young to have a driver's license. After I mastered the route from home to school, up Princess Margaret Boulevard, a quick left and another one, I got really bold one spring afternoon. I tried to impress some friends by driving them to McDonald's with the top down, and Oscar Peterson's *Tristeza on Piano* blasting from the eight-track. Five minutes out of the school parking lot, a police cruiser pulled me over. The cops found a roach clip and a dime bag of pot in my jacket pocket. I was taken in to get a good scare from a cop in the juvenile crime unit, a Lieutenant Hand, who let me go with a warning. I promised my sobbing mother never to touch drugs again, and as soon as I got home, I even tossed a pipe hidden in my bedroom into the backyard bushes. But it wasn't long before I was back at it again.

Somehow I kept getting rescued from myself. One day I was cruising downtown, along Yonge Street, hoping someone would offer to sell me something. A guy on the sidewalk with a clipboard, who must have had a pretty good eye for losers, stopped me and asked if I wanted to take a personality test. It sounded like a healthy diversion, so I started following him to the "test center."

Suddenly a middle-aged man—a guardian angel in a brown corduroy jacket with elbow patches—bolted toward us from across the street, dodging traffic to catch up. "Excuse me," he said, catching his breath as the personality tester tried to quicken the pace. "I am a professor from the University of Toronto. Do you know where this man is taking you?"

"He's going to give a personality test," I replied. The professor pushed in front of me and made eye contact.

"No, he isn't. He's taking you to the Scientology office. It's a cult that steals people's minds, and everything they own."

The Scientologist who had picked me out of the crowd sensed me drifting toward the professor. He felt a good catch slipping the hook. "Don't pay any attention to this old fool," he said, smiling like my best friend. "Let's go do the test."

And then the professor put his hand in front of my eyes and snapped his fingers. It was like a spark had jolted my mind back to life.

"I think I'll pass," I told the personality tester, and escaped into the traffic.

It was a high school history teacher named Mr. Robert Scott who got me turned around in time to find a purpose to life. He didn't tell me how wrong I was, or give any lectures on drug abuse. I don't know if he ever knew how stoned I was half the time. He worked to inspire everyone. In Mr. Scott's class, an underachiever like me could banter with the smartest kid in school, and become friends. That's how I ended up in a canoe with Stephen Harper, future prime minister of Canada, when Mr. Scott took a small group of students paddling in Algonquin Provincial Park. Under a bright canopy of stars, I felt wonder again, without the drug haze. My mind opened to an endless universe of real possibilities. Adolescent nihilism suddenly sounded pretty stupid.

Harper always took the conservative side of the debate and I the liberal. He was straight-laced and bookish, I was a drug user and a big talker. But Richview Collegiate didn't have the impermeable teen cliques that would normally keep a nerd and a dope freak far apart. We used to talk current events and argue politics for the fun of it. I'm not sure what Stephen got out of it, but I liked the mental exercise of trying to score points against brilliance.

We sat near each other in Ed Warda's tenth grade geography class. Mr. Warda gave weekly tests to see how well we had memorized the latest slew of facts. He handed the marked papers back in order, from top grade to bottom, and Harper's name was always called first, with a perfect ten out of ten—until one day, when Mr. Warda's quiz included the question: How many moons does Jupiter have? The answer Mr. Warda had taught, the one in the textbook, was eleven, and that's what he expected his students to repeat back to him. But Harper had read the latest issue of *Science* magazine, which reported the discovery of a twelfth moon, and that's what he wrote on the test. "Class, what's our best answer?" Mr. Warda asked when Harper politely protested his first and only error. "The answer in the text," Mr. Warda replied to his own question. Had it been me, the injustice would have been answered with intemperate words, followed by a trip to the principal's office. At my previous school, I'd threatened to blow up the science teacher's car after he gave me a failing grade even though I'd been in hospital for three weeks, recovering from an injury suffered in a classroom chalk fight, just before the exam. But Harper always looked at the long term. He took the hit quietly, returned to official perfection the next week, and left no doubt who was the smartest person in the room.

In twelfth grade, the pressure was on to pick a career path. I had toyed with the idea of becoming a lawyer and took tenth grade Latin thinking it would give me a leg up into law school. I got about as far as mastering the conjugation of *wini, widi, wici* before admitting I wasn't cut out for dead languages.

It was the mid-1970s, the golden age of newspaper journalism, when Carl Bernstein and Bob Woodward's Watergate reporting brought down President Richard Nixon and combat journalists in Vietnam had exposed the war for what it was—an unwinnable blood-bath that was sapping American military strength and moral author-ity. To a teenager ready to conquer the world, journalism seemed just the ticket. I went from delivering newspapers to founding one, a com-pendium of my views that I pecked out on a manual typewriter and ran off on the school's mimeograph machine. I called it *The Final Edition*, and within a few issues, I got bored and the name became a self-fulfilling prophecy.

At our high school graduation ceremony, the master of ceremonies told the audience of our future plans. Mostly, it was a dull recitation of the same business schools, pre-med courses, and university names that parents politely applauded year after year. When it was Stephen Harper's turn, the emcee announced: "Taking a year off to go out west and find himself." I thought it was a joke. The smartest kid in the school had dropped out of university to soul search? It sounded like something I'd do after one spliff too many. Yet I had somehow been elected the graduating class valedictorian, and droned on from the lectern about how it was up to us to make things better, a naive reporter-in-waiting who thought the printed word was powerful enough to change the world.

5

COMBAT TOURIST

If I had a chance to visit another planet . . . I'd want to see the planet's principal features—what makes it tick. Well, the planet I've got a chance to visit is Earth, and Earth's principal features are chaos and war. I think I'd be a fool to spend years here and never have a look.

P. J. O'ROURKE, *HOLIDAYS IN HELL*

In my earliest memory of wanting to be a journalist, I'm in the back seat of our car, crawling slowly past a bad accident on the highway, wishing I could get out and take a closer look. I wanted the reporter's license to stick my nose where it wasn't welcome. On an aptitude test in high school, I forgot to fill in one of the bubbles beside sex, so the computer spit out results for both male and female. From the rest of my answers, it concluded I was most suited to be a female marketing executive. But suits and sales bored me. I wanted to stir things up, and after Watergate had made newspaper reporters seem so noble, I knew I had to be one.

The first journalism school to reply to my applications was Ryerson Polytechnic Institute, which my guidance counselor advised was a fine place to learn real newspaper work. It wasn't a university, which meant it wouldn't please my family, so when I was accepted, I planned to tell them "No thanks," but they checked out prospects carefully and told me to attend an interview, so I decided to go. I wanted to impress, to look serious and mature, the opposite of a drug-addled teen—my TV sense of a true newsman—so I wore a new suit and tie. That was my first mistake. An instructor with greasy hair, an ashtray overflowing with unfiltered Gauloise cigarette butts, and his feet propped up on his desk smirked as I took a seat in front of him, with a clear view of his worn-out soles.

He started by reviewing my spelling test, which only deepened his disgust. I hadn't heard the instructions right and assumed there was an error to be corrected in each sentence. So I misspelled a lot of words. He harrumphed and tossed the test over his feet, blowing cigarette ashes across his desk. He scowled reading the second test. It told me to imagine I was a news editor at a small-town paper and I had to choose which of two stories belonged on the front page: the closing of a local post office or a famine in Africa. Of course I picked the foreign catastrophe. It was dramatic and exotic, an obvious grabber. And also the wrong answer.

"Local always leads," the instructor said, and he told me to send the next applicant in on my way out.

Ryerson sent a rejection letter, but I got into Carleton University's journalism school in Ottawa. My guidance counselor had told me it was more into theory, but also had an excellent reputation. It just wasn't very *practical*. I soon discovered it also had clunky old manual typewriters. The keys were always popping off on deadline in reporting class and I'd have to crawl around on the floor searching for the *p* or the *s* or, as the clock ran out, just press ahead with metal levers stabbing into my fingertips to get my copy in on time. Dreams of safari suits and gunfire kept me going.

At Carleton, our student newspaper was called *The Charlatan*, which seemed fitting, so I volunteered to write for it in my first year. It was in the late 1970s, and I was bummed about missing Vietnam and obsessed with figuring out where the next big war would be. One night in the newsroom, my mind was drifting and I found myself staring up at a wall plastered with posters trumpeting various causes of the day. One caught my eye. It showed two African guerrilla fighters, running hunched down with assault rifles, as if they were coming over a rise, advancing under fire. It was celebrating the freedom struggle against apartheid white rule in Namibia, which neighboring South Africa controlled in defiance of the United Nations, and referred to by its colonial name: South West Africa. The guerrillas were from SWAPO, the South West Africa People's Organization. Across the top of the poster was the slogan: *SWAPO: The People Armed.* And it came to me, like a voice from above: That is where I must go.

I worried editors early. As a summer intern at the *Vancouver Sun* in the early 1980s, I drew the plum assignment of covering the Abbotsford Air Show. The organizers offered reporters various rides for stories that would provide free publicity, and the assignment editor who handed me the promotional pamphlet, along with the number to call to reserve my place, said the choice was up to me. "But whatever you do, no wing-walking," he barked.

I read down the list: flying with the Canadian air force's Snowbirds aerobatic team, or pulling heavy Gs in a fighter jet. Walking on the wing of a biplane called Ol' Thunder Pumper sounded to me like the only one that would make much of a story, so I called the air show flack and asked her to put me down for wing-walking. I was off shift when she called back to confirm, so she talked to the assignment editor. Within minutes, he was dialing my number. "The managing editor wants to see you. Get in a taxi and get down here now," he said, and hung up.

From across his desk, Bruce Larsen leaned closer and sized me up with eyes that were filming over with what looked like early signs of cataracts. He wanted me to cancel the wing-walking flight, and wasn't buying my insistence that it was perfectly safe, or my offer to sign a waiver releasing the newspaper, its editors, and shareholders, from any liability. "I don't want to be the first managing editor of the *Vancouver Sun* to kill a summer student," Larsen said.

I made up something about being enclosed in a cage that would ensure I couldn't fall off the wing, and agreed to wear a helmet normally handed out to reporters covering riots or other terrestrial dangers. The managing editor finally relented. I would get a ten-minute shot at being an amateur daredevil, standing on the top wing of Ol' Thunder Pumper as it flew into the sunset at 125 miles per hour, two thousand feet above the countryside.

As promised, I showed up for the flight with the newspaper's crash helmet under one arm. John Kazian, the real wingwalker, sniggered: "Wear it if ya like. But it's only going to make it look dangerous. Whatever makes you happy is fine with me."

Kazian didn't have much time for chest-puffers. He'd seen his share in Hollywood, where he did stunt work on *The Great Waldo Pepper* and *The Stunt Man*. His solo credits included wing-walking above Niagara Falls in 1971. I got the feeling I annoyed him, that he thought I was a putz ready to put a foot through a soft spot in his wing, and it made me nervous. He assured me his fourteen-year-old son wing-walked with the leather cap and goggles he'd suggested I try. I wasn't going to be outdone by an adolescent, so I quickly put them on, thinking I looked like a World War I flying ace instead of a dork.

Kazian helped me up onto the wing, where I pressed the small of my back against the strip of padding atop a narrow steel stand wired to the plane like a waist-high mast. I was afraid that if I pressed too hard, the cables would snap. Kazian locked the thin safety belt webbing around my waist, gave the thumbs up, and pilot Hank Schmel fired up the propeller. The single engine sputtered a little and stopped.

"It's just hot," Kazian shouted up from the tarmac. I nodded knowingly and forced my shoes further into the wing stirrups.

"It's just a gas lock," Kazian tried to reassure me. "You'll be up in a jiffy . . . and make sure you don't dirty up my airplane!"

After getting the engine going, we taxied to the end of the runway only to turn back again because the second plane that was supposed to carry a photographer up to record my brief stunt wouldn't start. When Ol' Thunder Pumper finally got airborne, the warm wind blew my cheeks up like a balloon, and splayed my legs open. I spent most of the flight fighting to get my right arm forward, elbow pressed into my gut, so I could wave at the photographer as we did a low pass over the airfield.

The *Vancouver Sun* printed that one, and a smaller silhouette of me flying into the sunset. When editors laying out the paper saw it, they figured the sun had to be above the plane, so they ran it on the front page with me flying upside down, legs bowed in the breeze like a swaggering cowboy's.

A staffer tacked a clipping of it to the union's space on the newsroom bulletin board, with a question written in ballpoint: "Is this what a summer student has to do to get a job?"

The next day, someone added a second clipping of our report on Ol' Thunder Pumper's crash on takeoff as Kazian was getting ready to do his act on the air show's opening day. The plane lost power because of a vapor lock, and to avoid smashing into fighter planes and other aircraft on display on the tarmac, the pilot swerved and flipped the biplane, which came to rest on its upper wing. Kazian was sitting in the front seat, and suffered only a minor neck injury. I would have been squished and scraped across the tarmac, but I'd taken a risk, gotten away with it, and the newsroom backslapping only cranked up my craving for the buzz.

I was accepted into the master's program at Columbia University's School of International and Public Affairs in New York, a global crossroads where so many experts passed through that you could get a fine education by crashing some of the many free seminars that the school hosted as brown-bag lunches. I wanted the seal of approval I thought an Ivy League diploma would impart, so I did all I could to get to Columbia even though I couldn't afford it. My grandmother came up with some of the money, and I was able to get a full scholarship for my second year, but I was short on the initial tuition and housing costs. So I had to defer my acceptance for a couple of years, with fingers crossed that the dollar exchange rate would shift in my favor. Instead of grad school, I went to Africa for some real-life lessons as a volunteer teacher in the small, desperately poor country of Malawi.

By the time I had enough for the first year's tuition at Columbia, I'd also learned something about real life, and about poverty. In Manhattan, I spent more time with books than I ever had before, trying to block out the city, the late-night moans coming from neighbors' rooms in residence, knowing that if I didn't buckle down and get a scholarship, I wouldn't be back for the second and final year.

After graduating from Columbia in 1987, I got a job as a city

reporter at the *Toronto Star*. I did my time writing police blotter stories and obituaries, and covering local politicians, while saving up
money for a working holiday in a war zone. The *Star* had few foreign
bureaus, and the competition to get posted to one was fierce. I was too
low on the pecking order to have any hope of going abroad on the
newspaper's bill. By the time I was ready to go on my own, it was
1989, the eve of Namibia's independence. I'd missed another good
war, so I scanned the map of the world and settled on Eritrea, far to
the northeast in the Horn of Africa.

Their war wasn't getting much coverage, and nobody seemed to
care, so the ego risks were minimal. If I failed to get in, or came back
with worthless stories, who would notice? The Eritreans had been
fighting for independence since 1961, when Emperor Haile Selassie
revoked the former Italian colony's autonomy and declared it a province of Ethiopia. Like neighboring Somalia, Ethiopia was a strategic
spot on the Cold War map, but it was Soviet competition, not Eritrean
rebellion, that made news in the Horn of Africa. It was just the sort of
obscure place I needed to test myself and see if I was fit to be a foreign
correspondent. Eritrea had another, more important advantage. The
main guerrilla group, the Eritrean People's Liberation Front (EPLF),
had offices and a guest house in neighboring Sudan. If I could hook
up with the rebels' representatives there, and convince them that I
really was a war reporter and not some errant backpacker, I'd get a
guided tour of their conflict.

First, I had to get a visa, which meant a detour to Egypt. Sudan's
army had seized power just a few months earlier and the junta did not
like nosy foreign journalists. So when I walked down a dark alley in
Cairo and joined the crush against the rusty window bars of the small
visa office with my application form, I needed something other than
"journalist" to write under Profession. I chose "mailman." I figured

that if it ever came to interrogation, I could easily talk about a phony mail delivery route. I was once a paperboy. Under Purpose of Visit, I wrote tourism. The visa officer gave me a skeptical once-over. "No tourists Sudan," he snapped, and the swarm of shouting laborers, traders, and other visa-hunters pressed in again, pushing me aside.

I kept going back for several days, fighting my way through to the window bars, where I tried to persuade the clerk of the depths of my sincerest passion—a lifelong dream, I shouted—to experience the beauties of Sudan. He looked even more skeptical. But for some reason, maybe to get rid of me, or perhaps to punish me, he finally relented.

I got my visa just in time to arrive in the blowing dust and trash and crippling heat of Khartoum for the Muslim Friday Sabbath in the holy month of Ramadan. Everything was closed tight. A taxi dropped me at a budget hotel on a deserted street and the front deskman escorted me into my room through low, double-slatted doors that reminded me of a linen closet. I had to duck to get through. Lying on the bed, listening to the moaning air conditioner blow hot air, I felt trapped. Maybe I wasn't such a genius. I had only two weeks' vacation, and I was barely halfway to the war zone.

The next day, I found the rebels' office, and they agreed to take me to Eritrea. (I'd been warned by Eritreans in Toronto never to utter the name of where I was going—even to Eritreans. Mentioning Eritrea to the wrong person could get me arrested and deported. So I immediately adopted the standard code: I wasn't headed for Eritrea but "into the field.") I convinced the officious Sudanese officer in charge of travel permits that an infidel mailman on holiday in the middle of Ramadan had a reason to visit Port Sudan, the rebels' transit point into neighboring Eritrea, for something other than spying. The EPLF wanted publicity for their forgotten war, so the guerrillas' local representative greased a few palms, and within a few days, I was in a jaw-rattling Land Rover following the dry riverbeds that the rebels used as roads. The vehicle barely got above a crawl as the driver rolled the Land Rover up and down rocks and boulders, stopping every hour or so to listen for the distant drone of the Soviet-built Antonov cargo planes. The Ethiopian air force crews opened rear cargo doors in flight and rolled bombs out the back. They weren't big on accuracy, which meant schools, clinics, and homes were more vulnerable to attack than the guerrillas.

We were well into the middle of an Eritrean nowhere when malaria parasites that I must have picked up from a Khartoum mosquito went to work. I was bouncing flat out in the back seat, swinging from uncontrollable shivers to a raging fever and back again, trying not to throw up my dinner of sourdough bread, boiled eggs, and goat. The ever-efficient EPLF guerrillas had doubled me up with a pair of Australian eye doctors scouting for a location to start an aid project. They had met Thomas Keneally at a book signing for his novel *Towards Asmara*, a story about an Australian journalist traveling through Eritrea's war with a feminist aid worker who was searching for her father. They told Keneally how much they loved his book and he told them they should go help the Eritreans, which, fortunately for me, they promptly did. They traveled with cases full of equipment and medicine that included Chloroquine tablets to treat malaria, so before they could do anything for Eritrean eyesight, they treated me for the week that we traveled through barren mountains.

We drove only at night, with lights out, to avoid the Ethiopian bombers and the mind-warping heat. The Eritreans were in their twenty-eighth year of a war for independence, yet the EPLF had an incredible certainty that victory was inevitable. The dawn of the age of live war as television entertainment was still two years off, and Eritreans had spent a generation fighting battles that rarely registered in the outside world. Theirs was not a small-time hit-and-run guerrilla war. They were dug into almost two hundred miles of meandering mountain trenches, just three hundred yards from their Ethiopian enemies at some points. Rebel men and women fought alongside each other, lithe warriors with trademark puffy Afros that made them look like some lost disco civilization. They were fighting the largest army in Africa, in some of the biggest land battles since World War II. In just one offensive in 1982, the EPLF killed forty thousand Ethiopian troops. Yet few outsiders had ever heard of a rebel army that had built itself, largely with Soviet-made tanks and other weapons captured in battle, into one of the best in the history of guerrilla warfare.

When the rebels finally won their war in 1991, it had taken them thirty years. They fought on just two plates of lentils a day. The war zone also suffered from chronic famine, and foreign donors insisted on giving most of the aid to the Ethiopian government. They didn't want to be accused of feeding guerrillas. The EPLF fighters wore shorts, bush shirts, and plastic sandals made in rebel factories dug deep into the mountainsides, safe from Ethiopian bombers. They also had surgery wards in mountain tunnels able to withstand direct hits from thousand-pound bombs. The rebels had even built a drug plant out of old shipping containers, fitted it with imported equipment such as ultra-violet lights and air purifiers to keep the lab sterile, and produced essential drugs like Chloroquine, antibiotics, and birth control pills.

The rebels didn't seem to care whether the rest of the world knew about them or not. They weren't pawns deployed by some far-off super-power, only to be dumped like spent weapons when the policy changed and they were no longer useful. Their strategy wasn't to provoke a fight, get television coverage of civilian casualties, and demand foreign intervention to win their war for them. They understood freedom to be a right that's taken, not a gift that's granted. They were in it to win.

Still fighting the malaria, I climbed a mountainside to the rebels' trenches overlooking the town of Keren. There was supposed to be a ceasefire, but Ethiopian warplanes droned overhead, dropping bombs here or there to keep up their skills. At the top of the ridge, I met Solomon Iyassu, a twenty-year-old farmer's son who had joined the EPLF when he was fourteen. The guerillas taught him how to read and write so that he could learn about the unstoppable march of revolution. Listening to his story in a cramped observation post, it was the first time I'd heard an ordinary person talk of surrendering to something bigger than himself, a power that wasn't a God I refused to believe in. "If I die, that's the price I pay for independence," he said simply. "I know the rest will continue to victory."

I would have happily given my life on the spot if I could live the heroism of his words for just one moment.

I returned to Toronto from my trip with enough pictures and notes for a few stories that I freelanced to the *Star*. But I was quickly back on the midnight shift, on the far edge of the newsroom, longing for the sounds of mountain wind, spoons against tin plates, and rebel laughter in the African darkness. Behind the glass walls of the police radio room, where I was supposed to be listening for hints of news in the squawk and squelch of more than a dozen police, fire, and ambulance scanners, I planned my next vacation in a war zone. I chose Angola, largely because the UNITA (The National Union for the Total Independence of Angola) guerrillas were backed by Washington, so the travel arrangements were easier to make—and a lot more comfortable.

For years, successive administrations in Washington had condemned white rule in South Africa, yet the Central Intelligence Agency cooperated closely with apartheid leaders in support of the secret war in Angola.

During the Cold War, beating the Soviets was more important than promoting democracy and rights for the black majorities in South Africa and Angola. When I set out for my summer holiday visit in 1990, Angola had been independent, but locked in a vicious civil war, for fifteen years. South African president F.W. de Klerk was starting to dismantle apartheid, and the Cold War was ending. Yet South Africa and the CIA were keeping Angolan rebel leader Jonas Savimbi and his UNITA forces alive in their war against a Marxist government that controlled a vast supply of oil, diamonds, and other valuable resources. Four years earlier, President Ronald Reagan had hosted Savimbi at the White House and heralded him as a hero in a global war for freedom. Most other governments treated him as a power-hungry rebel whose refusal to compromise had condemned a potentially rich country to ruin.

UNITA's public relations consultants in Washington were as efficient as they were discreet. They told me to fly to South Africa and leave the rest to them. In early August, I landed on another tourist visa at Johannesburg's Jan Smuts Airport, where I was met by a man in a safari shirt, tight khaki shorts, beige woolen knee socks, and desert boots—the basic Afrikaner uniform. He was holding a sign welcoming, in black felt marker, "Mr. Wartson." I was new to the etiquette of covert war, and nervous about slipping up, so without a word between us, I followed and got into his four-wheel-drive. He dropped me off at a nearby Holiday Inn. "Wait in your room until you are contacted," he said as I stepped out of the car.

Jet-lagged, I went to sleep. A day passed. No call. Another day passed. No call. I was starting to think they really had been waiting for Mr. Wartson, realized their mistake, and dumped me. On the third day, the phone rang and the voice told me to be ready by mid-afternoon. Another man in a safari shirt, short shorts, woolen knee socks, and desert boots picked me up and dropped me at northern Johannesburg's

Lanseria Airport, next to a silver DC-3 Dakota. The twin-engine plane looked like the one Humphrey Bogart and Ingrid Bergman kissed next to in *Casablanca*, so I felt a tingle of a romantic war adventure. Not for long. The pilot and copilot, also in standard khaki Afrikaner bush dress, showed me to a single seat in the plane carrying supplies to Savimbi's forces. They pointed to some cold sandwiches and cans of beer in a plastic cooler. The loud hum of the engines, and the soothing beer, lulled me to sleep. A buzzer and flashing light next to the cockpit woke me when we were on approach to Savimbi's airstrip. I unbuckled my seat belt and stood to look out a small forward window from where I could just make out the ground as the plane circled in the dim light of a waning moon. Dozens of oil lamps illuminated an outline of the grass airstrip so the Dakota could land.

"This is a cool war," I thought.

Savimbi and his foreign advisers ran a tight ship, so I was welcome to see what they wanted me to see, but little else. My handlers wouldn't let me go far from Savimbi's main camp at Jamba, north of the Namibian border. But I got an interview with the rebel leader, to the accompaniment of soft classical music playing on his bunker stereo. Savimbi was a heavyweight autocrat prone to bizarre rants and binge drinking, which gave rise to speculation that he was either psychotic or syphilitic—or both. Our encounter produced a brief, guileless story in the *Star* about Savimbi's desire for peace in Angola, which would have to wait another eleven years. His death in early 2002 allowed an end to more than three decades of war. The rebels' PR people also took me to see badly burned villagers and insisted they were victims of chemical warfare, which was widely dismissed in North America as propaganda. Saddam Hussein had sent Iraqi forces into Kuwait earlier that month, so there was little interest in the West about stories from the African bush.

83

WHERE WAR LIVES

The trip was not a total bust, though. About thirty-five miles east of the bombed-out town of Mavinga, I visited a rehab center for mine victims and other disabled Angolans. When the propaganda tour was almost over, I got to chatting about life and war with the director, Lieutenant Colonel Antonio Chassanha. He was the Angolan-born son of Portuguese settlers who decided to stay when his parents fled to the motherland. He joined the colonial army that brutally defended Portuguese rule until the end in 1974. Chassanha fought against all three guerrilla movements, proxies of the United States, South Africa, the Soviet Union, and China, during the independence war. When the Portuguese lost, he joined UNITA, which quickly turned against a transitional government that was supposed to unite the liberation forces.

Like many of the guerrilla fighters I had met, Chassanha thought I'd lost my left hand to war. When I told him it was actually an act of God, the thirty-eight-year-old colonel explained why that might not be such a good thing for someone planning a career in war zones. He had been wounded seven times by shrapnel and bullets, one of which destroyed nerves in his leg in 1984. Each wound was a charm to him. "I've learned one thing in war," Chassanha said. "If you go many years without getting wounded, the first time is going to be fatal. But many wounds over time are safe. It's a certainty of survival."

To this day, I repeat his war wisdom in my mind whenever I'm on a back road in someplace like Afghanistan, wondering whether the ambush is just around the corner. And I hope the colonel was wrong because I've gone so long without getting hit.

By my third war zone vacation, I was ready for the big time: Somalia. It was one of the places in the world where a reporter could type the word *anarchy* and only be guilty of understatement. It was January 1992, and Somalis were already embroiled in a civil war. The only way in was on one of the daily flights that delivered tons of *qat*, the

84

Somalis' favorite chew. For a regular addict, its buzz is slightly stronger than what you would feel after knocking back a few double espressos. Qat, pronounced *chat*, kept the militia fighters in kill mode through the night. They usually broke for siestas in the afternoon.

To get a seat on a qat flight, I simply showed up at dawn at Wilson Airport on the outskirts of Nairobi, Kenya, found a willing pilot and paid him for the amount of qat he had to leave behind to fit me in. It looked like the twin-engine plane that I'd dreamed of flying in as a kid stretched out on the rec-room floor, watching *Sky King* reruns on TV in the 1960s. There was just enough space between the stacks of burlap sacks and the ceiling for me to crawl up to the copilot's seat. We landed at K-50, an airstrip south of Mogadishu, so named because it's fifty kilometers from the capital, on a road pockmarked with shell craters and littered with shrapnel that made it virtually impossible to reach Mogadishu without at least one flat tire.

The pilot stayed just long enough to drop his load of qat, and me, into the hands of crazed Somali gunmen. They were wearing wraparound shades, cradling rocket-propelled grenade launchers and heavy machine guns, and wearing bandoliers of glistening bullets over their shoulders with the style of starlets in mink stoles. They didn't like unannounced guests, but the sight of U.S. dollars warmed them up a little. For a few hundred more than it cost me to fly there, the gunmen agreed to drive me to Mogadishu. It was my first lesson in the extortion that passed as Somali negotiations: take it or die.

We got two flat tires on the way, but we made it to Mogadishu without the gunmen firing a single shot in anger, just warning bursts here and there to keep bandits at bay. I had no idea where I could stay, so the driver dropped me at the one place he'd seen foreign guests wander into out of nowhere: the home of Raymond Marchand, the only foreign oil worker still toughing it out in Somalia.

He wasn't in when I knocked, but his Somali housekeeper must have assumed I belonged there because he showed me to a bedroom. I was exhausted after the qat flight and the drive from the K-50 airstrip, so I quickly fell asleep.

Later, the housekeeper woke me up and said Mr. Raymond would like me to be his guest for a late lunch. Groggy, I took a seat at one end of a long dining table, and my host sat at the other. Marchand told me he was Belgian, although I later heard he was French.

"Do you mind if I ask what you're doing in Somalia?" I said, trying to be careful not to offend. I needed the room.

"I'm the country manager for Conoco," he replied. "It's an oil company. You've heard of it?"

I asked him why he hadn't fled with everyone else. Somali clans were still battling in the streets with tanks, anti-aircraft guns, and rockets fired down long boulevards. Surely oil prospecting wasn't a priority in all of that.

"I'm trying to get our drilling equipment out," he said.

Naively, I asked whether that was worth risking his life.

"My company doesn't like leaving things behind," Marchand told me.

Somehow Marchand's interests seemed to run a lot deeper than crude, but it would be years before I saw declassified U.S. documents that showed how closely the oilman worked with the American government.

6

GUARDIAN ANGEL

We should not forget to entertain strangers,
lest we entertain angels unawares.
HEBREWS 13:2

Just before the Gulf War started in 1991, the *Star*'s Middle East correspondent left Iraq on the last flight out. I was pulled off the city desk in Toronto just in time to fly halfway around the world and get into Baghdad hours before the airspace closed.

"Maybe you should go back to your country and visit us another time," an Iraqi Airways flight attendant said to me as an almost empty Boeing 747 sat waiting for takeoff from Amman, Jordan, to Baghdad. Wistfully, she added: "If I come out again, maybe I will stay here."

At Baghdad's airport, a customs agent confiscated the shortwave radio that was supposed to be my lifeline to the outside world. Watching him scribble a chit, and attach half to my radio with an elastic band, I imagined it sitting on the officer's shelf, in a Baghdad market, or in fragments in the rubble of a bombed building. I was glad I'd ditched my copy of *Republic of Fear*, a catalog of the Hussein regime's horrors by Iraqi expatriate Kanan Makiya, somewhere en route. At least I couldn't be arrested as a subversive smuggling anti-Saddam literature. But without the BBC on shortwave, or Makiya's insight as a handy primer on Saddam's propaganda, I was pretty much a novice walking blind into the biggest, most dangerous story I'd ever covered.

And I was overjoyed to have made it in time.

The white-and-orange taxi dropped me off at my assigned hotel, the five-star, eighteen-story Al-Rasheed, built in 1983 on the west bank of the Tigris River. Iran and Iraq had begun firing Scud missiles at each other's capitals in the mid-1980s, so it was comforting that the Al-Rasheed's defenses were battle tested when I checked into room 630. The guest rooms had double-glazed bulletproof windows and, it was rumored, hidden cameras in the TV sets so that Saddam's sadistic Mukhabarat intelligence agents could keep a close eye on visitors. I changed in the bathroom.

The hotel had none of the romance I'd read about in stories of other legendary war correspondents' haunts, like the Continental in Saigon or Beirut's Commodore. The Al-Rasheed had the concrete-cage look one would expect from the headquarters of some powerful government agency, say, the intelligence service. In reality, the undercover Mukhabarat agents on duty in the Al-Rasheed's lobby seemed to spend most of their time slouched in boxy armchairs, chain-smoking, and glowering at anyone who passed. Instead of the classic war correspondent's bar, with the single malt and Cuban cigars, the Al-Rasheed had the One Thousand and One Nights Disco, where Saddam's son Udhay used to shake his groove thang before he was disabled in a failed assassination attempt. The Al-Rasheed had another, more troubling distinction: the U.S. military claimed that Saddam had a bunker and command-and-control center, complete with fiber optic cable links, beneath the hotel, which was a not-so-subtle way of saying we were living in what might be deemed a legitimate target. The thought left a knot in my stomach. My only concept of U.S. air strikes on an enemy city came from newsreel footage of the 1972 Christmas bombing, when some seven hundred U.S. B-52s carpet-bombed Hanoi and Haiphong. I assumed the Al-Rasheed's neighborhood would be a smoking ruin not long after the first air-raid sirens sounded.

Precision strikes with bombs that followed laser light to their targets, or cruise missiles that could be programmed to fly low and long toward a designated window, were little more than intriguing notions to most of us on the eve of the first Gulf War. The new reality of high-tech air war was still waiting for its live debut, just hours away, on CNN. And I was still trying to figure out how to work the Telex machine.

It sat behind a counter in the Al-Rasheed's lobby, where a kind Iraqi woman waited for reporters who wanted to file stories, or to send messages about the latest rumors of war to editors around the world. First, they had to type their copy on a teletype machine that spit out a yellow paper tape full of holes. That was rolled up, held closed with a paperclip, and delivered to the Telex lady, who fed it into her own machine and transmitted the messages and stories when she could. I had trouble getting mine to go through to Toronto, so I spent a lot of time chatting with her over the counter as she worked her way down my list of numbers. She quietly typed each one out on her machine, waited for connections that didn't come, and apologized with a weak smile. She told me she would rather be home with her family. She was afraid the bombing would start and she wouldn't be able to reach them. I nodded in sympathy and asked her to try sending my yellow tape again.

As darkness fell on January 16, 1991, the attack rumors were coming fast and furious, and I still couldn't get through to my editors.

That morning, the 8 a.m. deadline for Saddam to pull his troops out of neighboring Kuwait had come and gone, and Baghdad remained quiet, shrouded in thick fog. But French radio had reported B-52 bombers taking off from the Indian Ocean island of Diego Garcia, and a slammed car door was enough to make me jump. By sunset, journalists were rushing in and out of the lobby, some making plans to be on the streets when the first bombs fell, others trying to figure out how to escape, or at least haggling with the desk clerks for new rooms on lower floors. I had the woozy feeling of being on the deck of a slowly sinking cruise ship when the call goes out to don life jackets.

By this point, word had spread through the Al-Rasheed that White House spokesman Marlin Fitzwater had made a personal appeal for journalists to leave Iraq, something along the lines that as a friend of some of the reporters in Baghdad, he feared for their safety. I was relatively new to the mind games of war then, unaware of the Pentagon's tendency to push independent reporters out, so I assumed the worst. In fact, the use of cruise missiles and laser-guided bombs gave foreign journalists holed up in a five-star hotel good odds of surviving the air war. That would only be obvious to me in hindsight.

"Why don't you go up to the CBS suite and ask Allen Pizzey if you can use his phone?" someone hurrying onto the elevator suggested. "He's Canadian too."

I only knew what I'd seen on TV, a seasoned, Emmy-award-winning war correspondent for what was then America's most respected network. Naturally, I assumed he was American. But he was from Brantford, Ontario, and I was desperate to make a phone call, so I strode into his suite and played the Canadian card. Pizzey let me call Toronto, which sorted out my Telex number problem. Then he invited me to take all the beer I wanted from his ice-filled bathtub. He and his crew were packing up, planning to head for the Jordanian border as soon as possible. Trying to sound like I knew what I was getting into, I chugged my first beer and told Pizzey I was staying. He looked at me like I was crazy.

"I just got here," I told him. "I can't leave now."

Pizzey started pulling various emergency supplies out of boxes and tossing them next to me on the couch. Plop. A package of large pressure bandages. He explained that they might help if I got a sucking chest wound. Plop. Packages of dried food. Pizzey said I should expect to be feeding myself for a while. Plop. A jar of water purification tablets. Pizzey warned that the hotel's water supply would be cut off early in the bombing. I got up and pulled another beer from the bathtub. As I sat getting drunk, slowly surrendering to the truth that I didn't have the first clue what I was getting into, the phone rang.

It was the network's Pentagon correspondent calling from Washington. He told Pizzey something like: "I talked to your family, and they're all fine, but two of the kids have colds." That was the prearranged code to let the correspondent and his crew know how much time they had left before zero hour. It was around midnight Baghdad time and the bombing was a little over two hours away, Pizzey announced to a collective groan from the crew, who kept on packing. I finished off another bottle of beer, thanked Pizzey for his help, dropped the pressure bandages and other stuff in my room, and headed down to the lobby to see if the Telex lady was still on duty behind the counter.

She was gathering her things, getting ready to leave, but took pity on me and broke the rules by allowing me to sit at a keyboard next to her and have a teletyped conversation with Bill Schiller, the *Star*'s Johannesburg bureau chief. As we talked by Telex, Schiller kept foreign editor Paul Warnick on the phone and relayed to him what I was saying. I told him about CBS's coded message, and Warnick said I should leave Iraq by Saturday. It was in the first hour of Thursday morning and I was just getting the hang of things. I asked for permission to stay longer.

"SHOULD ADD THAT VARIOUS SPANISH PEOPLE HOLDING ON, AND OH YES, A FAIRLY FINE YOUNG THANG FROM IRELAND," I typed.

"HOLD ON," Schiller replied. "WARNICK NOW ORDERS YOU OUT TOMORROW. BUT HE WISHES YOU THE BEST OF LUCK ON THE IRISH LASSIE IN THE NEXT 24 HOURS."

I wanted to type back and, like a teenager bucking curfew, argue with the foreign editor's exit order. But I remembered one of the first lessons I'd learned as a foreign correspondent: say nothing, and you can always claim you didn't hear the order. Just blame a bad line.

"PAUL ARE YOU THERE," Schiller typed, followed by twenty-three bells, ringing out the urgency.

"PAUL," and twenty-seven bells. A long pause and I stared at the machine as it rang another cold, anguished string of forty bells.

"COULD YOU PLEASE CALL PAUL WATSON TO THE MACHINE?" And fifteen bells. Then silence.

It was 12:38 a.m. on January 17, and the final preparations to bomb Iraq into submission were underway.

I was a little drunk, and very tired, so I went back to the sixth floor to sleep. I was just about dead to the world when a furious knocking at the door startled me awake. I opened it a crack. It was a European woman, a guest in a nearby room, I supposed, whom I couldn't recall meeting. "You'd better get an overnight case packed," she said. "For the bomb shelter."

I thanked her for the tip and tried to go back to sleep, but I could hear people rushing up and down the hallway, sounding anxious. I decided the scene would make good color for my story, so I got dressed and went back down to the lobby. My heart sank. The Telex lady was gone and her spot behind the counter was dark. Part of me was glad. When zero hour struck, at least she'd be with her family, and not surrounded by a bunch of screaming reporters thrusting yellow paper tapes at her. The other part of me was angry. How the hell was I supposed to send my story? I doubted Pizzey would be so generous with his phone when the war was on.

I sat down in the Telex lady's chair and looked for the machine's "On" button. Several attempts, and it just sat there, dead. I tried a few more button and key combinations and then suddenly the machine whirred to life. I typed Schiller's number: 428613. Nothing happened. It took me a while to figure out that I needed a country code in front of that. I searched through the Telex lady's drawers for a directory, scraps of paper, anything that might have the right code on it. I found a copy of an earlier message with the complete number.

I typed in 095428613 and hit return. The machine paused and spit back some numbers again. Nothing. No connection. Well over ninety minutes passed, and I'd retyped strings of numbers again and again, trying different speeds, going faster or slower, hoping for a link. Still I couldn't get through. Then it came to me. Each time the Telex lady typed a number to connect, she followed it with a plus sign. I typed in 095428613+.

"428613 TSTAR SA," the machine replied. I was connected. It was 2:01 a.m.

"HELLO BILL. ANYBODY THERE?" I hit the bell key fifteen times in case Schiller was asleep.

"YEAH I'M HERE," he replied. "GO AHEAD." I read the words with such a rush, it was as if I'd just been linked up from the dark side of the moon.

I felt guilty about leaving Schiller hanging the last time, so I got chatty and tried to talk my way out of the order to leave. I might not be able to get out if the Iraqis insisted I get an exit permit, I typed. Warnick wanted to know if I was being censored by Iraqi officials, which I wasn't. I had pirated the Al-Rasheed's Telex line, so the information ministry minders had no idea what I was transmitting.

We had just called it a night, and agreed to talk again after sunrise, when panic broke out in the lobby.

"ANYONE AWAKE?" I frantically typed, followed by five bells. It was 2:31 a.m.

"OF COURSE," Schiller responded. "WE WORK FOR A LIVING."

"PEOPLE RUNNING THROUGH LOBBY NOW FEAR COULD BE REAL THING MUST GO. ASSUME BOMBS DROPPING. OK?"

"OK LET ME HAVE A READ OF THIS," Schiller came back. "NO HANG ON . . ."

"BILL, BOMBS DROPPING AS I WRITE. COMPLETE PANIC HERE. AIR RAID SIRENS GOING OFF AND LIGHTS GOING OUT. WOMEN SCREAMING. ONPASS PLEASE."

The lobby's tall plate glass widows were vibrating with thunderous explosions. I shouted from behind the counter at one of the hotel staff members, who were running past, pulling on powder blue flak jackets. "Has the war started?"

It was just anti-aircraft fire, not bombs, he insisted. As people streamed down the stairs to the Al-Rasheed's bomb shelter, next to the bowling alley, I typed to Schiller that it was probably a false alarm.

"PLEASE ALSO ADD THAT HOTEL STAFF HANDING OUT GAS MASKS."

The line went dead.

I shifted to the next Telex machine and got Schiller again. He wanted to confirm: Was I saying the war was on or wasn't I? I had no fucking idea. Peering over the Al-Rasheed's front counter, seeing intensely bright flashes and hearing cannonading booms that shook the lobby windows, it sure seemed like war. But I couldn't get a clear enough look at it from the Telex lady's chair and I didn't want to get up and risk losing the link. Fortunately, several floors above me, CNN's Bernard Shaw was telling the world on live television: "The skies over Baghdad have been illuminated. This is thunder, this is lightning, this is death—this is hell."

As the anti-aircraft fire picked up again, and the explosions intensified, the Telex clicked back to life.

"OKAY. JUST GOT A CALL FROM T.O. THEY SAY CNN REPORTING IT HAS STARTED."

And the old journalism was blown away by the new.

At 2:55 a.m., what sounded like low-flying jets streaked across the sky and two heavy blasts rocked the whole neighborhood. Iraqi anti-aircraft gunners on nearby buildings opened fire, but I know now they were probably shooting blindly at stealth fighters or at cruise missiles that were streaking down Baghdad's broad streets, making sharp turns and crashing with massive blast force into their targets. Seconds before 3 a.m., after I helped a Canadian Press reporter file her brief dispatch, I tried one last time to catch up with history.

"PAUL WATSON TORONTO STAR," I typed. "PASS ON BOMBS DROPPING NOW." I stared at the teletype, waiting for a reply.

The teletype machine didn't move. An air strike had knocked out the Telex link precisely at the top of the hour.

I wanted to get back to my room to watch the mesmerizing explosions, but security people in the stairwell forced me to follow the crowd of 150 people down into the hot, stuffy bomb shelter. The sign outside said it was the Ali Baba Room. It had heavy, airtight steel doors that closed with long handle latches. Standing next to an elevator shaft, I recalled seeing pre-war TV graphics of bombs aimed directly down stairwells. Listening to the heavy concussions rumble through reinforced concrete and steel, I wished I could find an escape to my sixth-floor room. Most of the people huddled inside the bomb shelter were Iraqis in pajamas and housecoats. People were sharing water or taking belts of Jack Daniel's. A baby cradled in the arms of an Iraqi woman fed from a bottle. When the shelter walls trembled with a long, loud rumble, and the dim lights flickered out, Iraqis began dancing under the white glare of a TV spotlight, chanting: "Palestine is Arab! Palestine is Arab! Down, down Bush!" A group of reporters listening to the BBC on a smuggled shortwave radio broke out laughing when an announcer said the Foreign Office was advising citizens of the United Kingdom now in the Middle East "to keep your heads down and keep listening to the BBC."

When the long, mournful wail of an air-raid siren sounded the all-clear at 5:45 a.m., I went straight to the Telex machine to see if I could make it work. I still hadn't filed a story on the start of the war. But the machine didn't even have power, let alone a working line to connect. So I climbed the stairs to my room, where I looked out through the bulletproof glass over a city blanketed in fog and the haze of bomb dust and smoke. I was shocked to see most of it was still intact. The air strikes had taken out single buildings, even bored out the cores of some, leaving scorched walls still standing, while others nearby were barely touched. The morning traffic was already starting to build. I collapsed half-naked on my bed, lulled into sleep by the distant thud of bombs and jet rasp.

I don't know how long I slept, only that I woke up dazed. The air was still alive with jet noise and intermittent explosions, and the toilet reeked because the water had been cut off. I walked down to the lobby feeling frantic and defeated. The best story of my career, and I still had no way to file it to my newspaper. A few TV networks had set up satellite phones on the patio by the swimming pool, but they were tied up with twenty-four-hour live coverage. The BBC World Service radio crew offered to read my story to an operator in London during a break, but anything longer than a minute wouldn't make it, and they gave no guarantees that the operator would have time to pass to Toronto whatever she captured on her tape recorder.

I sank deeper into a funk and wandered back through the lobby. Out of the corner of my eye, through an open door, I saw a dark-haired woman sitting in a chair with her back to the wall of a small office, talking to someone I couldn't see. I don't know what made me turn her way, but I did. When I stopped at the doorway, I saw two men behind a desk interrogating the woman and I asked her: "Would you like some help?"

She nodded yes, so I sat down in the chair next to her.

The men were Iraqi intelligence agents and the woman, I would learn later, was Jana Schneider, a farm girl who grew up to become a Wisconsin beauty queen, and then a Broadway actress, before she took a sudden turn and became a combat photographer. The Iraqis had marked her as a dangerous spy because she was caught in the middle of Baghdad, in the dead of night, taking pictures of the air strikes. Iraq's security forces came down hard on journalists who looked to them like spies. Later, three Western photographers, obeying an order to leave the country, were arrested, blindfolded, handcuffed, and beaten before they were handed over to an information ministry official who hugged them and apologized. A British reporter who headed to the abandoned U.S. embassy hoping to find a phone to file his report at the start of the war was beaten and interrogated in jail for three days.

Jana had gone to the same place, where she called her mom in Wisconsin to assure her Iraqis weren't anything like the ruthless enemy depicted on TV. Her father, her *hero*, ran down to the local tavern to tell his friends he'd just gotten off the phone with Jana and the war had started when CNN broadcast the same newsflash. After that, he always bragged that his daughter beat CNN. Jana went up to the embassy's roof and photographed Iraqi tracer fire as it arced across the night sky, and after getting her sweater caught several times on the concertina wire, headed down into the street where she set up her tripod in front of a mosque.

That's where the police picked her up, a little over an hour after the war started. They took her to a dark room, yelled at her, and started to stroke her with their guns, rubbing them up and down her legs, poking them in her mouth. She bolted and ran to a senior officer down the hall. He asked her to undress and said he wouldn't hurt her. She said he could pat her down for any weapons, and he settled for that, before tying her up. The neighborhood was bombed through the night, and when she was able to calm a crying Iraqi child whose parents were killed in an air raid, the Iraqi police eased up on Jana and delivered her to the Al-Rasheed hotel in the morning. When I finally saw her being interrogated, I had no idea who she was, or why she had been detained, so I could hardly defend her.

"We know who you work for, we know what you're doing here,"

the Iraqis kept repeating. Each time, Jana calmly insisted she was a photographer on contract with the SIPA photo agency, Save the Children, and UNICEF.

I just sat there, speechless, staring at the Mukhabarat agents, letting them know, in case they cared, that I had seen their faces.

That was enough to break their rhythm, and the fierce anger in the air quickly dissipated. Before long, Jana told me I could go, and as I walked back through the lobby, she sat chatting with her interrogators, winning them over as only Jana could. The skills she had developed on the stage served her well as a journalist.

Around noon on the war's first full day, a cruise missile shrieked low past the hotel on its way to the Iraqi national defense headquarters, where it exploded and set the building on fire for the third time. With no sure way to file the story to Toronto, I finally decided I'd better leave Baghdad.

Sadoun al-Janabi, head of the Iraqi government minders assigned to keep foreign reporters in line, set up a desk in the hotel lobby to register anyone who wanted to leave in a guarded convoy. He issued exit permits on the spot and assured me that anyone on the list would be welcome to return. I took the bait, figuring I could make a quick trip to Jordan, phone in my story from there, and hurry back to the war.

The BBC had hired four taxis to move its crew and equipment, and the front passenger seat was empty. For one thousand dollars U.S., I bought the seat but had to sit cross-legged, like a Buddha statue, on a large black case. The driver, Mr. Ramadan, had a healthy stock of whiskey to steady his shaking hands, and several cassettes of Beatles music, which he replayed constantly during the fifteen-hour journey to the border, on a superhighway that was targeted by U.S. warplanes trying to prevent Iraqi troops from moving Scud missiles closer to Israel.

Mr. Ramadan was especially proud of his keychain, a wrinkly plastic George Bush head. He'd written "DOWN" in black felt pen above the president's eyes. At 75 mph, with one hand on the wheel and the other on his whiskey bottle, Mr. Ramadan raced us through the desert to a blaring soundtrack of "Yellow Submarine," "Can't Buy Me Love," and my favorite, "Help!" The songs almost drowned out the jet noise, bomb blasts, and anti-aircraft fire all around us.

At the border, I paid another five hundred dollars to a Jordanian taxi driver to speed me through immigration and get me to Amman, where, too tired to think, I called the rewrite desk in Toronto and read scraps from my notes to a reporter who wrote the front-page story of what the headline writer called my "Escape from Iraq." In the peaceful light of a new day, it felt to me more like a chicken run from the biggest story I'd ever had.

I spent the rest of the war stuck in Jordan, standing for hours each morning at the "window of shame," the small, barred portal on an outside wall at the Iraq embassy in Amman, where foreign journalists pushed, shoved, and shouted, trying to find out if their applications for visas had been approved. Each evening, I joined the same crowd at a hotel bar, schmoozing with Mr. Adnan the Iraqi visa man, a short thug with a cruel, pockmarked face, who sucked down free drinks and made passes at women as fawning journalists tried to cajole him into letting them into Iraq.

I eventually gave up and bided my time covering riots in Palestinian refugee camps, getting knocked down by angry old ladies or teargassed by Jordanian security forces. And I hung out in cold rain on the border interviewing Iraqi refugees, trying to figure out what was going on in a conflict tantalizingly out of reach. Leaving the war too soon had been a big mistake. I swore to myself it wouldn't happen again.

7

FOR THE LOVE OF WAR

Men love war because it allows them to look serious. Because they imagine it is the one thing that stops women laughing at them.
JOHN FOWLES, *THE MAGUS*

The lucky break of figuring out the Telex machine just in time for the first air strike created the impression I had the one thing a foreign correspondent can't succeed without: the knack for being in the right place at the right time. I got promoted from city side to the foreign staff and the *Star* sent me to Johannesburg to be its Africa Bureau Chief in 1992.

Leaving the Gulf War early made me feel like a failure, but it also taught me the importance of sticking around. Of course, it was sticking around that led me to take the photo of Cleveland. As haunted as I was by it, I also felt flush with my new fame as a combat photographer. Within a few days of taking the photograph, I was jumping into bed with a friend after doing a live rooftop shoot with CNN. The self-deceit of heroism tends to last longer than the public's interest, so months later, I was still feeling much more impressive than I was. At a party at a colleague's home, I sat obsessing over a young woman across the room who was getting drunk next to her best friend, the daughter of a powerful agency bureau chief. All the media attention, the face time on CNN, had given me a new confidence with attractive women. I summoned the courage to go over and introduce myself, and somehow talked Khareen into giving me her phone number. She wrote it on the palm of my hand, and sweat had smudged the ink by the time I got home. After dialing a few wrong numbers, I got lucky, or so I thought, and we spoke again.

Soon we were on our first date, driving to her father's eucalyptus oil farm for the weekend. We skinny-dipped in the creek, had homemade knudles and beer for dinner, and listened to a tape I had made of George Gershwin's piano rolls. Khareen and her father were shocked that I knew nothing of rococo art and tried to enlighten me. The picture of the dead American soldier also came up, and Khareen's German-born father was displeased. He recalled being a child in a column of refugees during World War II, walking from the front as Allied troops advanced along the same road. "I can feel it now," he said, his eyes welling up. "I was so thirsty, all I could think of was water. I was crying for a drink of water. And then a black American broke away from the other soldiers and told me to sip from his canteen.

"I can still see his face," he said, smiling now. "Until the day I die, that will be the face of America for me."

I took it as a less than subtle dig. Real heroes stand up and help. I had only stood by and watched.

We retired to the living room for brandy, and Khareen stretched out on her father's lap. She stayed there for what I found an uncomfortably long time, with her arm across his shoulders, being cute. I got the strangest feeling I was supposed to be jealous. That night Khareen sat on the end of my bed talking about how her favorite grandmother's ghost often visited her there. As she left for her room, she turned at the end of the hall and raised her blouse to flash her breasts.

Some nights later in Johannesburg, we gorged on sushi, got drunk on sake, and went back to my place. We ended up naked in bed, touching but not having.

Soon after, I talked Khareen into sharing a house, which she kept warning was a bad idea. She agreed only after we found a place behind high walls, with two buildings: the main house and a separate office attached to a small bedroom and a kitchenette. In between, there was a swimming pool and tropical garden. I paid the rent and lived in the small room next to the office; Khareen got the real house, with my stereo and TV. When she didn't have guests, or she needed me to help her write a story that was way past deadline—or if she just felt like screwing with my mind—I was welcome to visit her wing. Strange as it seems, I was happy. I obediently went when she summoned me to sit next to her bath, or her bed, to share a joint and a drink in the candlelight while I listened to her talk about her lovers as she satisfied herself beneath the foam or the covers. "This isn't sex," she would say, in case I was getting ideas. "It's only for comfort."

One night, she secretly let a former boyfriend, a bass player in a popular rock band, sit on the garden step, peering through the glass door that led to her bedroom, while she screwed another man. She worked out a system with the ex-boyfriend, who called from a cell phone when it was time for her to buzz him in for the show through our electronic gate. Khareen made sure to tell me all about it, in excruciating detail, the next morning over breakfast.

Khareen was struggling to get started as a freelance journalist, so I would be her teacher, her housemate, a fellow traveler—everything but her lover. That, she promised, would come in good time. Our first reporting trip together was in Kathlehong, where leaders of Nelson Mandela's African National Congress went to see the devastation from one of the worst township wars fomented by government agents in the dying days of apartheid. Daily clashes between rival militias based in workers' hostels in Kathlehong and neighboring Thokoza townships had killed some twelve hundred people in the space of a year, and driven three thousand more from their homes. As the ANC leaders approached a hostel controlled by Zulu supporters of the rival Inkhata Freedom Party, with forty journalists and peace monitors in tow, shots rang out from the hostel. The ANC guards fired back with pistols and AK-47s. "Buya!" they shouted at the Inkhata supporters as firearms popped and clattered. "Come! We will kill you all!"

In the mad scramble of people running for cover through tall grass and climbing over wire fences, I lost track of Khareen. For a while, I thought I'd gotten her killed on our first working day. But she found me at my car. She was trembling and cursed me for not protecting her, and I saw her point. One journalist died in the fire-fight: Associated Press freelance photographer Abdul Shariffe, who was shot in the back as he fled. Two others were injured. Khareen was a sobbing wreck, but I thought this baptism by fire had prepared us for a road trip.

The next month, in February 1994, I bought Khareen a plane ticket and we flew to Rwanda, sharing a hotel room on the *Star*'s tab. The foreign editor wasn't all that interested in what from afar seemed like endless cycles of mindless tribal violence. But a Canadian, Brigadier General Roméo Dallaire, was commanding the 2,500-member U.N. force in Rwanda, so there was enough of a local hook to justify the cost of a couple of news stories and some features on Rwanda and neighboring Burundi.

It seemed the perfect place to get Khareen alone. At the time, Rwanda looked like a pretty straightforward peacekeeping problem, a state neither at war nor at peace, with just enough risk in the air that I could seduce her a little more. Hutu extremists were murdering minority Tutsis and moderate Hutus each night in the capital, Kigali. Tutsi rebels were violating a ceasefire in the countryside. But U.N. troops were managing to keep a lid on things.

In the two days before we met with Dallaire, Hutu extremists wielding sticks, machetes, and hand grenades had killed up to forty people, and wounded fifty more, in Kigali alone. The city's streets were mostly deserted because people were too afraid to leave their homes and go to work or open up their shops. Khareen and I were trying to find a souvenir store that wasn't shuttered when a group of *interahamwe*, the Hutu extremists who would soon lead one of the worst genocides in modern times, came marching down a main street. We took cover in one of the few shops that wasn't shuttered and locked up as the mob approached. The owner bolted the door behind us, and in a whisper told us to stay away from the windows.

After the mob passed, we bought a couple of grinning clay gorillas, painted black with glass bead eyes, and thanked the worried shopkeeper. He didn't smile back. If the shit really hit the fan, Rwandans knew foreigners like us would be gone in a flash, leaving them to face the massacres alone. Thinking back, I know I could have seen what was coming in the eyes of that terrified man—if only I'd paid attention.

When we met with Dallaire, he told us that a U.N. mandate allowed his troops to kill in order to save someone's life, but so far they had fired only two warning shots. The extremists were getting bolder by the day, tossing a grenade into a marketplace here, rolling another into a sleeping family's house there. Publicly, at least, Dallaire was still putting his faith in negotiations. "We were very close to an agreement twelve days ago," he told me. "So, if we were close, we can get close again. I'm an eternal optimist. If I see people still talking, I think there is a chance."

A little over a month later, the mass murder would begin, but I was too busy fantasizing about Khareen to get more than a vague sense that trouble was coming. As I listened to Dallaire, I thought he was naive and weak. I had no idea that he knew precisely what was on the way, and that he was fighting a secret battle with U.N. bureaucrats in New York because he wanted to do the right thing and use force to stop the killers before they really got started. As Khareen and I sat in Dallaire's office, I couldn't help but wonder if my four-month-old picture of the dead American soldier being dragged through the streets of Mogadishu had helped to ensure that Dallaire would be powerless, left to stand by and watch Rwanda's massacres while American, French, and Belgian troops came in just long enough to evacuate their citizens and leave the genocidaires to their work.

On January 11, just six weeks before I spoke with Dallaire, he had sent a secret cable to Kofi Annan, then head of U.N. peacekeeping operations in New York, warning that Hutu extremists were preparing massacres and requesting authority to raid their arms caches. The reply told him to work through the national police, who were among the genocide's plotters. Dallaire sent five more cables insisting it was time for U.N. forces to act, but the soldier was effectively ordered to do the diplomatic job of gentle nudging and prodding. Still feeling the political sting of the Somalia debacle, President Bill Clinton's administration issued a directive that the killings in Rwanda must not be called what they obviously were—genocide—because acknowledging the fact would then oblige the United States to intervene under a 1948 U.N. convention on genocide.

For weeks, in a bizarre display of oral acrobatics, U.S. officials called the mass murder in Rwanda everything but the genocide that it clearly was, because telling the truth would have obliged Clinton to send troops back to Africa. He was afraid of another Somalia. State Department officials in Washington were getting tied in rhetorical knots trying to avoid saying what anyone who could read a newspaper could already see.

"Well, as I think you know, the use of the term genocide has a very precise legal meaning, although it is not strictly a legal determination," State Department spokesperson Christine Shelly told a press briefing, three weeks into the genocide. "There are other factors in there as well. When, in looking at a situation to make a determination about that, before we begin to use that term, we have to know as much as possible about the facts of the situation."

The Clinton administration wasn't satisfied with simply blocking foreign intervention in Rwanda. It went further and instead of giving Dallaire the five thousand extra troops he had requested, *cut* his U.N. force to just 270 soldiers as the genocide picked up speed. Clinton later rewarded Annan for running interference, and helping him keep U.S. troops out of Rwanda, by ensuring his promotion to U.N. Secretary-General. Dallaire was thrown to the ghosts. Diagnosed with post-traumatic stress disorder, he had to retire from the Canadian military a broken and haunted man. Six years after the genocide, he was found passed out drunk in a suburb across the river from Canada's capital, curled up in a ball, hiding under a park bench.

If Rwanda was teetering on the edge in early 1994, Burundi had fallen off the cliff. Burundi's Hutus were killing Tutsis in a civil war that had killed fifty thousand people, which sounded like a lot at the time. So a few days after meeting with Dallaire, Khareen and I headed to the border by road from Kigali, to the Burenge refugee camp just inside Rwanda. A French team of relief workers from Médecins Sans Frontières was struggling to save the lives of children who were slowly starving to death. At least twenty-five people died each day in a camp of four thousand refugees. Three children died at its feeding center in the three hours that I was there.

In that same, short morning, Khareen fell in love with Laurent, a tall, muscular French aid worker with a sharp Gallic face and Mediterranean passions. He was building latrines for the refugees, working to save lives, and I was on the sidelines, watching. By mid-afternoon, Khareen was lying on Laurent's cot, demurely veiled beneath the soft white mesh of his mosquito net, writing in her diary.

The border area was a dangerous place, where armed militias roamed and killed at will, so I didn't want to be in Burenge long. I had planned for us to be safely back in our Kigali hotel by nightfall, when the grenade blasts started. Khareen was chasing a different thrill. I left her in Laurent's tent.

When she finally caught up with me in Kigali a few days later, Laurent was with her. He took a room below ours at the five-star Hôtel des Milles Collines, and after Khareen got cleaned up, she went down for dinner. The grenades were exploding in shanties close to the hotel all that night as death squads worked their rounds. After each blast, I'd phone down to Laurent's room and ask for Khareen to make sure she was keeping up with events. She was giggling, and whispering to Laurent to stop it, and I was going on about hand grenades. A horrible evil was descending over Rwanda, and I couldn't stop wondering what position Khareen and Laurent were enjoying in bed. The hotel complicated the love triangle by giving me a bad case of culture shock as I stewed. Managed by Belgian's Sabena airline, it was an island of European refinement in a rising sea of African chaos. Far removed from the risks in the top-floor restaurant, I had a panoramic view of the city over crepes or steak, grilled perfectly to medium rare, with a selection from the well-stocked wine cellar. A large, beautiful garden sheltered the grounds from Kigali's sinister atmosphere, and if reality still managed to intrude, I only needed to wave my hand and a waiter in a crisply pressed uniform would deliver another round of well-chilled bottles of imported Amstel beer poolside.

The aphrodisiac of simmering war had backfired on me, and I hoped that a trek up the side of a volcano to sit in the Rwandan rain forest, in the shadow of the powerful mountain gorillas who lived there, would provide the charm I needed. I hiked with Khareen and several porters for more than three hours along a muddy path up Mount Visoke, fighting to catch my breath as the air thinned, clutching at needle-sharp nettles to keep from sliding back.

It felt like I knew this place from movies, and the depths of my imagination. *King Kong. Gorillas in the Mist.* Tales of Tarzan and the African jungle. They were part of the media mythology. We were the top primate on evolution's ladder after more than 2 million years of climbing, and we couldn't resist a look down the rungs to see the creatures just behind us.

Our interpreter for a family of mountain gorillas, among the less than five hundred left, would be Dr. Pascale Sicotte, a Canadian primatologist who was then the director of the Karisoke Research Center.

I went to meet the mountain gorillas I'd wondered about for so long, and to write a profile of Sicotte. Dian Fossey, the American pioneer of mountain gorilla research, founded Karisoke in 1967 by pitching two small tents in a clearing on Mount Visoke, and allowing the gorillas to accept her on their terms. Karisoke is at an altitude of more than ten thousand feet, where Fossey noticed that many of her visitors suffered from what she called "astronaut blues" because the symptoms were similar to those experienced by astronauts undergoing isolation training for space missions. They include sweating, uncontrollable shaking, short-term fevers, loss of appetite, and severe depression accompanied by prolonged crying spells. Which could have described me on an average day at any altitude.

Karisoke made me nervous. I found it a spooky place. The canopy of trees towering forty feet or more above the cabins filtered out most of the sun, whose rays sliced through the mist like blades of light piercing the dust in a musty old mansion. Long, stringy strands of gray lichen hung from the tree limbs like witches' hair. On the edge of the clearing, there was a row of small crosses of rough-hewn wood rising from the red-brown earth. Dented metal plates nailed to all but one cross identified the bodies lying beneath: fifteen gorillas and Fossey, the human who sacrificed her life trying to save theirs. Rwandans had called her Nyiramachabelli, or "The old lady who lives in the forest without a man." She had had little time for outsiders, especially journalists, who arrived in this mountain refuge without good reason to disturb her gorillas. I wondered whether she was watching me, and what she might think. I wanted to be welcome, but I felt like an intruder.

During eighteen years in Rwanda's Virunga mountains, Fossey won international acclaim for her detailed study of the gorillas and her efforts to protect them from poachers. Her stubborn defense of the animals she loved probably got her murdered in her Karisoke cabin on the day after Christmas in 1985. She was fifty-three, struck down with a blow from a machete knife that split her skull.

Before we left Johannesburg, Khareen had discovered that a strain of malaria resistant to the standard drugs was spreading through Central Africa. She immediately started popping Larium to make her bloodstream as poisonous as possible for malaria parasites, even after reading the manufacturer's warning that the drug could, in rare cases, cause disabling attacks of anxiety, depression, confusion, hallucinations, restlessness, forgetfulness, psychosis and paranoia, emotional instability, aggression, and agitation. Which pretty much summed up Khareen without Larium. She was nothing if not unique, so sure enough, after the long climb to Karisoke, Khareen collapsed in a psychotic fit. She was convinced that she had encephalitis. We'd been strictly forewarned that anyone with a hint of illness wouldn't be allowed near the gorillas, to prevent the spread of an epidemic that could wipe them out. Without asking, I figured encephalitis was just the kind of infectious disease the gorillas' protectors might be worried about. Like a frat boy shouldering a drunken friend, I tried to walk and talk Khareen back to sanity, looking frantically over my shoulder to see if anyone was watching, pleading with her not to destroy this dream.

After she was a little more leveled out, we persuaded Sicotte that nothing was physically wrong, at least not anything that a gorilla could catch, and she agreed to guide us through the cold, misty forest to the gorillas. First, she briefed us on how to behave to make sure we didn't scare them. Rule Number One: Never look a gorilla straight in the eye. And don't point. No sudden, quick movements. And never stand above a gorilla. I already had those down pat. They were among the survival techniques I'd learned riding the New York subway as a graduate student at Columbia. We also weren't allowed to talk except in a few brief, whispered exchanges with Sicotte as we observed the gorillas from just a few yards away. There was one last rule of survival: if a gorilla felt so threatened that it charged us, we had to remain still, and cower, so the animal could firmly establish its dominance without having to attack.

While we hiked for several hours through the dense vegetation and deep ravines that are the gorillas' last sanctuary, Sicotte taught us a little of what it was that made her admire fellow primates so deeply. Rwandan trackers helped trace the gorillas' movements by spotting knuckle marks in the dirt, reading subtle changes in the vegetation, and remembering the animals' individual quirks. They led us to a group of fifteen gorillas, huge animals weighing up to 375 pounds, lazily lounging among dense bushes, munching on leaves and insects, and dozing. A large male charged a smaller male, baring his teeth and beating his chest with cupped hands that sent a loud, rapid-fire pok-pok-pok-pok-pok warning echoing through the jungle. He made his point without a fight, and the group was soon at ease again.

We'd been sitting next to the lounging gorillas for several minutes before I realized a bushbuck, smaller than a dog, was lying quietly among them. I couldn't see the tiny antelope until it struggled to its feet and walked off into the forest. It had been content, and safe, resting with primates that terrify their human cousins. The bushbuck feared us. Sicotte saw that I was stunned by the peaceful nature of beasts powerful enough to break a bushbuck's neck with a single swat. In a hushed voice, she said something that would take on powerful meaning weeks later, when I witnessed humans commit mass murder in the hills and valleys below.

"If they had been chimpanzees, they would have killed and eaten the bushbuck quite happily," Sicotte whispered. And then she explained the evolutionary chain that linked us, as humans, to the vicious top end of the primate family.

Gorillas are not the killer beasts conjured up in filmmakers' imaginations. They eat mainly leaves, stems, and roots, along with bamboo shoots, berries, insects, and the soft insides of the giant senecio tree. Mountain gorillas also like their privacy, and after sleeping in individual nests, they usually rise with the sun and spend each day quietly foraging. Genetically, gorillas are 92 percent similar to humans, Sicotte pointed out. Our closest primate cousins are chimpanzees, who share 99 percent of our genetic code.

Like humans, chimpanzees seem to have a taste for war. Pioneering primatologist Jane Goodall described in detail how one group of chimpanzees with a defined territory exterminated another in a series of attacks over several months in 1977. When the losing side was down to just one male, named Sniff, six males from the rival camp crossed a border stream and converged on him, pulling at his limbs and biting his face and head. After a prolonged attack, Sniff "was bleeding from wounds on the mouth, nose, forehead and back, and his left leg seemed to be broken," Goodall wrote. "As he crouched, Satan grabbed him by the neck and sucked blood from his nose. Satan and Sherry then grabbed a leg and, screaming, dragged him down the slope."

Goodall concluded from her long study of chimpanzees that they are capable of hostile and territorial behavior "not unlike certain forms of primitive human warfare." Some scientists' views of human evolution suggest that warfare played a key role in natural selection. According to their theories, early forms of combat could have allowed hominids with greater intelligence, courage, and language skills to wipe out their more dull, cowardly, and disorganized competitors and so advance the rise of *Homo sapiens*. Farther down the primate hierarchy, mountain gorillas sometimes fight and hurt, and may even kill, but Sicotte told me she believed that gorillas normally only kill one another by accident. They certainly do not share humans' lust for violence.

"I don't think they have the will to kill, not at all," Sicotte said.

Unlike most of their human cousins, mountain gorillas show overwhelming grace in self-restrained power. They can easily take life, but they must be pushed to an extreme limit first. Before she was murdered, Fossey's close study of them in their habitat found that violent aggression is rare in stable groups. Silverbacks, the graying patriarchs of gorilla clans, can fight to the death if two groups meet and compete for territory, but their conflicts are usually resolved by ritual displays unique to mountain gorillas, the animal world's proof that the truly powerful don't have to use force to get what they want.

A mountain gorilla normally goes through nine escalating steps in a charge display before violence becomes a final option. He starts by hooting, slowly, then faster. Then he performs a feeding ritual. If he needs to say more, he rises up on two feet, throws vegetation around, and pounds his chests with cupped hands. If the matter is still unresolved, he kicks the air with one leg, then runs sideways, thrashes at the vegetation, and finally, thumps the ground with his palms. We saw that escalation during our visit, when a large male went through the ritual and then bared his canines, as if he were about to bite another member of the group. But he stopped. Whatever the dispute was, it passed as suddenly as it erupted, and everyone was quickly foraging again.

We, the intruders, were mostly ignored. Mountain gorillas, it seemed, were way ahead of us in anger management.

When an animal as perceptive as a primate has been hunted by humans to the edge of extinction, yet decides to trust you—chooses not to fear you—it has bestowed a quiet honor. That's how I felt when the parents of a six-month-old baby named Vuba allowed him to come up and almost sit in my lap. He had a comical little mesa of frizzy hair rising atop his head, which reminded me of the guy in the college cult movie *Eraserhead*. He had big, inquisitive eyes that spotted anything new around him, such as my camera and my watch. From a safe distance, he studied them. And then, like any shy human child, he came a little closer to test my reaction—and probably his parents', before beating a quick retreat. When he felt confident enough, he let his curiosity take over and he knuckle-walked right up to my crossed legs, gently touching and sniffing my camera and watch, and then playfully somersaulting off into the bushes.

Later that day, I knelt at Fossey's grave behind the cabin where she had lived and died. She lay about ten yards away from Digit, a magnificent silverback who was closest to Fossey's heart before poachers killed him on New Year's Eve 1977. Digit was his group's sentry and when six poachers attacked with dogs, he held them off as long as he could so that his relatives, including his pregnant mate Simba, could escape. Digit managed to kill one of the poachers' dogs before he died from five spear wounds. Fossey's colleague and friend Ian Redmond found Digit's bloodied corpse. His head and hands had been cut off, probably to be sold as a trophy and ashtrays.

"There are times when one cannot accept facts for fear of shattering one's being," Fossey wrote six years later in *Gorillas in the Mist*. "As I listened to Ian's news, all of Digit's life, since my first meeting with him as a playful little ball of black fluff ten years earlier, passed through my mind. From that moment on, I came to live within an insulated part of myself. . . . I have tried not to allow myself to think of Digit's anguish, pain, and the total comprehension he must have suffered in knowing what humans were doing to him."

As Fossey battled the poachers, the row of gorilla graves grew longer, and with them the crosses made from the wood of saplings and battered aluminum nameplates. In the cabin, shivering a bit at the thought that Fossey was with me, I scanned the shelves that still held some of her old books. There was a copy of Robert Frost's *In the Clearing*. It was the poet's last book of new verse, published in 1962, on the same day that he received the Congressional Medal of Honor. He died the following year. Inside the first edition copy at Karisoke, he wrote in black fountain pen: "Robert Frost to Dian Fossey."

In "From Iron," one of the book's final verses, Frost wrote:

Nature within her inmost self divides
To trouble men with having to take sides

"Of course, she didn't make friends with poachers, but she didn't make friends with others, either," Sicotte told me. "She died for it."

The reason for Fossey's murder is still murky, the perpetrators unknown. Rwandan police arrested one of her research center's trackers, who then died in jail in suspicious circumstances. Authorities say he hanged himself. Many believe he was killed to cover up a murder plot. The government then tried to blame Fossey's American research assistant, who managed to flee the country before he was arrested. After genocidal killers rampaged through Rwanda in 1994, attention turned to a more likely suspect, former provincial governor Protais Zigiranyirazo, whom Fossey was reportedly close to exposing as a leading poacher and trafficker in endangered species and gold. He was charged with being a leading organizer of one of the twentieth century's most horrific human slaughters.

8

LIFE AMONG THE DEAD

My retrospective anger and dismay is not that we made a wrong
decision, but that we didn't make any decision.
FORMER NATIONAL SECURITY ADVISER ANTHONY LAKE,
ON THE CLINTON ADMINISTRATION'S FAILURE
TO INTERVENE IN RWANDA

In the early days of the Rwandan genocide, I was battling the *Star*'s
foreign editor over which story was more important: mass murder in
Rwanda or the first democratic elections in South Africa. I couldn't
persuade him that the vote could be left to another reporter sent in as
backup because its outcome was predictable: Nelson Mandela's ANC
would win, and a few white extremists would set off some bombs but
fail to ignite a civil war. From the comfortable distance of Toronto,
Rwanda's unfolding crimes against humanity seemed like the same old
tribal warfare. When I finally made it back to Rwanda in early May
1994, the Interahamwe were murdering at the rate of more than three
hundred people an hour. The killers hadn't even reached the halfway
mark in their hundred-day genocide that would kill some eight hundred thousand people. There was no way the world would intervene, so
the genocidaires took their time, savoring each death. They beat many

of their victims to a bloody pulp with large wooden clubs, like something out of a Flintstones acid trip. The prehistoric weapons had hundreds of nails and heavy spikes protruding from them at all angles, the better to turn human flesh into raw meat. A few thousand well-armed soldiers with air support could have chased away the murderers like scrawny rats in a few days, and saved several hundred thousand lives.

One day, standing on the bridge overlooking Rusomo Falls, on Rwanda's border with Tanzania, I lit up a joint and got high with Khareen as we watched the evidence of genocide spill across the border. Beneath a misty rainbow of yellow, blue, and red, around thirty-five swollen corpses swirled in a roiling whirlpool and smashed against the rocks. As we watched, trying to keep an accurate count, two more corpses spilled over the falls, and we had to start over again. The water had bleached their black skin to a ghostly grayish-white. One of the dead looked like a woman, but the body was bloated to twice its size, so it was hard to tell. The corpse was still wearing a red sweater, and what looked like the shredded remains of a skirt. The naked bodies of three children, two no older than five, were trapped in the whirlpool too, sliding up and down against the rocks like rag dolls. They looked like a family together, caught in the same swirl of foam and green plant stalks, going round and round in some macabre game of Ring around the Rosie.

The Hutu extremists' propaganda said Tutsis were foreign interlopers who had invaded the territory centuries earlier from somewhere in North Africa. The genocidaires urged the pure to send them back to where they came from. Some of the faithful took their leaders literally, and after massacring Tutsis, dumped the bodies in the muddy Kagera River that flowed down to Lake Victoria, a source of the Nile. The journey of the dead stopped in the expansive lake, where Ugandan authorities had collected 10,700 bodies by mid-June of 1994, and were still counting.

Aid workers told us that just days before we arrived at the border they had counted more than seven hundred bodies coming over Rusomo Falls during daylight. This was not just another African horror, but a sin of deliberate political choice in Washington, one that left a legacy of death in Central Africa that is still playing out to this day. At Clinton's urging, the world turned its back on Rwanda and guerrillas were left to stop it on their own. We moved west across the country with mainly Tutsi guerrillas of the Rwandan Patriotic Front (RPF) as they battled government forces and extremist militias. Anywhere we stopped, there were hundreds more corpses to count, and documents to sort through in a choking stench of rotting flesh and clouds of buzzing flies, trying to put names to the dead.

In the deserted town of Kigarama, behind a row of shops, we found dozens of corpses, several with their hands bound behind their backs. Across the street, in a two-room house, we discovered the bodies of children heaped on the bed in a small room where they had apparently tried to hide. A gunman had killed them with a burst from an assault rifle. Several spent shell casings littered the floor. A baby was at the bottom of the pile, and only its tiny bloated hand, its severed head, and its legs were visible, as if the older kids had tried to hide the youngest among them from killers with AK-47s who sprayed the room. Just outside the open wooden door of their house, scattered in the dirt, was a small stack of school notebooks neatly covered with pages pulled from magazines. One of them was perfectly wrapped in a color publicity shot showing the cast of *Dynasty*, with the face of John Forsythe grinning out from the center. A folded piece of graph paper, a report card stamped by the Episcopal Church of Rwanda,

Rukira Parish, listed a pupil's subjects, including French, math, hygiene, religion, civics, and sport, with each term's grades marked in blue ink beside them. This student, one of the bodies on the bed nearby, earned a final grade of 80.7 percent overall. I thought of my own teachers' assessments: Good effort. Can do better.

In Gahini, sixteen-year-old François Sempundu sat on the grimy brown foam of a hospital mattress laid out on a patio, nervously sweeping his bandaged hand over the bits of dried grass and dirt on his bed. A week after the genocide began, attackers tossed a grenade into his house, blasting hot shrapnel into his knees. Then Hutu extremists murdered his mother and seven other children as they went house-to-house in Kitazigurwa village in the middle of the afternoon. Only François and two of his brothers survived. He hid in the kitchen for five days, among his family's decaying corpses, too terrified to go out in case the killers came back for the ones they missed. He was waiting to die. "After all the others were killed, if anybody came I didn't mind if I was killed, too," he told me.

Even amid mass death, there was the overwhelming power of the will to live. For weeks, some three hundred people took refuge in swamps near the southern town of Nyamata, until the killers tracked them down and hacked to death as many as they could. Those who weren't killed straightaway were left to bleed to death among the reeds. Many simply refused to die although that would have been easier. Several were children whose hands or feet were cut off. One woman lived almost a month hiding in the muck of the swamp with bone-deep machete wounds. In the guerrillas' makeshift hospital, her untreated wounds were suppurating feasts for maggots. Her sunken eyes rolled back until only the whites stared up at the doctor who didn't have enough medicine to help her fight the sepsis slowly coursing through her body.

The RPF guerrillas chased the perpetrators, their followers, and their families into neighboring Zaire, where more than 1 million refugees camped out on ancient, razor-sharp lava rock from Nyiragongo Volcano. After sundown, we could see Nyiragongo's throbbing red glow on the black horizon. The refugees drew water from a nearby lake and stagnant ponds, and now they were dying of cholera, suffering a holocaust of their own making. It was here that Clinton decided he had to send in U.S. troops—safe from the fighting just across the border in Rwanda—to deliver water, food, and medicine to many of the Hutu militiamen who had committed some of the century's worst crimes against humanity.

At Rwanda's Nyarabuye Church, and its small Catholic school, I walked among as many as one thousand corpses, most lying shoulder to shoulder in a courtyard. Villagers had come here thinking that God's house would protect them from the genocidaires, but it only corralled them and made their slaughter more convenient. In another room, which looked like an office, I found a child's body in a corner behind a filing cabinet, where he must have tried to hide, hoping the killers would pass him by. A four-inch knife wound across his forehead had slashed right through the bone.

The faster things spun out of control, the more blurred morality became. Sorting out the innocent from the guilty was getting harder by the day. Even children had joined in the massacres, sometimes to save their own lives. But there was at least some innocence in young faces, so I tried to focus on them. One day in Zaire, I was standing at the roadside near a fresh row of corpses in a Rwandan refugee camp the size of a small city when I noticed a girl, about five years old, start across the road, alone. She was dressed in a man's sooty work shirt, and a dirty black T-shirt, but nothing else. She was looking for the toilet, which consisted of an open field on the fringes of the camp where hundreds of thousands of people went to shit or piss or die. The stench was easy to follow. Frightened and lost, she walked straight into a dumping ground of more than twenty bodies, most of them lying uncovered, dressed in the rags in which they had died. A few others were rolled up in straw mats, bound at the head with rough twine. Their cold, bare feet poked out the other end.

The girl stopped right next to the corpses, standing on scattered straw. Bewildered, she began to cry until she was wailing for someone to come and help her. No one did. A falling tear etched a line down the dust on her cheek. I saw a picture and raised my camera to shoot it, and as I stepped back to frame the child among a few more corpses, I put my foot down on the bony arm of an old woman's dead body. It snapped like a dry stick.

And then I knew I was lost, too.

Days later, in late May, I left Rwanda to fly to New York to accept a Pulitzer Prize for the picture of the dead American soldier. It was only then that I could feel my mind cracking under half a year of nonstop trauma, and Khareen's torment. Laurent had become her frequent houseguest. From my bedroom across the garden, I could hear the long buildup to screaming matches, objects smashing against walls, and then raucous sex. I felt like a kid hiding in the dark from horrible parents, trying to will them to go away.

"If you want me," Khareen said one especially difficult day, "you have to see a psychiatrist."

I'm sure she meant it as a new precondition, not an ironic comment on the mess we were in, but as her hold on me diminished, Khareen was the one who broke down and landed in the hospital. I was packing to leave for New York, for the Pulitzer ceremony, when she collapsed with some kind of mysterious ailment. She self-diagnosed as encephalitic, and in the emergency ward, she thrashed about and screamed at doctors who couldn't find anything wrong. No fever. Blood pressure fine. No physical symptoms of disease. To calm her down, they admitted her anyway and doped her up with tranquilizers. She wanted me to cancel my trip and stay at her bedside. I was actually thinking of doing it, when the phone rang. After hanging up, she told me to go ahead, just leave. Laurent would take care of her. But she had one more duty for me before I was free. I must go back to the house and bring her some clean underwear. Specifically, a black thong. With a tiny pink ribbon in a bow and a fake pearl on the front. Then, with a scornful glare, she dismissed me.

The Pulitzer luncheon was held in the august rotunda of Columbia University's Low Memorial Library, a late-nineteenth-century mélange of Rome's Pantheon and Greece's Parthenon, a few blocks away from Harlem, on Manhattan's Upper West Side. A marble bust of Athena, goddess of wisdom and military victory, stood beneath columns of green Irish marble, surrounded by the twelve signs of the Zodiac. After making sure my name was really on the winners' list, a young woman behind the reception desk brusquely recited the rules: "No speeches," she said. I took it personally. With the stench of Rwanda's dead still hanging about me, I was in the mood to vent. I figured she saw a rant coming on, and didn't want to spoil lunch.

A greeter steered me into a side room where hors d'oeuvres were laid out on a long table. I put a few on a small plate, and nervously picked away at them, thinking that I should be back among the dying in Rwanda, not standing here in tight new shoes, a blue blazer, and charcoal-gray pants selected by the man at Brooks Brothers, trying desperately to look like I belonged among the winners in Manhattan.

John Honderich, the *Star*'s publisher, must have sensed I was slipping. "How are you handling everything?" he asked. He sounded worried.

"Not very well, to be honest," I replied, and a lump rose in my throat. I thought I was going to choke on a canapé.

Then Honderich offered the advice that would eat away at me for more than a decade. "Have you thought about finding the widow or parents of the dead soldier?" he asked. "I'm sure it would help you find closure."

"I can't," I said, staring down at my plate.

"Why not?"

"I'm too scared."

Just in time, the greeter told us to take our seats for lunch in the rotunda. I followed Kevin Carter, a colleague from South Africa who once snorted ground-up Mandrax from my apartment floor, to the stage. His searing photograph of a vulture waiting for a starving Sudanese girl to die won the Pulitzer for feature photography. Mine won in the spot news category. Carter was certain that he'd received the loudest applause. I couldn't see why it mattered.

Two months later, when I was back on the Rwandan border watching thousands more people die from a raging cholera epidemic, my satellite phone rang. It was an editor calling with news of Carter. The night before, he had parked his pickup truck in Johannesburg, ducttaped a garden hose to the exhaust pipe, and committed suicide.

"Why are you telling me this?" I thought. With all the people fighting to live around me, I couldn't care less about someone who had given up and taken his own life. Like the rest of us, Carter was chased by a lot of demons. People wanted to know what he'd done to help the starving Sudanese child. Carter said all he could do was sit under a nearby tree, light a cigarette, and weep, which didn't satisfy the public's demand for a hero. But something much less complicated finally killed him. The Pulitzer aura had helped Carter land his first major magazine assignment, in Mozambique. Messed up on drugs, he lost the film on the flight back. Rather than face that final embarrassment, he committed suicide.

"I feel alienated from normal people," he had written months earlier. "The shutters come down and I recede into a dark place with dark images of blood and death in godforsaken, dusty places."

Carter was thirty-three, just two years younger than me, and as much as I wanted to blame him for the suicide, I knew I'd thought several times of doing the same thing. I just didn't have his strength.

In mid-August 1994, as Rwanda's genocide was finally coming to an end, its mountain gorillas were still at risk of being wiped out. When Khareen and I followed the genocidaires and their families into Zaire's refugee camps, we also found some of the gorilla trackers whom we had met at Karisoke months earlier. We persuaded a couple to cross back with us into Rwanda and lead us to the abandoned research center and the gorillas deep in the forest.

We were being reckless with the lives of the trackers who agreed to lead us. It was a stupid thing to do. We went back and forth from the trackers' camp, high up a hillside, trying to persuade one or two to join us. Most of them wanted nothing to do with us. They were terrified of going back and of either being arrested by the RPF guerrillas as suspected genocidaires, or killed by them, poachers, or any number of other possible predators in the jungle. But we got official approval from one of the guerrilla officers with whom we'd traveled across Rwanda as the RPF battled the government forces and their genocidaires allies. And we promised not to let anyone separate us. They were brave, empty words because in truth, we would have been powerless to protect anyone. We didn't have a pocket knife between us. We climbed again up the volcano, through dense fog that crept up the valleys like giant fingers, certain that humans, not gorillas, were the jungle's real beasts.

We found the research center's eight wooden cabins looted and damaged. Windows were smashed, filing cabinets overturned and emptied. Scientific files, cataloging years of research data, were scattered everywhere. Fossey's books, her volume of Frost's poetry, were torn and dumped on the floor. On the edge of the small cemetery where she lay buried, a new cross rose above a patch of loosely packed, red-brown earth. Unlike the other crosses, this one didn't have an identifying metal plate. It belonged to Effie, a female gorilla who died at around thirty-nine years old, apparently from old age, the Rwandan trackers told us. They hadn't had time to give her a proper burial. They had been in a rush to get down the volcano so that they wouldn't get caught between the genocidaires and the advancing Tutsi guerrillas.

As Rwanda's war escalated and the government collapsed, the national park that was supposed to be the gorillas' sanctuary became a busy transit route for mass murderers, poachers, and various other thugs who used the forest cover to sneak in and out of the country while rebel forces pressed their offensive. On my last night at Karisoke, as I lay in my sleeping bag next to Khareen on the floor of a looted office, a group of men came through the camp, angrily shouting words we couldn't understand and banging on doors. We doused the kerosene lamp, and in the faint glow of the dying embers in the wood stove, we froze, saying nothing, willing them to leave. If they found us, or the Rwandan trackers we'd persuaded to come with us, we would likely be next in line for graves.

"They're going to kill us," Khareen whispered. I told her to keep quiet or we wouldn't have a chance.

The voices came closer, and they sounded wildly drunk. There was pounding on our door, and then a pause, and I thought I could hear my heart beating. Then more pounding, and silence, and footsteps walking away. I fell asleep wondering what the voices would have done if they had broken down the door, and whether they would come back again, or sate their blood lust elsewhere.

9

SHRINKING

A bit of shooting takes your mind off your troubles—it makes you forget the cost of living.
BRENDAN BEHAN, *THE HOSTAGE*

Weeks later, I went back home to Johannesburg, hoping to decompress, clean some clothes, and return to Rwanda. I usually didn't need more than a few days away from war to calm down, get over the nightmares, and be eager to jump back into the madness again. But my recovery time was suddenly slowing. I felt lost among the posh bungalows of Johannesburg's white northern suburbs, where, in those early days of freedom, most blacks on my neighborhood's streets were still maids, gardeners, and other servants walking to and from work. I was slowly going crazy at home, a syndrome familiar to the listless middle-class housewives who lived all around me. My angst had this twist: I was thinking of guns and wondering why I was still alive.

Whenever Africa intruded too close to the walled compounds of the northern suburbs, the quickest escape was through the gleaming corridors of Sandton City shopping mall. There were faux European cafés, potted plants carefully selected to evoke somewhere else, and a dream world of shop windows filled with Japanese electronics, Swiss watches, and American jeans. Newspaper reporting, even on a foreign correspondent's expense account, didn't pay enough for me to be welcome at the preferred white refuge: the neighborhood country club. I doubt I could have found sponsors to swear I was the right kind of white to share in their poolside reverie anyway. And I still had enough of a mind left to know that Mandrax pills, South Africa's version of Quaaludes, and the downer of choice for lost young males, were just cocktail nuts for the demons. Which left me with the sedative mix of mall walking and Muzak.

As I often did when I was afraid of being alone, this day I joined the midday migration, at the wheel of my white Toyota Corolla four-door with the hint-of-coconut rental car scent, rock radio thumping from the dashboard. The air conditioning was set to anesthetic chill, and I was in a depressive haze, drawn like a bug from the darkness to bash my head against Sandton City's fluorescent lights. Mine was the second car stopped in the fast lane, waiting for red to turn green. I spotted a white pickup slowing to a stop at my right. Out of the corner of my eye, I saw a pile of black-skinned corpses, rolled in reed mats and stacked up in the back. I focused in on the cracked, dusty soles of bare feet sticking out one end, and the dried mud and tattered edges of men's pants. It felt like a fist was tightening around my throat.

"Fuck, not here too."

I blinked, and tried to shake it off, straining to see more clearly. In a couple of seconds, I realized I was staring at rolled-up carpets. I felt like I was falling. I gripped the steering wheel as tightly as I could. I was crying so hard that I couldn't keep my head up, and I slumped against the wheel. When car horns started to blare all around me, I could hardly see to drive. I still can't remember how I made it back home, or where I got the number of Dr. Larry Grinker.

In the psychiatrist's reception room, I sat alone by the front door, ready to turn and run. The walls were inching in. I tried to calm myself down by reading a magazine, but everything was a blur. I was flipping pages without seeing anything but a psychedelic mélange of colors melting into black type. With each swallow, I choked, and like a noose, the panic pulled tighter. The receptionists sat behind a high counter, chatting and laughing, and I could feel them taking turns peering at me. It was like all the times I'd sat outside the principal's office, waiting to spin some clever defense and be punished anyway, and the secretaries scowled and tsk-tsked. I was getting ready to bolt when Dr. Grinker walked out and welcomed me into his office.

Following his professional routine, the psychiatrist took his seat and addressed me across a desk, in a soft, clinical monotone, reviewing items on the white patient detail card I'd filled out at reception. Age: 35. Sex: Male. Employer: The Toronto Star. Insurance: Company plan. Marital status: Single. Next of kin: Mother. There was no line that said: Describe what haunts you. The basics established, Dr. Grinker led me from his desk to the therapy corner. I expected him to point to a couch, but he offered a high-backed brown leather chair, which I took as a good sign. The scene looked more marketing executive, or sixties TV talk show, than shrink's office. Sitting upright, instead of sniveling flat on my back, I would at least feel more in control.

I was shaking, but still wondered whether I was making too much of nothing. The doctor sat across from me, with a clipboard propped up on a crossed leg, and said he had to ask a few things before making his diagnosis. My confessor was a short man with solemn eyes and close-cropped hair. I tried to make eye contact and he glanced away, his chin resting on a fist, staring at an upper corner of the room for so long that I wanted him to stop looking there and acknowledge my despair. He began to ask me questions, and with each one, another crack opened in the dam until finally I was slouched in the chair, sobbing.

I wanted help, yet the thought of being in a psychiatrist's office scared the hell out of me. For one thing, I was afraid of losing my edge. Being a little crazy has its advantages in my line of work. And it provides a certain cachet. If I got well, my bent mind reasoned, I'd be too sane to keep doing what I loved. I was also wary of letting a psychiatrist rummage around inside my mind. It had taken me a lifetime to lock a lot of things away in psychic boxes and I didn't want a meddling shrink probing around in there and making a mess.

All I was really looking for now from Dr. Grinker was his signature on a prescription for some fix-all pills and a quick way out of what I figured was a big mistake. I didn't think he'd have any idea what was twisting my mind. How could he, sitting here in one of Johannesburg's privileged white enclaves? Dr. Grinker didn't exactly build confidence by asking how I felt about my father, my mother, and whether I was in a stable relationship. I thought he'd been counseling conflicted white South Africans for too long. In fact, he wanted to know if I had someone to go home to, anyone who could make sure I didn't kill myself.

At the end of our first session, Dr. Grinker came to an immediate diagnosis: chronic depression and post-traumatic stress disorder that had been building for an extended period, as I self-medicated with beer, single-malt Scotch, pot, hash, and cocaine cut with God knows what.

War reporters, like soldiers, are supposed to be tough-skinned, inured to the madness that surrounds them. The unwritten code of honor, passed down through generations of wars more bloody than any I could imagine, doesn't allow reporters to let all the killing, the relentless gnawing fear that they can't admit, get to them. But in a conflict or catastrophe, a journalist is alone with this distinct disadvantage: his professional code demands that he not act, that he strictly maintain an objective distance. A soldier can stand up to his enemy and shoot. An aid worker can pick up a starving child and feed it. Journalists are condemned to watch, listen, and report.

Long after any big war story is old news, it festers and a psychic pus swells the mind. Good sense tells the reporter to be a professional and just live with it. If a construction worker drops a beam on his foot, he sees a doctor, goes to rehab, gets worker's compensation, and heals. If a war correspondent fries a few circuits, he sedates himself with whatever booze, drug, or quick lay is at hand and gets ready for the next deadline. After all, if he can't take it, there are lots of fresh bodies waiting in line to take his place.

By one model for the treatment of post-traumatic stress, intervention is most effective if it is carried out soon after the trauma, and close to where it was suffered, when the brain is undergoing chemical changes that can effect long-term damage. But I'd suffered so many shocks to the mind, in numerous places, over several years, that I was a chronic case by the time I sat in Dr. Grinker's chair.

The symptoms accumulated gradually over the years, and so were easy for me to ignore. They are obvious to me now, but in the early months and years, when treatment would have had a better chance, I believed the retreat of my once cheerful, outgoing personality was an intelligent, logical reaction to a horrible, dangerous world. In some ways, I still do. The constant killing, whether sanctioned as war or condemned as war crimes, dampened my faith in humanity. My social bonds broke down. I felt betrayed not just by individuals, but by human nature itself.

I withdrew. Unanswered letters piled up. Invitations stopped coming. Old friends got sick of leaving messages on my answering machine, and they stopped calling. I didn't mind. Friends can't hurt you, or die on you, if you have no friends at all. I gradually lost interest in meeting new people because I knew that meant engaging in torturous social graces such as witty banter, nasty gossip, and white lies. And today, I have withdrawn so far into a protective shell that the only people I care to spend time with, the only humans I truly trust not to hurt me, are my wife and son.

Long after war's traumas recede, the fear and anger still burn, like red-hot embers that cool to gray only to flare into a raging fire without warning. Even now, when time has smoothed the edges of old war memories, I often wake with my hand balled in a tight fist, fingernails digging into my thumb muscle, leaving deep, crescent-moon dents. The nightmare flickers and is forgotten before I can remember what made me so scared. I have maddening gaps in long-term memory, yet shocking images remain as vivid as the day they burned themselves into my brain, like flashes of bright light on film. I can still see that baby's hand, exactly as it poked out from under a pile of murdered children's corpses in a Rwandan bedroom. But to remember the route we took to get there, or the names of the people I lived and ate with for many days on the journey, I have to trawl through scribblings in old notebooks. I can see movies, or read books, over again because the plotline fades from memory within days. My concentration is shot.

No matter how good I feel, I know that grief comes stinging out of nowhere. I can be sitting quietly, thinking of nothing, really, and suddenly the sadness creeps up and overwhelms me. I begin to cry with no reason. Sometimes I give up, lose the fight to get out of bed, leave the house or hotel room; I just want to pull the blackness over me like a blanket and disappear.

Outside the safety of my home, pure joy is mostly a memory. When I catch sudden glimpses of myself in a mirror, I see a furrowed brow and an aura of deep, quiet rage. When I see a similar expression reflecting from the face of my seven-year-old son, I ask him why he is angry, and he remains silent for a moment and says, "I'm not angry. I'm thinking." It scares me.

Dr. Grinker immediately put me on an antidepressant, 450 milligrams of moclobemide per day. Gradually, the drug built up its forces in my body, slowly strengthening my ability to feel a hint of happiness. It boosted the levels of serotonin, epinephrine, norepinephrine, and dopamine that help control some of the most primeval forces in human personality, the compulsion to flee or fight, feelings of anxiety or pleasure, or a range of urges, from the most mundane motivation to get up and do something to the hunger for sex.

It was years later that I read about the pioneering research of Dr. Joseph LeDoux, who investigated how the brain processes and stores emotional memories, especially fear, in two almond-shaped lumps of neurons called the amygdala. I flew to New York to visit LeDoux's lab at New York University's Center for Neural Science. It was a March day, and Manhattan was shivering in a spring cold snap. The son of a Louisiana butcher, LeDoux was wearing a red small-checked shirt and blue jeans. There was sadness about him. His eyes were hooded. He had recently lost his teenage son to a heroin overdose, and as the neuroscientist worked to understand the mysteries of the mind, a father's sense of guilt was eating away at his heart.

LeDoux showed me some of his lab rats in dimly lit Plexiglas enclosures called conditioning boxes, with floors of metal tubes that deliver a mild, half-second shock to the rats' feet as they hear a ten-second tone. A video camera recorded their reaction, which LeDoux imitated by hunching his back and curling his fingers into gripping claws. Once shocked, a rat only has to hear the tone again and it reacts precisely the same way. "This is simulating a rat in the wild that's being attacked by a cat," LeDoux said. "The cat growls as he scratches, and so the tone is the simulated, anticipatory sound that warns, 'The next time you hear a growl, you better freeze or do whatever you have to in order to protect yourself.' You can't practice that until you get it perfect. You have to get it right the first time and you have to remember it forever. And that's why it doesn't go away."

It's strange, I told LeDoux. As much as I hate going to war zones, and feel my luck running out, I'm less anxious once I'm in a dangerous place than, say, I was walking down Fifth Avenue to his office. I told LeDoux about the illogical feeling of blame I still felt over the desecration of Cleveland's corpse in Somalia and asked if science had discovered where guilt resides in the brain. "I wish I knew that," LeDoux sighed, fighting back tears.

After my initial crisis passed and the antidepressants slowly began to buoy my spirits, Dr. Grinker and I got to what I thought was the heart of the problem: the picture. I brought a framed, eight-by-ten print of my October 1993 photograph of the Somali mob triumphantly dragging and beating Cleveland to the psychiatrist's office. Dr. Grinker studied it carefully. I told him about the voice that I'd heard that day, and his warning: "*If you do this,* I will own you forever."

Dr. Grinker said it was the voice of my superego, my mind talking to itself.

No, I told him, I know my inner voice very well. We speak often. This was something very different: a sound so clear and strong that it seemed to come from outside and inside, from all directions, all at once. And I've heard it since, felt him next to me. Feared his presence.

The drugs didn't deliver a sudden surge of joy, just a slow retreat of desperation, which would fight back for dominance as the chemical battle raged in my brain. It was now almost a year to the day that I had heard the voice, and true to its word, Staff Sergeant William David Cleveland still had his grip on me. I needed otherworldly intervention.

Dr. Grinker boosted the moclobemide to three tablets a day, which made me more dizzy and nauseated just as Khareen and Laurent's relationship reached its breaking point. I could hear them constantly: shouting invectives, hurling things across rooms, insisting that it was over, that they were leaving. And then they jumped into bed to hump like jungle beasts. As their fights got more vicious, and the making up less satisfying, Laurent climaxed with the ritual's highest display stage, reminding me of the gorillas on Virunga. Once, he pursued me onto the driveway, where I cowered by the car as he grabbed fistfuls of his hair and yanked and beat his chest and let out a long primordial scream. He wanted to know what I thought he should do.

I was rescued by a long-forgotten friend from the Gulf War: Jana Schneider, whom I'd met in Baghdad's Al-Rasheed Hotel, just hours after the Mother of All Battles began.

After the Gulf War, Jana alighted in the former Yugoslavia, where she covered its collapse. The first time I heard Jana's name again was when a South African photographer, back from the Balkans, was dissing her at his kitchen table. In June 1992, Jana and Slovenian newspaper reporter Ivo Standeker were among the first to get through Serbian lines into the Sarajevo suburb of Dobrinje. As they were crossing a field, the Serbs started firing mortar bombs. One explosion threw Jana fifteen yards and she landed on her neck, and the back of her head, with hot shards of steel shrapnel burning in her legs. She later told me it was louder than anything she had ever heard or felt, a force so powerful that it felt like her whole body was exploding. As she screamed at her colleague to run, a second mortar bomb tore open his back, killing him. Jana suffered a heart attack and went into cardiac arrest.

Some photographers, like the one I was listening to in Johannesburg, blamed Jana. She was reckless. I'd heard the same accusation leveled at me, usually by people who had missed the news. I think it was their way of claiming some deeper wisdom about the vagaries of war, as if they knew the secret to getting away with the insane risks that come with the job.

Another photographer, who had stood by the military ambulance door as Jana was loaded in, unconscious, was stunned to hear she had survived. He was certain she was dead. No, I told him, she's alive, all right. I've talked to her. A few weeks earlier, the phone had rung at my Johannesburg home. "Do you know who this is, honey?" the voice asked.

"Uh, not really," I said, guessing it was a crank.

"It's Jana, hon," and I still didn't really believe it. Then I wondered what she wanted.

Jana is a woman with an implausible life that happens to be true. She once had a recording contract. She had wowed the critics on Broadway and gotten a Tony Award nomination for Best Supporting Actress in a musical in 1986. She shot images of war that appeared on the covers of *Time* and *Newsweek*. She'd come back from the dead. Ed Bradley had done a piece on her for his CBS newsmagazine "Street Stories."

Still, when she explained what had brought her to South Africa so suddenly, I thought I knew better. I rolled my eyes as Jana babbled on about how she was in South Africa to star in a ninety-second Volvo ad being shot in a game park. She would be at the wheel, speeding after a Dakota plane. Sure. "I need to borrow a blanket," she said. "I'm sleeping in my car."

It sounded like an oddly low-budget production for such a high-end, practical automobile.

But I was wrong to doubt her. The storyboard went like this: Jana takes the wheel of the Volvo 850, pursues the plane as a real-life dare-devil in black and white in the African wilderness, while doing many of her own stunts. To showcase the 850's "toughness and durability," the daring escapade is interspersed with color images of war.

Jana dropped by to pick up the blanket, and as soon as she walked through the door, Khareen was circling her, like a lioness sizing up another that had overstepped her scent marker. I ended up in between them, feeling one pull me this way, and then the other back again. I felt that Jana had come to free me, and Khareen somehow sensed it right away.

They each spoke to me in short back-and-forth bursts that came so fast the words didn't register. I was drawn to both of them, but found myself slipping into Khareen's field of gravity because that was the easiest thing to do. As Jana felt me drifting away, she snapped her fingers right in front of my eyes. It was precisely the same as the finger snap, years earlier, of the Toronto professor who kept me from follow-ing the Scientology recruiter—an electric spark of clarity. Khareen's spell was broken, and no matter what she tried after that, whether it was a psychotic fit or a naked dip in the pool, she no longer held the same sway.

That night, Jana and I had a meal of cold sushi and warm sake. The same meal that had consummated Khareen's hold over me was now confirming my release.

"You're ruining your career, you know," Jana said. I knew she was right, but it was eerie to hear it from someone who had come out of nowhere.

"How did you know that?" I asked, astonished.

"Honey," she smiled, "Jana knows everything."

She left that night with the blanket. A few days later, it reappeared, neatly folded on my doorstep. But no Jana. No note either. And no phone call to say goodbye. She simply vanished, like an angel ascending.

Almost a decade later, in early 2004, Kit Roane, a senior editor at *U.S. News & World Report*, published a lengthy profile about Jana. He sent me a link to the story, and as I read it, my stomach tightened. On December 10, 2003, at the age of fifty-two, she was smoking a cigarillo on the steps of a Manhattan brownstone, surrounded by several plastic bags stuffed with her clothes, clogs, and other debris of a troubled life: the cardboard that sheltered her against the cold, a zipper bag with change panhandled from pedestrians, and a scrap of pizza, when three police officers pulled up in two squad cars. A fire truck pulled up behind them. They were responding to a complaint that a woman was being "boisterously loud."

Stuffed down the front of her pants, in a manila envelope wrapped in a plastic bag that contained her most important documents, including copies of her passport, press cards, and an expired New Hampshire pistol permit, was an August 17, 1992, copy of *People* magazine. It called her "Calamity Jana," and in just over fourteen hundred words left no doubt that this broken woman in front of the police, a bag lady with rotting teeth, was not muttering delusions of grandeur. "If they ever make a movie of Jana Schneider's life (and someone probably will)," the *People* article began, "the hard part will be to cram the whole incredible story into two hours."

Convinced she was crazy, the cops hustled Jana into a squad car and drove her to Bellevue Hospital Center in Lower Manhattan. The doctors concluded that she suffered "paranoid ideations" and locked her up involuntarily on the psychiatric ward. For three months, doctors there treated Jana for depression, and what they diagnosed as psychotic episodes possibly triggered by schizophrenia. Feeling like she had landed a part in a real-life *One Flew Over the Cuckoo's Nest*, she was heavily medicated on anti-psychotic drugs, with pills dispensed three times a day, and put in a room with three other patients. They slept on wooden beds with air mattresses on plywood boards.

She finally persuaded a judge to release her into the care of her mother in McFarland, a village in Wisconsin, where I flew to see her. It was an awkward reunion. I smiled as best I could through my guilt over not having been there for her when she had for me. We hugged, but neither of us was truly happy.

Jana told me about her time in the psychiatric ward, and how doctors there had misunderstood symptoms from a witch's brew of ailments including post-traumatic stress disorder, the lingering effects of a contra-coup concussion that she suffered from the mortar blasts in Bosnia. She also had epilepsy linked to that brain trauma, and the early stages of Parkinson's disease. After the explosions, she had to relearn her own language, in sheer terror when she opened a dictionary and read the word *should*, knowing she could build a sentence around it, but having no idea what it meant. She couldn't even remember the alphabet. She had spent years relearning, but there were still enormous gaps in her memory and her ability to communicate. To the psychiatric ward doctors, this was symptomatic of psychosis, perhaps brought on by schizophrenia.

The doctors wanted her to attend a class on how to read a newspaper. They said to her, a photojournalist with credits in some of the world's best newspapers and magazines, "'Miss Schneider, can you answer this question about newspapers? Now we're doing pictures. What is this picture of? Can you tell me? Is that a cowboy?"

In time, Jana finally persuaded a judge to listen to reason. "In one hearing, the court officer stood up and said, 'Her name is Janet Ann Schneider—my birth name,'" Jana told me. "'She *has* received a nomination for a Tony in New York, and she also has been verified as an international photojournalist.'" And they continued with proceedings as if none of it had occurred.

10

DOWN AND OUT

*"I am alive," I said, "and if you seek fame, it may be precious to you
above all else that my notes on this descent include your name."*
DANTE ALIGHIERI, UPON HIS ENTRY INTO THE
NINTH CIRCLE OF HELL, *THE INFERNO*

I knew I had to get out of Africa fast. It had been years since I'd
been charmed by the simple pleasures of Malawi, where I went to
teach. The country was ruled by a quirky dictator, a physician
brought in from London as a figurehead for the independence movement, who quickly eliminated his top backers once the British left.
Officially, he was His Excellency the Life President of the Republic
of Malawi Ngwazi Dr. Hastings Kamuzu Banda, but most people
called him H.E. for short. The dictator wore Savile Row suits and a
homburg hat, carried a lion's tail fly whisk, and liked to dance with
circles of women bused in to ululate at his speeches. He declared bell-
bottom pants illegal, prohibited men from wearing their hair long
enough to touch their shirt collars, and refused to speak Chichewa,
the national language, or anything else but English, Ancient Greek,
and Latin. His speeches were translated live by the uncle of the Official Hostess, whom Banda lived with in his six palaces in lieu of a

wife. My introduction to life under an African tyrant had a certain comic charm.

I was posted to Providence Secondary School, a girls' boarding school run by Catholic nuns in the village of Chisitu, where the head-mistress was Sister Mary Joy Magombo, a tough disciplinarian. She had a mischievous side, a naughty sense of humor that she picked up during studies at an American college, which was revealed when she removed her starched white wimple. She enjoyed getting me worked up over one trivial matter or another and watching my face turn red. It was a playful diversion from dealing with the head of the English department, a lonely British widow who had lost two husbands to accidents, and seemed to be fighting some kind of curse. She spent evenings and weekends getting drunk in her house on the hill and chasing the neighbors' kids with the gardener's machete knife.

I'd lived just outside the compound's front gate, in a whitewashed bungalow with polished concrete floors and a corrugated iron roof. It was shaded by towering mahogany trees, from which a troop of monkeys launched raids on the banana plants in my backyard. It was a magical place for a young man straight out of his teens and hungry for adventure. From my living-room window, I could see the Mulanje massif, a broad finger of rock some sixteen miles long that rises 9,855 feet above rolling green tea fields that carpet the plains below. The first European to set eyes on it was the Scottish missionary David Livingstone, whose name had stirred romantic images of Africa in my imagination since I searched for him as a kid while playing American reporter Henry Morton Stanley in our primary school play.

In a way, I guess I was still acting out the fantasy of the noble white man in Africa at Providence. I had a barefoot cook and cleaner named Neverson, who insisted on addressing me as *bwana*, or sir. At first it embarrassed me, and I told Neverson to call me by my first name. That embarrassed him, so I learned to enjoy his subservience and unqualified respect. I had two drinking buddies, Mr. Banda, a beanpole-thin commerce teacher who indulged his sexual obsessions while his young wife was away studying at an agricultural college, and Mr. Chakwanira, an elfin, snuff-snorting biology teacher with a wispy beard, who was so saddened by the death of his first child that he gave the second a Chichewa name that meant, "We Are Still Crying."

Almost every day after school, the three of us would stroll along the strip road that ran past the school to the bottle store, where I'd buy rounds of Carlsberg Greens chilled to tepid in a kerosene-powered cooler. We sat there on a rickety bench, with beer bottles the size of bowling pins, waiting for a car to pass and provide a new topic of conversation. A woman driving alone stirred gossip about who might need the services of a local witch doctor famous for providing love potions to lure back wayward husbands. A car with young men from the city suggested a run to buy some of the potent local pot. Villagers rolled it in banana leaves wrapped in homemade twine, which they pulled tighter each day as the marijuana dried. The process compacted the pot into a dense "cob" so powerful that when I mixed a few tablespoons into a brownie mix, and ate just a few baked squares, I hallucinated and passed out for several hours. My African descent began long before she tempted me with war.

Mr. Banda fretted that I was lonely and arrived at my front door one Saturday morning with the bottle store owner's teenaged daughter and her friend. They were in their best dresses, sewn in the village style with puffy shoulders, and they were wearing plastic slip-on shoes. Mr. Banda asked if I had two bars of soap to give them as gifts. I knew where he was going with this, and I knew Sister Mary Joy would throw a fit if she found girls in my house, but Mr. Banda kept telling me to relax and enjoy myself. The girls sat giggling in the living room, watching us smoke a joint, and then Mr. Banda disappeared into the guest room with one. The bottle store owner's daughter led me to my bed. I lay there with her for less than a minute, dizzy from the pot, guilt, and her musky scent. Suddenly I leapt up, shouting: "Get out. Everyone get out. Now."

I banged on the guest room door, and Mr. Banda emerged, half-dressed, looking down at me with his bright, charming smile. "What's wrong?" he asked. "Don't you like her?"

"I told you, just get out. *Now.*"

He brought the girls together, apologized for my behavior, and made them promise to keep our secret. Then he glared at me. "You should still give them some soap," he whispered.

I opened the linen closet, grabbed two bars of Lux, and handed one to each girl as Mr. Banda hustled them out the back door.

Moral dilemmas only got more difficult to resolve the longer I lived in Africa. At least as a teacher, I felt like I was doing something for positive change. As a reporter, I felt more like a scavenger feeding off the decay. I needed a clean break, somewhere to start over again. After Jana disappeared, I put in for a transfer to become Asia bureau chief in Hong Kong, and when it was approved, I decided to make one last trip to Somalia. Part of me wanted to say goodbye, but mostly I just couldn't let go.

My boss had approved my move to Hong Kong at the start of the New Year, so there wasn't anything to gain by going to Somalia in December. But the last U.N. peacekeepers were getting ready to pull out, and that was a good enough excuse for me to go back one last time. Khareen came with me.

One night, it was getting too weird watching her snort Ritalin off the floor and flirt with every male in the room but me, so I went to bed. I'd been staring through the darkness for some time, waiting for her to come back to the room we were sharing in separate beds when I heard her outside making out with one of the photographers. I could hear the giggling and whispering and kissing as clearly as if it were coming from the bed next to mine.

After a while, the sounds of imminent sex disappeared down the hall and in the quiet I wished, harder than I ever had, someone would just shoot me. To improve my chances, I got up early the next morning and started out with my friend and interpreter Harun on a three-hundred-mile journey south in the desert and down the coast, through some of Somalia's most dangerous bandit country, to the city of Kismayu. I went on the pretext that I had to cover the latest shoot-out between the local warlord and one of his rivals. Everyone told me I was nuts. That it was suicide. But it turned out to be one of the most peaceful trips I'd ever had in Somalia. I just couldn't catch a break.

In Kismayu, I checked at the local hospital for a body count to gauge how serious the fighting had been. A nurse with Médecins Sans Frontières was astonished to see another foreigner wandering in.

"How did you get here?" she asked.

"We drove," I replied.

"Are you crazy?" she asked.

"Sometimes," I said, and left it at that.

When I got back to Mogadishu, Harun had a surprise for me. A group called Al-Ittihad al-Islami, which was Al Qaeda's affiliate in Somalia, was meting out medieval forms of punishment in sharia courts in its stronghold of Gedo on the Ethiopian border. Now they had spread to north Mogadishu. Across the Green Line that divided the city, north Mogadishu was under the control of Aideed's chief rival, Ali Mahdi Mohammed. A favorite of the Italian government who claimed to be the rightful ruler of Somalia, he enjoyed the luxuries of his European sponsors in his Italianate villa, and had bought into the radical Islamists' argument that the best way to rebuild Somalia's fractured society was to impose an especially cruel form of Islamic sharia law. The most serious offenses would be punished by death by stoning. The sharia court wanted to know if I'd like to witness a trial and execution, Harun said. Of course, the answer was obvious.

We raced safely through no man's land, and across the Green Line, to reach the court, but the local officials were disappointed. I had no cameras.

"I can go back and get them," Harun offered. "The judges will wait for us before they begin."

"No," I told him. "If they want me to take pictures, I'm not going to."

Maybe I was still feeling the backlash from the dead soldier picture. Maybe I was just being difficult for the sake of it. Whatever the motive, I know I did the right thing. I was not going to watch again through a camera lens as people killed just so they could send the message of their great victory to the world. And so the trial of Abdulahi Weheliye Omar and Gelle Omar Ali, both twenty-five and accused in the rape of eighteen-year-old Maryan Hussein Amir, began in the stifling heat of a cramped, bullet-scarred office on the second floor of a looted import-export company. They would be judged by twelve sheikhs, who sat in upholstered dining chairs in a semicircle behind an old office desk. They held copies of the Koran in their laps. Two guards flanked them with AK-47s at the ready. One also held a hand grenade.

The trial was brief. Both men admitted they had raped Amir three months earlier near the village of Mahadey, some sixty miles north of Mogadishu. The men had promised to help the teenager find her sister in the town of Johar. But after they met at the agreed time, around nine o'clock in the morning, the men led Amir into the bush, put a knife to her throat, and raped her for four hours. They also stole one hundred thousand Somali schillings, or about twenty dollars, which Amir had earned selling qat.

Since the details of the allegations were admitted as fact, the judges had only to decide the punishment. The outcome had been decided long before the trial began—as my invitation made clear. There was no suspense among the hundred or so spectators, all men, who sat cross-legged on a carpet, waiting for the judges to pronounce sentences stipulated by sharia law. They, too, knew what was coming, and with sweat dripping down their foreheads, and several elders struggling to stay awake, everyone was in a hurry to cut to the chase. Amir stood less than a yard from the men who had raped her, and they refused to look at her as the head judge took up a megaphone to announce the verdict.

As a bachelor, Ali would suffer one hundred lashes for the rape. But his accomplice, Omar, was married and therefore had compounded his crime by being at once a thief, a rapist, and an adulterer. And so his punishment would be suitably severe: death by stoning. Amir was pleased with the sentences, and refused to forgive the men. "They didn't do *me* any favors," she hissed, and then counted the greasy bank notes returned by the chief justice, to make sure all one hundred thousand schillings were in the stack bound by an elastic band.

Her rapists were led out of the court by a dozen gunmen into the shimmering midday heat, to a once grand public square that now looked more like a dirt parking lot, where a statue too heavy for the looters to cart off, and too solid for them to dismember and melt down, showed two Somalis of another age holding high the nation's flag. Beneath them, three hundred people, mostly women and children, were waiting to see justice done.

149

As I followed the courtroom spectators to the killing ground, one of them asked me, in halting English: "What do you do to a man in your country who has raped?"

"We put them in jail," I replied. "We don't kill them."

"But then they will rape again," the man countered, in righteous anger.

Omar and Ali were handcuffed together and forced to sit in the middle of the square, encircled by excited spectators standing forty yards away, chatting and laughing, eagerly awaiting the first blow. But they would have to wait still longer for the main event. First, an elderly man convicted of drinking beer in public would get forty lashes, a reduced sentence out of respect for his age. It was an uncommon bit of mercy from the sharia court sheikhs of north Mogadishu. In just the four months since the court opened on August 11, 1994, the judges had sentenced 182 convicts to lashings, amputations, or for the fortunate few, simple prison terms. Most of the amputees were thieves who had a hand and a leg cut off with any long knife that was available. Their wounds were cauterized by shoving the raw stumps of their amputated limbs into boiling oil, Chief Justice Sheikh Ali Sheikh Mohammed told me. Today the court would graduate to its first execution.

The lashing of the old man proved to be an excellent warm-up for the crowd. With each snap of leather against his skin, he twisted, trying in vain to block the blows with hands that were cuffed behind his back. It looked like he was dancing, and the crowd laughed.

The punishment of forty lashes complete, he was dragged away semi-conscious and drenched with a bucket of water to ensure he was awake to the pain. The whole time, the two rapists sat in the dirt, shackled together, awaiting their turns.

Then, the guards unlocked Ali from the cuff that held him to Omar's left ankle. They stripped off his shirt and blindfolded him with it. A sheikh counted off each lash, one through one hundred, over a megaphone, pausing only for the guards to adjust the blindfold. Ali was choking on it. *"Laa ilaaha illa laah, Mohammed Rasuulu laah,"* Ali chanted as each lash cut a new, bleeding welt in the crisscross pattern across his back. "I believe there is no rightfully worshipped God in the world save Allah, and Mohammed is his prophet."

The crowd laughed some more. After the hundredth lash, Ali stopped stumbling and writhing and lay unconscious in the dirt. Several men dragged Ali away and tried to revive him with water and camel's milk.

Then the spectators got what they had come for: Omar's life. Just behind him, a couple of guards tore open a tattered grain sack packed with chunks of broken concrete, which spilled onto the dirt. Omar's left wrist was handcuffed to his left ankle. He pleaded quietly with the guards, rocking slightly, unable to see how close his punishment now was. His only hope was that, at this last minute, someone would believe his claim that he was never married and commute his death sentence to one hundred lashes. Omar was still repeating, just above a whisper, that he was a single man when around twenty men fired the first jagged rocks, most of them about the size of softballs, at his back. I was standing in a VIP spot, yards behind him, unable to look into his eyes. The image of Cleveland flashed before me. In the face of the mob, I felt as helpless now as I had then.

Only men were permitted to stone someone to death. The women and children egged them on and heckled. The crowd laughed and cheered at the sharpest hits, like the one delivered by an elderly man who raised a hunk of concrete with both hands, high above his head, and smashed it down on Omar's. That opened a gaping wound near Omar's neck, and his body suddenly went still, except for his free foot, which quivered for about a minute and then stopped.

A guard craned over him to check his breathing, like a wary hunter searching for life in his wounded prey, afraid that it might lunge and bite. Even though his face was a swollen mess, Omar's chest was still heaving and he coughed a few times. Another guard unlocked his handcuffs and the barrage resumed. "Kill him. Don't make it difficult for him to die," Abdi Ali Alasow, the court's deputy chairman, shouted over the megaphone. "Each one of you take a stone. Continue until he is dead. Don't show any mercy."

Fifteen minutes after the first rock fell, Omar was still breathing, blood streaming from his nose and gurgling in his throat. He finally died after about twenty minutes, and the guards left the bloodstained rocks where they lay, piled up against the corpse of Amir's adulterous rapist.

"It's a big victory for the Muslims, especially in Somalia," Alasow announced to the satisfied crowd. "Take a lesson, those men and women who walk the streets embracing with their arms over each other's shoulder. Take a lesson."

As the crowd dispersed, I asked the court chairman if he knew that most of the world condemned such ruthless justice. Of course, he said, and quickly shrugged off any criticism as foreign meddling. No one should feel sorry for Omar, not after what he did to an innocent woman, Sheikh Mohammed added. "Not even one," he insisted. "We took a vote and they are all happy. The Muslim religion supports this. Even those who were amputated are happy. They told us so."

Afterwards, I wrote a piece on the execution for the *Star*. If there was much revulsion among newspaper readers back home, the letters to the editor didn't reflect it. Seven letters were printed, the last one on Christmas Eve, and only one condemned the execution. Both Muslims and non-Muslims supported the stoning. One of the latter, a woman, wrote: "Watson goes into great detail describing the 'barbaric' punishment 'meted' out to the rapists, while leaving little said about the brutal four-hour rape the victim endured. It is obvious that he has more sympathy for the rapists than the victim. Views like this help to place the criminal's rights above the rights of the victim." Another pointed out: "While the stoning to death of a self-confessed rapist appears abhorrent to us in the West, it must be recognized that this punishment is rooted in all revealed faiths. The Judeo-Christian tradition asks that the body of an adulterer be given to Satan while his soul awaits the Day of Judgment. Adultery is a sin condemned in the Ten Commandments." The letter condemning the killing came from a man who wanted to point out that the hard-line mullahs ruling Iran were delivering equally cruel justice. When I read the letters, I was glad that I had denied the Somali court sheikhs the publicity photos they had wanted. They could only have fed the bloodlust, I thought. If nothing else, maybe I had allowed a condemned man to die without the click and whirr of cameras taunting him, along with the laughter and cheers of unseen strangers.

I traveled home to Johannesburg through Nairobi, where I learned that another colleague had died. Hitoshi Numasawa, bureau chief for Japan's Kyodo News Agency, was killed December 6, 1994, along with five other people when their small chartered plane hit a television transmission tower, shortly after taking off in bad weather from Nairobi's Wilson Airport. It was the same airport where I'd boarded my first qat flight to Somalia on a vacation/reporting trip almost three years earlier. Hitoshi and the other journalists were flying to the

Rwandan refugee camps in Goma, Zaire, to find out how the genocidaires and their families were getting on.

Kyodo's top bosses flew in with Hitoshi's wife and their two young sons to join his closest friends and colleagues at his funeral. There wasn't a Buddhist temple in Nairobi, so the next best cremation ground was at a local Hindu temple, where Hitoshi's body lay encased in logs, smeared with sandalwood paste. Standing in the small circle of mourners, watching the Hindu priest prepare the pyre for lighting, my mind drifted back to the day I met Hitoshi, in a ground-floor room across from the front desk of the newly renovated Sahafi Hotel in Mogadishu. It was just days before U.S. Marines landed on the beach in 1993. There were no hotels to meet the needs of the gathering legions of journalists, so an American TV crew paid a local businessman to fix up the Sahafi.

By the time I arrived, there were no rooms left, so I begged him to let me have the storage room. It was either that, or sleep on the street, I told him. He relented and gave me two cans of cockroach spray to address a slight problem in the cupboards. I slowly opened one a crack, and a shaft of light fell on a skittering mass of bugs the size of mice. I gassed hundreds of them with both cans, and was cleaning up their carcasses and the rest of the room when Hitoshi knocked at the door. Would I mind, he asked, if he and a few other Japanese journalists moved in? They had no place else to go. I really wished they would just go away, but I knew they couldn't so I let them in. Soon they were feeding me ramen noodle soup in a plastic cup and we were friends.

Months later, when we bumped into each other in the Rwandan refugee camps, I told Hitoshi I was being transferred to Hong Kong and we made a date to meet in Tokyo. And now here I was watching his two young sons honoring an ancient tradition by trying to put the first flame to their father's funeral pyre. They each had a disposable lighter, and as hard as they flicked them, the flame quickly went out. It made them laugh, and while everyone else stood silent, a man in a dark suit stepped forward to help the boys light the fire that would burn their father to ashes. Their laughter turned to tears. It took a long time for the pyre to burn, and I stared into the flames, thinking of Hitoshi and myself and Somalia—what it had done to us.

As the dwindling pyre continued to pop and crackle, the mourners dispersed and one of Hitoshi's colleagues approached me. He gently shook my hand and thanked me for coming. "He wanted so much to be like you," the Japanese journalist said. He meant it as a compliment, but I felt obscene. What kind of game were we playing that left young boys behind to face life without a father, in the vain hope that we might enlighten people who chose not to understand each other.

When I got back to Johannesburg, a woman called from Amnesty International's headquarters in London. She had seen my death-by-stoning article, the first eyewitness account of Somalia's sharia courts in the Western press, and she wanted to confirm some of the details. "That was an incredible story," she said excitedly. "Do you have any pictures?"

"No," I told her. "They wanted me to take some, so I didn't." There were a few seconds of dead air on the long-distance line.

"Oh," she finally replied, and I could hear the eager anticipation leak from her voice.

No pictures, no proof. Which meant mine was just another uncorroborated story of African brutality. There were a lot of those. So the Amnesty woman asked a few polite questions and then hung up.

Back in Johannesburg, as my time in Africa ran out, I paid up the rent and the utilities for the house and spent an afternoon tripping on magic mushrooms with a photographer friend. I was hoping for a hallucinogenic sendoff, and all I got was intense, frightening paranoia. It made me even more eager to flee the place. I didn't want a long goodbye with old friends, but a quick getaway. Dr. Grinker was the only person I expected to miss. While the movers packed my things for shipment to Hong Kong, I stopped by his office for what I thought would be a final session. I really just wanted to thank him and say goodbye. He renewed my prescription for antidepressants, gave me a referral note, and urged me to find a good psychiatrist in Hong Kong to pick up where he had left off. Dr. Grinker also wrote out his home number and told me to call if I ran into trouble. My hour was up, but I lingered at his office door, afraid to leave.

It would be a long time before I attempted the journey again.

11

MISSING MASSOUD

Nothing is more seductive for man than his freedom of conscience,
but nothing is a greater cause of suffering.
IVAN KARAMAZOV, IN FYODOR DOSTOYEVSKY'S
THE BROTHERS KARAMAZOV

The way I imagined it, Asia was the perfect antidote for Africa. I could break out of the rut of starvation and civil war and write about economic miracles and emerging powers. Memories of gagging on the stench of rotting flesh would give way to dreams of breathing in the mystical scent of incense. If I didn't find spiritual enlighten-ment, at least I'd have a fair chance at a better outlook on life.

Khareen followed me to Hong Kong, and when I told her to leave, she got one leg up over my twenty-sixth-floor balcony railing and threatened to jump. I told her to go ahead. She left the apartment screaming, and hours later I got a call from the police saying they had picked her up in a delusional state and taken her to hospital. They let her go on the promise that she would board the next available flight back to South Africa. When I woke up, she had gone for good, along with my favorite Swiss watch.

From my new base in Hong Kong, I worked a beat that ran from northern China down across the Equator to Australia, and all the way west to Pakistan. A third of the world was mine. I had more than enough room to steer clear of combat, but its pull proved too strong for me to resist. Instead of seeing the light and writing something soft, say, a story about the Buddha's tooth preserved in a Sri Lankan temple, I hurried across the civil war's front line and hung out with the Tamil Tigers. It wasn't enough to sit and contemplate the transcendence of Cambodia's ancient Angkor Wat temple complex—I had to hop on the back of a guerrilla's motorcycle and go looking for the remnants of the genocidal Khmer Rouge. On the other side of an untamed frontier, where the Himalaya yielded to the Hindu Kush, I found Afghanistan to be the most wildly captivating of all.

After U.S.-backed mujahideen forced Soviet troops to end their almost decade-long occupation in 1989, Washington turned its back on Afghanistan as it collapsed into a ferocious civil war. Five years later, as local legend has it, members of a warlord's militia kidnapped and gang-raped two teenaged girls at a checkpoint in his home village of Singesar, in the dust-blown badlands an hour's drive from the southern city of Kandahar. It was a common crime, one that normally would have faded into the brutal monotony of violence that was strangling Afghanistan in 1994. But this time the atrocity changed the destiny not only of a country, but the world.

Mullah Mohammed Omar, an obscure country cleric and mujahideen veteran who lost an eye to shrapnel during the war against the Soviets, decided he had had enough. He mustered a small group of fighters, attacked the checkpoint, and then hanged the militia commander from a tank barrel. He then fled across the Pakistan border to the province of Baluchistan, where, with the help of military intelligence, he recruited fighters fired up for a new jihad by the puritanical Wahabi theology exported from Saudi Arabia and taught in hundreds

of Pakistan's madrassas, or Koranic schools. These students of religion, or Talibs, formed a militia called the Taliban, which used Pakistan army officers as front-line advisers, and war matériel and other
supplies from Pakistan, to win a series of stunning victories in their
sweep across southern Afghanistan.

As the Taliban advanced, Osama bin Laden was expelled from
Sudan and settled in the eastern Afghan city of Jalalabad. He provided financial support to the Taliban in return for bases to train
thousands of Al Qaeda militants, many of whom were, like bin Laden
and his new ally Mullah Omar, veterans of the war against the Soviets. Omar sealed the alliance by marrying off his daughter to one of
bin Laden's sons. By late September 1996, the Taliban had seized control of Kabul, the Afghan capital, and were again in the lynching
mood. They grabbed former Soviet-backed president Mohammad
Najibullah and his brother, Shapur Ahmadzai, who had sanctuary in
the United Nations' compound, and tortured and then hung them
from a police traffic tower with steel wire nooses.

It was just my kind of story, but I was far away in Hong Kong,
writing some forgettable piece about people smugglers. I was trying as
hard as I could to find significance in something other than war, and
missing a crucial turning point in history.

I finally set out for Afghanistan just over two months later, in
December 1996, when most journalists had moved on to some other
crisis. The mullah in charge of the Taliban's visa section in Islamabad
insisted I had to wait six weeks for approval from Kabul, but a Canadian diplomat persuaded the mullah to issue me a visa on the spot. A
taxi driver agreed to take me through the Khyber Pass to the Afghan
border without a permit. I refused to wear a burka as a disguise, so he
told me to lie down on the back seat and look asleep. We made it
through the first checkpoint, but got caught at the second by two

jubilant Pakistani police who seemed to think busting me was their ticket to a promotion. They loaded me into their pickup truck, and in broken English, went on about a trial and prison, grinning at me in the rear-view mirror.

We drove up a winding dirt track to a mudbrick compound on a mountainside. It looked like a fortress, and took me back to a Saturday matinee showing of *Gunga Din*. My fate was now in the hands of an Afridi tribal chieftain, whose people had little tolerance for interlopers who did not pay proper tribute in this smugglers' paradise, where the Afridis demanded a cut of any opium, heroin, rifle, or Sony Trinitron TV set that passed through their domain. For centuries, invading armies from Alexander the Great to Muslim conquerors and British imperialists had pushed their way along this same barren pass and failed to subdue the Pashtun tribesmen. As a British soldier remarked in the early twentieth century, "Every stone in the Khaibar has been soaked in blood." I was eager not to add a drop of my own.

The Afridi leader left me to sweat a bit in the corridor while he granted audience to various villagers who had come to resolve one dispute or another. When I was finally ushered in, a servant poured a cup of steaming green tea and put down a platter of nuts, raisins, and candies. The police, spitting with excitement, laid out the case against me. My taxi driver translated the chieftain's verdict, and about all I could understand was the word *jail*. I asked if I could pay a fine instead—the most polite word I could think of for bribe—and fumbled for a couple of twenty-dollar bills in my secret stash. We eventually settled on one hundred dollars, and with best wishes from the Afridis for a safe trip, I was back on the road in time to reach the Torkham border crossing by noon.

The tough tribesmen and dust-blown slopes on the Pakistani side of the frontier harked back to another era, but walking across to the

Afghan side, I was hurtled back to another century. The highway in from Pakistan, which passed bin Laden's new home of Jalalabad, had been reduced to mile after mile of craters and potholes. The taxi never got much over twenty miles an hour as the driver weaved around the jagged holes when he could, and inched his van through the rest.

Soviet bombs, civil war, and now the Taliban had all but destroyed the last vestiges of modernity, and ordinary Afghans were a broken people. The country's farmers were once the world's largest exporters of dried fruit, but most of the vineyards and orchards had withered in the war. Opium farmers and heroin traffickers were doing well, but the Taliban had put a stop to looters, who sold off all the wiring, doorknobs, window frames, and scrap they could steal across the border in Pakistan. Scrap exporters would now be decapitated. So scavengers took several steps down, and searched in graveyards and dumps for bones, which they bundled up in old sacks and sold to dealers for eight cents a kilo. The dealers exported them at a 20 percent profit to Pakistan, where Afghanistan's bones became ingredients in cheap soap and fertilizer. More than twenty-eight thousand children were living on the streets of Kabul, where government workers hadn't been paid a single Afghani note for months. The new Taliban regime had closed the banks and banned what had been the accepted currency, rendering any savings worthless.

The Talibs, with their black turbans and dark stares, had even banned music. Any cassette they sniffed out in a car, taxi van, or truck driver's cab was smashed on the rocks. They strung the tapes up from poles, decorating their checkpoints with what looked like thick streamers of shiny brown raffia blowing in the breeze.

In their rush to turn the ruins of Afghanistan into the leading example of Islamic perfection, the Talibs were cranking out decrees faster than anyone could keep up. Clean-shaven men were now criminals.

Enforcers from the Ministry for the Prevention of Vice and Promotion of Virtue went around tugging on men's beards to check if they were regulation length. If the religious police couldn't grab a fistful of facial hair, the beard was too short and a severe beating was in order. Waving hello was declared illegal, and in the only permissible greeting, a man was required to place his open right hand over his heart. The Talibs declared sports un-Islamic—even kite flying was banned. Photo shops were shut down because rendering an image of a human being was deemed an arrogant affront to God. Women were prohibited from working.

An exception was made for female doctors and nurses employed by foreign relief agencies. But the Talibs quickly overruled themselves and ordered female medical staff to go home, too. And so, as the Talibs spun an ever more complex and often contradictory web of diktats, they had to figure out how any doctor who was not the husband of a female patient could examine her without violating the strict rules on separation of sexes. Soon after I reached Kabul, Mofti Mohammad Masoom Afghani, acting minister of public health, issued a new decree that male doctors could not cross as they treated females. The female patient had to be enshrouded by a burka, while a male doctor could only reach under the head-to-toe veil to feel for what might ail her, always ensuring that he touched only the affected area. A simple look in the woman's eyes, or at her tongue, was difficult because they were reduced to a series of disconnected dots by the veil's heavy mesh.

Eventually, even the Talibs had to admit the medical system, already collapsing after years of war, couldn't function without women. So female doctors and nurses were called back to work, with strict orders to stay out of male patients' rooms. They weren't even allowed to be in the same room as a male staff member, so male doctors had to stop at the door of a female patient's room and try to guide their often less experienced female colleagues in a deadly game of blind man's bluff. Dr. Mohammed Hashem, director of Kabul's Malalai Maternity Hospital, later told me several of his patients bled to death as he struggled to figure out how to save their lives from a distance. The Talibs were certain in their faith that it was God's will. As Dr. Abdul Samay Hamed, a physician, poet, and closet political cartoonist, told me: the Taliban were "a puzzle that its creator was unable to solve."

When they weren't handcuffing doctors and nurses, the Taliban's edict writers did their best to make work difficult for most everyone else, including foreign journalists. Before the Taliban took over in Kabul, finding an Afghan interpreter was as easy as dropping by the Associated Press's house, and picking someone from the group waiting to be hired. The Talibs banned foreign reporters from working with any interpreter who had not been cleared by the foreign ministry.

When I arrived in Kabul, I went to the ministry's headquarters, a low-rise building with fading yellow paint, and trudged through the snow-covered grounds looking for a press office entrance. I searched the main building's first floor, knocking at each door, each time getting no response. I cracked every door to peek inside and every office was empty. It was the same on the second floor until I rounded a corner and found Najib Murshed sitting alone on a wooden chair in a bare room, staring out through an open door at the balcony in a freezing wind. He was next in line for work, patiently waiting for a journalist to arrive.

Najib had been an engineering student at Kabul University, which the Talibs had closed along with all the other schools while a special commission decided how to make the curriculum and dress code more properly Islamic. Najib also ran his own English school, so he did well on the Talibs' test for interpreters. He'd passed the foreign ministry's exam a month earlier, but didn't show up for work until the day we met; the Taliban had ordered him to use his accreditation or lose it. He had been sitting in the cold for a few hours before I arrived at the door. Wearing a thin white cotton shalwar kameez under a winter coat, he had a long, thick black beard, much more luxuriant than necessary to pass the Talibs' fist test. I assumed he must be a Taliban spy.

I had come for a month's assignment, hoping to be home in time for Christmas. Under another Taliban decree that was supposed to make it easier to keep an eye on foreign reporters, I couldn't stay at one of the comfortable guest houses run by aid workers. I had to take a room at the creepy Intercontinental Hotel that sat high on a hill overlooking Kabul. At the time, I was its only guest. It was so cold that hotel staff brought me six blankets and a gas heater, which only managed to warm the bone-chilling air within a six-inch radius of the flame. When I stuck my arm out from under the stack of blankets, my skin almost froze. Afraid that a Taliban informant might appear at my door at any moment, I was eager to flee to the countryside.

While I went through the motions of doing some reporting with Najib, I said as little as I could, and tried to dream up creative ways to shake him. And then, after working with him for a few days, the ice broke when we were riding in the back seat of a taxi. "I don't like the Taliban," he said, out of nowhere. "I just need work and this is the best job I can get."

Those few words formed a bond that grew into a deep trust as we began a long trip across Afghanistan. "What I really want to do is get out of Kabul and cross the front line into Northern Alliance territory," I told Najib. "I want to meet Ahmed Shah Massoud."

If Najib were an undercover Talib, he now had enough to turn me in as an enemy of the new Islamic state. But a broad smile spread across his face. Like Massoud, Najib was a Tajik, and his home village was in an area north of Kabul still under Northern Alliance control. Despite the enormous risks involved in taking me across the front line, Najib was as eager to go as I was. I formulated a plan: I would work with another approved translator and do a few interviews with Taliban officials, and then make it look like I was leaving the country by getting an exit permit stamped in my passport.

A few days later, at the foreign ministry, I told the Talib at the permit desk that I was going straight to the airport to catch a U.N. flight to Pakistan. Instead, I took a prearranged taxi to rendezvous with Najib at his house. We were now lawbreakers, enemies of the Taliban state, and if we got caught, the punishment would be severe.

I was willing to do whatever it took to get to Massoud because I had been intrigued by the legend of the Afghan warrior-philosopher since the war against the Soviets, when the Western media honored Massoud with the nickname "Lion of Panjshir." He and his forces had stopped the Soviets dead in their tracks at the southern end of the Panjshir Valley, where his guerrillas launched ambushes from steep mountain slopes. Some say Massoud's shrewd negotiating skills were even more important than his command of the battlefield, and that the Russians paid him handsomely in exchange for a ceasefire that left the Panjshir relatively safe from massive air assaults that destroyed much of Afghanistan. The image of Massoud in his round pakul hat, tilted like a beat poet's beret, an armed intellectual who could recall ancient Persian verse as easily as the range of any mortar bomb, had made a deep impression on me.

The only person who was willing to risk driving us across the front line of Taliban territory, and who had Najib's trust, was a truck driver named Mohammed Ayub, a rotund, middle-aged man with a pixie's grin. His moustache was shaved, and his best effort in the face of Taliban threats could only produce a wispy gray beard. He looked like a leprechaun. He called on a neighbor to borrow a car, a clunky yellow 1982 Lada, a battered survivor of the Soviet occupation. Behind front bucket seats upholstered in red velvet, a heavy black steel bar bolted to the doorframes ran the width of the car, to keep the vehicle from shaking itself to pieces. The dashboard was covered in gray fox fur and a tarnished silver serpent dangled from the rearview mirror in homage to the Afghan superstition that if a serpent slithers through your dream, you're about to get rich. I was paying Ayub fifty dollars a day, and the car was a mess: the heater that blew cold air, the windshield wipers were locked in the "Off" position, the crankcase leaked oil, the radiator spewed water, and the engine that died every few hours on roads where a stopped car was practically a flashing beacon to highway robbers.

As we chugged north out of Kabul, across the no man's land between Taliban and Northern Alliance forces on the Shomali Plain, the towering Hindu Kush mountains were a massive wall of white. In a dense morning fog, it was hard to know where the frozen earth ended and the sky began. Highway maintenance was not a Taliban priority, so the roads were covered in thick ice that gradually melted during the day only to refreeze each night. Across the plain, Taliban fighters were pounding Northern Alliance holdouts in the town of Qaliqan, and the ground was littered with dozens of corpses.

At the junction to the Bagram airbase road, Talibs stopped us at a checkpoint. I could tell from their voices that this was more than the usual hassle. When Najib grimly told me to get out of the car, I thought we'd been found out. But instead they asked for papers for the car. Ayub's neighbor hadn't handed over the Lada's registration documents. The Talibs said they were impounding it until Ayub produced the proper papers, so we caught a bus back to Kabul.

On a second try, we made it to Massoud's former stronghold of Jabal Saraj, which was now under Taliban control. Massoud was trained in guerrilla warfare in the early 1970s by the same Pakistani Inter-Services Intelligence Directorate, the military's omnipotent spy agency, that was teaching Taliban recruits how to defeat him. Known as a brilliant commander and a bad politician, Massoud had little time for the buying and selling that was central to warlord politics. His detractors said he hadn't had any qualms about making deals with the Soviets to hold on to the Panjshir, but geography strengthened his hand there. As the Taliban swept across the south and north, leaving Massoud's Northern Alliance in control of roughly 10 percent of the country, he was just beginning to make the necessary moves to present himself as the legitimate alternative to Mullah Omar's regime.

But he was up against stiff odds. Pakistan, Saudi Arabia, and the United Arab Emirates, the only countries to officially recognize Taliban rule, were working hard to persuade the United States to join them. As incentive, they dangled the prospect of building an oil and gas pipeline through Taliban-controlled territory for U.S. and other Western companies to export rich Central Asian reserves. Massoud had much less to offer.

A few months after he led a retreat into the Panjshir in late 1996, Massoud's Jabal Saraj house was much as he had left it. The Taliban who now lived there had gathered up some of Massoud's leftover ammunition—mortar bombs from China, land mines from Russia, and cases of rocket-propelled grenades and bullets from Iran—and piled them at his former compound's entrance. But they left his satellite dish, bench swing, push lawn mower, and milking machine in the backyard, along with his mini-gym. In his haste, the Lion of Panjshir was forced to abandon an electric treadmill, an exercise bike, a chin-up bar, parallel bars, and a swivel wheel I'd seen advertised on TV as the perfect way to work off love handles.

Massoud's library, said to contain some three thousand books, was also untouched. His close friend, diplomat Massood Khalili, later told me that whenever Massoud was forced to give up a base, he would pack his most loved books, like the Koran and volumes of ancient Persian poetry, and gradually build a new library around them. While the Talibs cleaned their Kalashnikovs on the verandah, I spent several minutes scanning Massoud's bookshelves, trying to get a glimpse of his mind. There were French romance novels, biographies of Enlightenment philosophers, numerous histories, and several books on American democracy and its icons, such as Thomas Jefferson.

I imagined Massoud studying the pages, trying to learn where great men had succeeded and failed, trying to map his own way to victory. From the titles on his shelves, I could only guess at who he was. But the men willing to die on his orders said he inspired sacrifice by example. He was such a disciplined Muslim, they insisted, that he wouldn't even let them smoke. I knew his militia was far from pure. It was accused of trafficking heroin, smuggling emeralds, and running other rackets. But among the thugs and war criminals that were Massoud's allies, he seemed the only one capable of making the transition from warrior to statesman. He was losing ground fast, though, and his aides said he was resisting U.S. pressure to surrender to the Taliban with all the strength he had left.

By the time Ayub got us back to Kabul, it was too late in the day to stay there because the Taliban would probably discover our ruse, deport me, and throw Najib and Ayub in jail as subversives. We decided that instead of pursuing Massoud across the front lines, it was safer for the moment to head southwest to Kandahar, the Taliban's spiritual capital, hoping the hardliners in the south didn't figure out we were lawbreakers, and would be willing to help us find the reclusive Mullah Omar, the Amir ul Momenim—the Prince of All Believers. We might as well have been searching for the Wizard of Oz. We left as the sun was setting, and without letting on how scared he was, Najib said a quiet prayer. Ayub whispered one too, and as he stroked his meager beard with one hand, he nudged the Lada into gear with the other. We headed down one of the worst, most dangerous routes in the country, through desert and barren mountains, along a road with shell craters and pond-sized potholes that made the car buck and fishtail over the ice.

After about an hour's drive, Ayub pulled over at a mudbrick restaurant where we would ask to sleep the night. Najib, who had survived countless rocket attacks and other close calls over the endless years of war, later told me he felt a shiver of terror worse than any he had felt before as we walked into the room, where half a dozen wild-eyed Talibs, each with his own assault rifle, glared at us. Najib didn't let on that he thought the men looked like killers who could rob us, shoot us, and dump our bodies in the snow and go back to their steaming cups of green tea as if we'd never been there. I thought they looked like any other Talibs and quickly fell asleep on the floor as the men argued. Najib lay next to me, keeping watch through the night as he prayed that we would live to see the dawn.

His prayers were answered, and I had one of the deepest sleeps of my adult life. We were back in the Lada at first light, making an average of twelve miles an hour. Even at parking-lot speed, Ayub bottomed out on an icy mogul. Oil was leaking out almost as fast as he could pour it in. We pressed on and stocked up on new cans of oil where we could, and as the sun set on the second night, I pulled my down-filled sleeping bag over the top of me, huddled in a tight cocoon, and fell asleep shivering in the back seat. Just half an hour outside

Kandahar, I awoke to the smell of burning rubber. I shouted to Najib, who translated to Ayub, who took a deep whiff, and then another, and said the engine block was just burning off some oil he'd spilled during the last refill stop. He kept going and the smell, and smoke, got thicker.

Najib finally persuaded Ayub to pull over and step out into the freezing darkness to look under the hood. He unscrewed the radiator cap, and from the faint trails of steam that he could make out, Ayub concluded the radiator was almost bone-dry. We were stranded in pitch darkness, stuck between mountains on one side and desert on the other. In the dead silence, Ayub had a stroke of genius. He asked for one of my empty Coke bottles and told us to piss in it.

Ayub and Najib each made their contributions, which were piddling. I'd just taken a leak an hour earlier, but somehow I summoned up a more substantial stream, aiming as sharply as I could to trap every drop. After laughing at my performance, Ayub emptied the bottle into the radiator with the rest and it disappeared into the engine like raindrops on desert sand. We needed more fluid—a lot more.

Then Najib heard the trickling of moving water somewhere in the darkness. The roadsides and desert outside Kandahar were littered with land mines, but the water sounded close, so Najib took a gamble. He told Ayub to follow him with my flashlight, which wasn't much brighter than a match flame. I pulled my sleeping bag back over my head and listened to the sound of my breathing, oblivious to the fact that the only two people with any hope of protecting me were walking blindly toward a very high cliff.

"Stop!" Najib suddenly shouted, just as Ayub was about to take a step over the edge, saving both of them from a fifteen-hundred-foot plunge. They came back to the car, terrified. We sat together in the fog of our own freezing breath, trying to figure out how to get something liquid into the radiator.

"We could melt snow," I offered. We didn't have matches. "How about spitting into it?"

"Shhhh," Najib said. "I think I hear a truck."

I strained to hear an engine. There was nothing, but Najib was certain now. And sure enough, after about ten minutes, I could hear the truck grinding in the distance as it crawled along the ice. Najib flagged it down, and I could see several plastic containers lashed to the side. The driver looked down at us from the cab and drove off into the darkness. We waited silently, and another truck came and went.

"They think we're thieves," Najib said. "They don't trust us."

I was starting to think that crying into the radiator might work, when another truck stopped and the driver gave us a little water. He was low and didn't want to risk running out himself. Then a convoy of trucks came, and we filled our radiator to overflowing. It was around midnight, and snow had given way to pouring rain, when we finally passed through the last Taliban checkpoint and entered Kandahar, where the hotels were locked up for the night. The streets were deserted except for a watchman with a lantern, who hammered on a metal door to wake the innkeeper.

I awoke just before dawn to a chorus of muezzins calling the faithful to prayer. "Allahu Akbar!" they cried over loudspeakers mounted on scores of minarets. "God is Great!"

We visited Mullah Omar's foreign relations office, where we were told his deputy on the Supreme Council, Mullah Hasan Akhund, might be willing to see us. While waiting for an appointment, we killed time by taking a tour of the city. In winter, it was several shades of brown and gray, a depressing place where bin Laden would soon build lavish villas for himself and Omar among the crumbling ruins of a once great city named after Alexander the Great, who founded it in the fourth century B.C.

During our ride around town, a man claiming to be a mullah stopped our car and said we were breaking the law. He'd heard a new edict, read out on the radio the night before, which decreed that it was illegal for foreigners to ride in private taxis. He seemed satisfied with the chance to scold a foreigner, and let us go, but I should have taken it as a hint that we were being watched. On the way back to our hotel, I noticed several photo shops with packages of Fujifilm stacked up in the window, even though a Taliban decree had shut down photo studios and printing shops in Kabul on the grounds that portraying the human form was idolatrous, and therefore blasphemy.

Our first-floor room looked out over Kandahar's broad main street. Several groups of men and boys were enjoying a sunny afternoon after the rain by playing rope tag, called *resman bazy*, in circles on the street's wide median, in front of large crowds of spectators. The player with the rope closed his eyes, and by swinging the rope, he tried to touch one of his opponents. It was tame as sports go in a country where *buzkashi*, a game in which two teams on horseback try to grab the headless carcass of a goat, is the national pastime. But since the Taliban had banned all sports everywhere else, I thought this bit of hypocrisy in Mullah Omar's spiritual capital would make a good picture. I sat on the floor, raised a telephoto lens to the open window, and shot a few quick frames of rope tag.

I thought I'd gotten away with it until Najib came back stunned from a visit to Mullah Akhund's office to check on our appointment. Two Taliban intelligence officers had stopped him. "You will be arrested in a few minutes' time," one said.

"Why?" Najib asked, fearing the Talibs had tracked our illegal journey.

"Well, I'll tell you this only so that you are informed: you were taking pictures from the window. Everybody knows about it now."

Najib hurried back up the stairs and was trembling when he told me a spy had spotted me taking pictures of the street games. I hadn't seen him so frightened before. As I told him not to worry, that if I'd done anything wrong, it couldn't possibly be serious, I realized I had no idea what I was talking about, and no business putting him in such grave danger. Najib wanted to make a run for it in Ayub's sputtering car once darkness fell.

"Najib, we can't do that," I told him. "We really haven't done anything wrong, and if we run like criminals, it will only make things worse."

"Paul, they won't do anything to you, but they'll put me in jail."

"I promise you, I won't leave Kandahar unless you're with me. Don't worry," I said, trying to sound confident. I knew that if the Talibs threw Najib behind bars, and ordered me to leave, I wouldn't be able to do anything about it. He knew they were weak words, but took heart anyway, thinking that at least I could get his name into the news and make sure he didn't disappear. I wasn't sure I had even that much power.

Najib wondered whether he should go back to Akhund's office and turn himself in or wait for the Talibs to come and arrest us. The sound of every car door slamming in the street below, and each footstep in the hallway outside our door, pulled the knot in my stomach tighter. The next morning, the Talib in charge of the local information ministry settled the debate by summoning us to his office.

"Tell me what to say to save us, and I'll say it—anything," I told Najib.

Mullah Haqani refused to shake my hand and remained sitting behind his bare desk, ignoring us as several of his men sat on the floor in a circle, eating flatbread and drinking tea. The mullah let us stew for a while before pointing out the spy who had turned us in, a man with a snitch's grin who was obviously very pleased with his catch. Mullah Haqani confirmed the basic points of my crime. As we'd agreed, Najib spoke first. "Sir, I'm very sorry," he said. "This journalist is doing things and not listening to me. He took some pictures of kids playing in the street, and I told him this was not allowed, but he didn't listen to me. So in your own words, sir, please explain it to him so that he understands."

"In our movement, it is a serious offense to photograph a complete human body," the mullah said, and he tapped the desk. "You are very lucky. Our soldiers are under orders to arrest anyone seen breaking this and other Islamic laws. They could have beaten you, broken your cameras, and put you in jail. Since you are our guest, out of respect to you, the soldier who witnessed this only reported the incident and did not take you to prison. But if you are caught again, you will be prosecuted. You can go now."

Najib asked the mullah to make our release formal, and put it in writing. That way, we'd have a senior Talib's signature on a piece of paper to wave at illiterate guards at checkpoints. Hardly a guarantee of safe passage, but better than nothing. We were already packed, and the Talibs didn't think to check my passport to make sure I was legal, so it didn't take us long to hightail it out of Kandahar.

On the long trip back to Kabul, on one of several detours around destroyed bridges, we got stuck behind a convoy of buses full of cartons of new Sony Trinitron TVs stacked to the ceilings and on the roofs. One of the buses had tipped over as it snaked up a muddy embankment. It crushed an assistant driver trying to guide his partner to a better stretch of road. When Ayub got out to dig us from the muck, he sank into it ankle-deep. The mud sucked both soles off his shoes with his first two steps. As usual, he was undaunted. Much like his country, Ayub kept struggling to move forward no matter what.

Near Ghazni, we slept in a kebab restaurant on a brick floor warmed by a fire burning beneath it. When we got up the next morning, it was so cold outside that the car was frozen solid in a crater filled with ice. Ayub simply poured down a puddle of gasoline and started a fire under the Lada to set it free.

When we reached Kabul again, it was even more risky to hang around because our run-in with the Talib spies in Kandahar could eventually get our names on a watch list. Fortunately, the Talibs were not efficient bureaucrats, and we slipped through Kabul undetected in a matter of hours. We were only there long enough to switch cars to a slightly more sturdy Volga before heading north for another try at finding Massoud. The front-line Taliban commander at the mouth of the Salang Pass was suspicious. "Where are you taking the foreigner?" he snapped.

"Dear Commander," Najib sweet-talked the Talib. "As you know, the Northern Alliance has blown up the tunnel and destroyed the bridges, and committed a lot of crimes. But the people do not believe. We want to go and see it for ourselves and reflect it in the media that these are truly crimes!"

The Talib smiled and snapped his fingers: "Let him go," he ordered his men.

We drove five hundred yards up the pass to a ruined bridge that Massoud had ordered destroyed as he retreated. Najib told our driver to return to Kabul without us, and we walked half an hour to the other side of the front line. In a quirk of Afghan warfare, thousands of traders kept up busy traffic, in both directions, across the front whenever there was a lull in fighting. As we walked north, a long caravan of porters passed us heading south carrying rolled-up carpets on their heads for export. In the nearby Panjshir Valley, where Massoud's forces had held out for decades against Soviet troops and now the Taliban, traders moved their goods on packhorses, donkeys, or in wheelbarrows. The better off simply drove their cars and trucks up to the pile of shattered boulders at the river's edge, where workers pushed logs through open windows so a crane could hook up and lift the vehicles over the chasm. After our hike across the front, we hired a cab, a newer Lada, and made fast progress north until three members of Uzbek warlord Abdul Rashid Dostum's militia stopped our car at a checkpoint and forced their way in for a free ride.

"Najib, where are these guys going?" I asked.

"They are going to Mazar-i-Sharif."

"What? All the way to Mazar? That's impossible. Either they go to Mazar or I do. Not both. Tell them I will report to General Dostum that his men are thugs and highway robbers."

Najib ordered the driver to stop and translated what I'd said. I could read the "You must be kidding" in their sheepish grins, which quickly turned to scowls as they weighed the advantages and disadvantages of shooting me and taking the car. They finally got out at the side of the road and sulked as they watched us drive off. When we reached Mazar, home to one of the holiest shrines in Islam, we were famished and went straight to a popular kebab place. The long tables were lined up in rows, and there was hardly an empty seat, but few of the patrons were eating. I followed their stares to a color TV mounted above a cassette deck near the front door. It was tuned into media baron Rupert Murdoch's Star TV satellite network, which was broadcasting *Baywatch*. It was a Friday, the Muslim Sabbath, and they were ogling nearly naked women bounding in slow motion along a beach.

I wondered if they realized how close the Taliban were.

We headed north again to Kunduz, still searching for someone who could take us to Massoud. (We never did find anyone who could. He was too busy defending Afghanistan, his people told us, and none of his allies seemed interested in anything more than lining their pockets.)

Instead we met with a local Northern Alliance commander who was in a funk, certain that his side was going to lose because it was too brutal and corrupt. I sat in the half-light and pulsing hiss of Mirza Mohammed Naseri's gas lamp. Most of the anti-Taliban alliance's soldiers hadn't been paid in months, he said, so they supported themselves by robbing people. Anyone who was arrested was usually freed within a few hours when his commander pressured police to let him go.

"And this helps the Taliban," Naseri said. "Being strict should be the first quality of the government in Afghanistan—like the Taliban."

He liked what others denounced as Taliban cruelty, especially their swift executions. Naseri had lost 367 relatives in the war against the Soviets, and at forty, he had lost most of his life to war. He spoke fondly of his three wives, and their ten children, longing for a peace that would allow them to have normal lives. Only a severe, honest government could save Afghanistan, he said, and so far, the Taliban struck him as the only faction with the strength and discipline to end the long agony. But I could tell from his voice that Naseri knew he would never see the day. He was killed months after he spoke to us, when the Taliban stormed north by buying off some warlords.

12

A CROSSROADS TO WAR

War is the greatest of all crimes; and yet there is no aggressor who does not color his crime with the pretext of justice.
VOLTAIRE

The *Star* was wearing me down by mincing in-depth features into short stories that said little more, and often less, than the wire reports. I was also still using cameras that I paid for myself because, even though I'd won the Pulitzer, the paper still refused to provide me with any camera equipment. I was a staff reporter, and the bosses didn't want to encourage any fantasies that I might be a photographer too.

One morning, after telling Toronto I'd quit, I was in the Hong Kong office of a French photo agency, borrowing the computer to update my resume. Suddenly, I saw in a different light a friend who helped run the operation. She was cute and a volunteer counselor on a suicide hotline, which in my state of mind was certainly a bonus. The bosses in Toronto talked me out of leaving, at least for a while, and over the next few months, I grew closer to Shum Sai Hung. If I kissed her, I knew I would soon want to marry her. I was afraid, and told her: "I don't want to ruin your life. I like you too much."

"Don't I have a say in the matter?" she asked.

I proposed at a quiet bend in a path on Victoria Peak, overlooking the twinkling neon rainbow of Hong Kong at night. Sai Hung wanted three good reasons why she should say yes. I remember only two: "I love you more than anyone else in the world," and "I promise you an adventure." We were legally married in a civil ceremony in Vancouver in October 1997, but we didn't consider ourselves properly wedded until our relatives and friends witnessed the union at a banquet in Hong Kong in the spring of 1998, the Year of the Tiger. Sai Hung gave me the greatest gift that any person could.

Our wedding gave some order to my personal life, and I knew it was time to get my career on a better track too.

I would have done just about anything to get a job on the *Los Angeles Times'* storied foreign staff, and I started pestering foreign editor Simon Li at an opportune time: he needed someone to cover the escalating slaughter in Kosovo. He had several good reasons not to hire me, but I persuaded him to at least give me a look. We met in the basement coffee shop of Hong Kong's legendary Foreign Correspondents' Club, a white, two-story colonial building surrounded by glass and steel office towers. It used to be the British colony's Ice House, but foreign journalists made it their watering hole in 1982. It had gone upmarket since the Vietnam era, when, as John le Carré wrote in *The Honorable Schoolboy*, correspondents "fooled and drank in a mood of violent idleness, a chorus without a hero." Upstairs, the walls of the reading room next to the main bar were shrines to some of the greatest names in combat photography, people like Eddie Adams, who shot the picture of Saigon's police chief firing a bullet into the head of a suspected Viet Cong, and Nick Ut, whose image of the naked, napalmed girl fleeing in terror is an icon of war's cruelty. I was glad Li was flipping through my scrapbook downstairs, where I only risked embarrassing myself in front of the coffee bar waiters and any lunch hour drunks who got lost staggering to the toilet.

"I'll be honest," Li said. "You scare me. You take too many risks."

"I take *calculated* risks," I parried. "I'm no more eager to get killed than anyone else." Which, at that moment, was true.

Li wanted to know what I would do if I were working for him in a war zone and he ordered me to leave. He'd had a problem with another correspondent in a similar situation. It was a painful thought, leaving a war early and hanging out on the sidelines with mobs of journalists, fighting over scraps. But I really wanted the job. "If you at least allowed a discussion, let me give you the reasons why I thought I should stay, and still insisted that I leave?" I replied, quietly cursing the thought. "Then I would go."

I got hired as Vienna bureau chief in the summer of 1998 and moved to Austria that fall with Sai Hung, and immediately left for Kosovo.

In time, I saw Kosovo differently than many other foreign reporters did. Most had come to its conflict by way of Bosnia, whose war began when the republic exercised its constitutional right to secede from the Yugoslav federation. Bosnia was not a country split by civil war, but the victim of a war of aggression fomented by outsiders, with Bosnian Serbs doing the bidding of Yugoslav president Slobodan Milosevic while Bosnian Croats took their lead from Croatian president Franjo Tudjman. Each tried to dismember a sovereign nation. But the battle lines were drawn differently in Kosovo, where an Orthodox Serbian minority had centuries-old religious and cultural roots in a land dominated by Muslim ethnic Albanians. The province was recognized by the world as part of Serbia, so its conflict fit the normal definition of a civil war, which made sorting out right from wrong more difficult—unless you simply carried on with the Bosnian plotline, retaining Milosevic as the evil instigator and the ethnic Albanians as the underdog good guys. And that is largely what the Western media did. At first, I, too, stuck to the stereotypes, but I learned that the situation in Kosovo was much more complicated than it appeared.

When Milosevic, Tudjman, and Bosnian president Alija Izetbegovic met on the Wright-Patterson Air Force Base to agree to end the Bosnian war in 1995, Kosovo Albanians were left at the gates protesting their exclusion. The following year, ethnic Albanian guerrillas in the Kosovo Liberation Army (KLA—also known by the Albanian acronym UCK) began killing Serbian police, civilians, and ethnic Albanians accused of collaborating with the government. Robert Gelbard, Clinton's special envoy to the region, said in February 1998, "We condemn very strongly terrorist actions in Kosovo. The UCK is, without any question, a terrorist group."

Milosevic apparently took Gelbard's statement as a green light for an offensive against the KLA, which was still a ragtag group of rebels mainly holed up in Drenica Valley. Five days after Gelbard spoke, the KLA ambushed and killed four Serbian police in Kosovo. It was the latest in a series of attacks that had left at least fifty police dead in a year, and the security forces went on a rampage, killing twenty-four ethnic Albanians in retaliation. All-out civil war had begun.

For years after Milosevic revoked Kosovo's autonomy in 1989, the United States and its European allies had backed a peaceful resistance movement led by Ibrahim Rugova, a Sorbonne graduate in an ascot whose Gandhian principles sounded good, but could hardly compete with the horrific images of war and genocide that kept the news focused on other parts of the former Yugoslavia. The KLA began to organize in 1991, but their early attacks were more harassment than war. Serbian forces surrounded the farmhouse of a KLA rebel leader, Adem Jashari, late that year. The Serbs pulled back when villagers rallied to defend Jashari outside his farmhouse command post in the village of Donji Prekaz.

Jashari, a forty-two-year-old farmer with a luxuriant gray beard and an ample reputation as a local thug, was left free to build up his rebel army for seven years. He was tried and convicted in absentia on terrorism charges before the security forces returned again to his house on March 5, 1998. According to the KLA's version of events, Jashari could see Serbian forces massing the night before, yet he stayed put with nineteen members of his family, many of them women and children. He knew what was coming and welcomed it because he thought a massacre was the spark that would wake up his nation, a close friend of Jashari's told me a year later. "He had a chance to be far from his house, but he wanted to show everybody that the best defense of your homeland starts from your own home," Gani Koci, a top KLA official, explained.

Jashari and his lieutenants had obviously learned one of the main lessons of war in the 1990s: Western politicians were moved to action by images of civilians suffering. The KLA needed foreign intervention against the Serbs, so they decided to generate the right pictures. Milosevic's forces obliged with a three-day assault by helicopter gunships and ground forces that killed Jashari and his family along with thirty-six relatives and neighbors, some of whom were shot at close range as they tried to flee.

It was precisely the Bosnia-style carnage that Jashari wanted, and it played in the world's media just as powerfully as he had imagined. The headline in the *New York Times* declared: "Gun Battles in Serbia Raise Fear of 'Another Bosnia.'" And the KLA, led by extremists and drug traffickers who were so recently labeled terrorists by the United States, were now vividly portrayed as the downtrodden victims of ruthless Serbs. Rugova had gotten Kosovo into the polite conversations of Western salons, but the KLA was forcing it onto ordinary people's TV screens. The shift from peaceful resistance to bloody rebellion would lead to NATO's first war. It was waged in the name of humanitarian intervention, but it tilted Western policy sharply behind the KLA guerrillas' goal, one that at first the West insisted it didn't support: independence for Kosovo.

It was sickening to see how well the strategy worked. Many times when I crossed through a Serbian police checkpoint and then drove a few hundred yards down a dirt track to enter KLA territory, my mind drifted back to Eritrea, where the guerrillas had long stopped caring what the outside world thought of their struggle. They were determined to fight Africa's biggest army and win independence on their own. And they did. The KLA wasn't strong enough, or sufficiently organized as a people's movement, to defeat Milosevic's forces by itself. So they attacked to provoke. Inevitably, the Serbs retaliated just as the KLA wanted, burning villages and killing civilians, and the drumbeat for NATO intervention grew steadily louder.

Milosevic wasn't the first to try to defeat a guerrilla army that hid among civilians by driving thousands of them from their homes. At the turn of the twentieth century, the British coined the term "concentration camp" in South Africa during the Boer War. They forced white Afrikaner civilians, and many of their black servants, into camps so that British troops could wage a scorched-earth policy and deny the guerrillas food and shelter. More than forty thousand innocent detainees, most of them children, died of illnesses born of hunger or from outright starvation.

Decades later, the French government forced more than a million Algerians into camps, and condoned torture and summary executions in a brutal war for independence that lasted from 1954 to 1962. And during the Vietnam War, U.S. forces frustrated by a guerrilla enemy well-entrenched in villages, unleashed the covert Phoenix program, under which CIA hit squads killed some eighteen hundred people a month, for a total of at least twenty thousand dead. When I watched Yugoslav army soldiers setting fire to ethnic Albanian homes one morning, I immediately thought of the TV images I'd seen as a kid of American GIs with Zippo lighters setting fire to thatched roofs so that Vietnamese villagers could be relocated to "strategic hamlets" while their villages became free-fire zones.

The Serbs committed their massacres, and when they had the upper hand, the ethnic Albanians executed Serbs and torched their villages. The morass made foreign condemnation, and claims that intervention was a moral imperative, hard for me to stomach. Before pulling out of Kosovo on the eve of the war, ceasefire monitors from the Organization for Security and Cooperation in Europe (OSCE) distributed satellite phones to trusted ethnic Albanians, who were asked to call in regular reports of what they saw, a long-distance human rights monitoring mission. To the Serbs, it was spying. KLA guerrillas had separate links to NATO forces to coordinate attacks, effectively adding the rebels to the alliance's strike force.

As a Yugoslav commander confided to me, it made no sense to fight one enemy in the air and another on the ground, so the army, police, and paramilitaries were quickly sent to deal with the KLA, and the rebels' village bases, before NATO bombs and cruise missiles began to strike. As brutal as it sounded, it made perfect military sense. And since Clinton had insisted that NATO's attack must only be from the air, to avoid any unpopular American casualties on the ground, the Serbs were left virtually free to burn, rape, and slaughter innocent villagers as they tried to flush out KLA rebels and deny them sanctuary.

I celebrated my first wedding anniversary alone, covering the worsening war in Kosovo. Like everyone else there, I had a bad feeling about what was coming. But I didn't really get it until I felt the breath of the monster as it peeked over a ridge of Cicavica mountain, a long massif that pierced like a dagger into the heart of rebel territory. I'd spent months watching the slow-motion destruction of Kosovo, small rebel assaults on police or Serbian farmers followed by ruthless revenge attacks on ethnic Albanians, usually by the thuggish interior ministry police, known by the Serbian acronym MUP. The pre-emptive offensive in the final days before NATO launched its air strikes was a horror of a different order.

To get a closer look at the forces mounting a pincer attack, I drove with British reporter Julius Strauss and his ethnic Albanian interpreter in an armored vehicle to the new Cicavica front on March 16, 1999, just over a week before NATO attacked. The car was a Land Rover fitted out with steel plate, which was too heavy for the transmission and engine, so it had an unnerving habit of dying at the most inopportune moments. It was painted white, with TV in large black letters on the sides and roof, which made it an irresistible target for Serbian snipers. Following a daily routine, we passed through a Serbian police checkpoint, and then a KLA post, and drove across a narrow valley toward the village of Lubovac, nestled in some trees at the base of Cicavica. The place was empty and deathly quiet, with some fresh laundry on a clothesline lifting gently in the breeze. Strauss quickly cranked the steering wheel, desperately trying to get the hard car to do an about-face in a three-point turn on the steep dirt track. We were just reaching the other side of the valley when the first mortar bomb struck, a few dozen yards from the bumper's front left corner. It exploded with an ear-piercing blast that made the armored car shudder, and sent a large spray of dirt and rock into the air.

"Shit," Strauss shouted as he stepped on the brake. The three of us were shoulder-to-shoulder in the front seat, and the interpreter was shrieking so loudly in my ear that I couldn't hear the engine sputtering out. "I don't want to die!" she screamed.

A second mortar bomb fell behind the car, shaking the ground and spitting out a plume of oily black smoke.

"Let's go, Julius," I said, trying to keep my voice level.

"The fucking thing is stalled," he snapped back. I immediately heard the voice of the British entrepreneur in London who had rented the vehicle to me over the phone from Pristina, with the caution that it should be driven gently. And not an inch of it was covered by insurance.

Another mortar bomb fell in front, this time much closer. The Yugoslav soldiers on the ridge were correcting fire, walking the mortars in to hit us. They must have been new to this, enjoying a slow kill, or simply stunned by their good fortune of a sitting target. They were taking their sweet time.

Julius got the engine to turn over, and another mortar bomb blew up behind us.

"Okay, do we go forward or backward?" he asked calmly, looking at me across his crying interpreter. I was flattered that he'd asked, terrified that our three lives probably rested on the answer. And then I remembered a war movie scene. "Wait," I told him.

After a few seconds of excruciating silence, another bomb exploded in front, still closer. "Now count," I said. We got to around eight seconds. The next bomb struck right behind us. The soldiers were close to finding their range. "You've got five seconds to get us the hell out of here!"

The Land Rover lurched forward, grinding and shuddering in first gear, as Julius struggled to keep it moving up the winding dirt track. There was a heavy, metallic thunk that sounded like a bullet glancing off the armor. The next bomb exploded seconds later, just behind us again. We'd broken free of the tightening noose, and the hard car kept running long enough to get us to cover at the KLA checkpoint, where several colleagues had been watching, waiting to see if the soldiers would hit us. I imagine a pool had already started on the number of rounds it would take to finish us off.

Over the next week, the crisis built to a frenzied crescendo. The threat of NATO air strikes had stirred the pot, and a low-intensity civil war was quickly boiling over into a vicious free-for-all. As Serbian forces stormed through the rebels' village strongholds and poured into towns and cities, ethnic Albanian and Serbian civilians were scrambling for cover. Any who could afford to get out of Kosovo altogether crammed their belongings into Yugos and trucks and either headed north to a safer part of Serbia or made a run for the international border.

One day, I followed the gray smoke of a dying house fire to the village of Novolan, overlooking the town of Vucitrn. Like most of the surrounding villages, it was deserted except for a couple of stragglers who had doubled back to collect a few cherished items after Yugoslav army soldiers and two Serbian police ordered everyone to leave within fifteen minutes, and to take nothing with them. As Nazmi Pliana, a grizzled old ethnic Albanian farmer, took cover behind a haystack to talk to us in a hushed voice, new fires began to consume three houses in the village on the next hill. A single rifle shot cracked the silence. "Anything they can't carry, they are destroying," Pliana said, watching the horizon in case the Serbs returned. And in a few moments time, they did, creeping up from the other direction in a camouflaged carrier from a special police unit.

The commander swaggered up the path with a bully's self-satisfied smirk, a look that was enough to make the villagers cower. He was known as Vucina, or The Wolf. Field radios poked out of both shoulder pockets of his blue-and-black camouflaged fatigues. A large army knife was strapped across his chest, and he was carrying a machine gun. A civilian, a Serb who spoke fluent Albanian, walked a half-step behind him.

After checking my papers and Pliana's, the commander gave Pliana a cold stare and suggested he let me know how well the police had treated him. "Tell them, did any of the police beat you?" the commander asked the old man. "Did you have any problems with Serbs?"

"No, I didn't," Pliana replied. His weathered hands were trembling, and the smoke was still rising from the remains of his neighbors' houses, no more than two hundred yards behind him.

The commander then turned to the old man's relative, Arsim Shahini. "I know this man's cousin," he said. "He is an honest man. I know these are good people."

When the APC was halfway back down the hill, heading toward Vucitrn, Pliana and Shahini rushed into a house, grabbed a treasured wall clock and as many plastic bags stuffed with clothes as they could carry, and fled.

With each day, the frantic exodus spread like a raging viral fever across Kosovo. Tens of thousands of people were on the move, many streaming into Pristina, the provincial capital, past others hurrying into the countryside.

It was a gamble to find the best refuge from the NATO bombs, KLA guerrillas, and the inevitable revenge killings by Serbian forces. A war that had cost just over two thousand Kosovo Albanian and Serb lives in its first year was about to explode and kill several times that in just over two months. Even Rugova, the "Gandhi of Kosovo," whose peaceful resistance movement had been neutralized by the shift of Western support to the KLA, was resigned to the violence that was spiraling beyond anyone's control. Sure innocent people will die, his aide Xhemail Mustafa, conceded to me. But there was no vote on which families should be martyred, no call for children who wanted to join the dead in the name of nationalism. War would make that choice for them. Mustafa assured me the people were united in their eager anticipation of what was about to hit. "Now they feel that the moment they will be free is very near," he said. "And they know they must pay a price to be free."

Journalists staying at the Grand Hotel started receiving threatening calls in their rooms. They should leave immediately, the male voice warned in broken English, if they wanted to stay alive. Zoran Cirjakovic, the *Los Angeles Times'* heroic Serbian fixer, who had bravely shepherded numerous journalists through the heartbreaking conflicts that had torn his country apart, was stepping off the elevator into the hotel lobby when another Serb, a stranger in civilian clothes, greeted him by name: "You see," the man said with a menacing smile, "we know who you are." Zoran took the hint, packed his bags, and left that night for Belgrade.

It was the eve of NATO's air war and Mahije Mala, the wife of one of Jashari's founding lieutenants in the KLA, was running out of places to hide. She and her five children had barely escaped with their lives when Yugoslav soldiers and Serbian police swarmed down from Cicavica and through the Drenica valley. Mala was abandoned to defend her children when KLA guerrillas fled the village of Prekaz, the very place where Kosovo's civil war had begun in earnest a little more than a year earlier with the assault on Jashari's house. When Serbian police stormed into Mala's home, she refused to answer their questions. So one grabbed her seventeen-year-old daughter, Iliriana, and put a knife to her throat. "Tell me, who is your father?" he asked.

To save her life, the girl admitted the truth. The police let the family go and turned to burn the house. Mala and the kids joined some twenty thousand people who fled into Pristina looking for some semblance of a safe haven. Local KLA supporters led them to a school in the Sunny Hill district overlooking the city. They couldn't risk going any farther because police at nearby checkpoints were screening everyone coming into the city center. The cops were rarely in a charitable mood, and now they were hungry for payback. Two nights earlier, KLA guerrillas had ambushed and killed four Serbian police at a checkpoint in the city.

Hordes of police, some of them disguised in black balaclavas, were racing through the city in blue armored vehicles. A unit had gunned down Kushtrim Gashi, shooting the eighteen-year-old student from thirty yards away with a single bullet in the back, as he tried to escape the neighborhood because the police were going door to door searching for KLA members. He was of fighting age, and that alone was enough for him to be hauled away.

Now Mala and her family didn't dare risk trying to leave the school. They were terrified even to look out the window.

Emina Berisha, an ethnic Albanian journalist who had taken over as my interpreter when Zoran was forced to pull out, heard about the school from sources on the street. She led me there on the afternoon of March 23, 1999, as the clock was ticking down to the first NATO air strikes that night. Mala and her kids had been given the luxury of their own classroom, where we found each member of the family on wooden benches or sitting at pupils' desks, exhausted from a series of sleepless nights. The concrete floor was freezing cold and their only warmth came from winter clothes they'd been wearing for days on the run. A few of the children lay their heads on the desks but were too scared to sleep. Their eyes were locked on the near distance, staring into nothing, with the same look I'd seen on so many.

"I'm afraid, very much afraid," Mala told me, gently rocking her five-year-old son in her lap as she began to cry. "Last night, there was shooting everywhere around us. I don't know what was happening."

After I'd finished asking questions, taken a few pictures of the forlorn family at their desks, and thanked Mala for her courage, she had a question for me. "She wants to know if we can help her escape," Emina said.

"We have no choice," I replied, afraid of what I was about to get us into, and worse, what would happen if I failed. "She has kids. We can't leave them here." I was breaking the cardinal rule against getting directly involved for the first time. For most of my career, I've carried around in my wallet a laminated magazine clipping of an Alexis de Tocqueville quote from the 19th century, which I think has gained relevance with age: "If one wishes to know the real power of the press," he wrote," one should pay attention, not to what it says, but to the way in which it is listened to. . . It only cries so loud because its audience is becoming deaf." In my work, I'd always tried to gather as many compelling facts as I could and let them speak for themselves to a jury of readers. As I went on, it became harder to figure out who, if anyone, was right, so taking one side or another made no sense anyway, and, now, standing with Mala and her kids, feeling the weight of their will prodding me to act, I wondered how telling their story in print could be anything more than a cop-out. I didn't want someone's death on my conscience, and I knew they had little chance of living if I turned my back on them.

We agreed that the best way to manage the risk of getting caught was to split up the family. If we got stopped at a checkpoint, or by a roving police patrol, a family of six with no local address, crammed into a foreign journalist's car, would be a dead giveaway. We took most of the luggage, and the two oldest children, first. They would be better able to fend for themselves if the second run went wrong and the family was split up. They hugged their mother, and she cried as they promised they would be together again soon.

Emina had long experience in dodging the cops in Kosovo, and as we made our way to the car, she was already gathering intelligence from locals on where the nearest checkpoints were, and which back roads and lanes offered the best hope of avoiding them. Still, we came dangerously close a few times. When we rounded a corner and a checkpoint came into view just down the hill, we made a sudden U-turn. Emina plotted a new route with information she gathered from young men loitering in front of shops, talking quickly and walking off to avoid detection from spies and snitches who were fingering suspects for the Serbs.

We finally made it to a neighborhood Emina knew well, and she asked people she could trust who would be the best person to shelter Mala and her kids. They pointed to the home of an elderly widow who lived alone, who came to the door dressed in black, with a matching kerchief covering her gray hair. She didn't strike me as the kind of person who could fend off marauding Serbs. She wasn't eager to take in boarders.

"I'm just an old woman," she said. "I have nothing, not even to take care of myself."

"Tell her I'll pay for everything the family needs," I said to Emina impatiently. It was late afternoon and we had to finish the second run and get off the streets before dark. I pulled five twenty-dollar bills from my stash. I didn't think the family would be hiding in this house long, either because the war would soon be over, or the police would find them well before that.

The old lady looked at the money and reluctantly agreed to hide the family. We left the two oldest kids with her, and she told us not to worry as we rushed off to get the rest. Mala looked surprised when we walked back into the classroom and was overjoyed when Emina told her the others were waiting at the widow's house. We packed Mala, her three kids, and the remaining bags into the car. She whispered again that no matter what happened, they must be quiet. They couldn't cry. Emina led us along the same route that had worked the first time. Serbian police were nothing if not predictable, and the checkpoints hadn't moved. They didn't find us worth chasing as we careened down dirt side roads, stirring up a long plume of dust.

When we reached the widow's house, she was waiting with the kids at the door. We quickly unloaded the car and begged the old woman again to do everything she could to protect the family. As we got ready to drive off, Mala and her kids waved from the window. I wondered whether I would ever see them again.

13

BLUE BODY BAG #4

*People who shut their eyes to reality simply invite their own destruction,
and anyone who insists on remaining in a state of innocence long after
that innocence is dead turns himself into a monster.*
JAMES BALDWIN

I was sitting in a friend's room at the Grand Hotel, scanning the
chill night sky through an open window, when the air strikes
started with pinpoint timing at 8 p.m. on March 24, 1999. The first
strike, from a bomb or a cruise missile, flashed bright orange about a
mile outside Pristina, where the Marshal Tito Army Barracks were
located. Then a second explosion sent a tremor rattling through the
windowpane. An ambulance raced past, blue emergency lights flashing, siren wailing. At 8:10, a shuddering boom, and suddenly the city
fell dark and silent. Through the night, bombs hammered the barracks, spewing great clouds of fiery sparks into the blackness. Some of
the explosions were so powerful that the blast waves, after traveling
several miles in seconds, felt like a puff of warm breeze as they gently
lifted the hotel curtains.

NATO had telegraphed its attack well in advance. The threat was
supposed to make Milosevic back down without a fight. NATO

insisted it only wanted to stop "ethnic cleansing," but Milosevic suspected a plot to break up what was left of his country and remove him from power. His commanders had prepared for the worst and dispersed their forces and equipment, camouflaging real hardware and deploying ingenious decoys to fool the pilots, in ways that would have made Tito's partisans proud. In small towns across Kosovo, hulking Yugoslav army tanks were backed into narrow alleyways between houses and shops, with barely an inch to spare on either side, where overhanging roofs cloaked them from prowling NATO warplanes. When dense fog rolled in each morning in the war's early days, the Serbs saw it as God's own camouflage and their armor roamed free through the countryside. Teams of soldiers were sent out into the fields to hammer together bits of wood and plastic tarps, with long protruding pipes meant to look like menacing barrels to pilots searching for targets from fifteen thousand feet. Driving by the decoys, I thought they looked foolish, like junkyard jungle gyms. But in NATO's daily slide show for journalists in Brussels, the blasted remnants of these phony weapons appeared along with other "kills" on colorful maps that tallied the alliance's progress.

Meanwhile, Serbian thugs had little to fear. Since NATO had also made it clear that no ground troops were coming, largely at Clinton's insistence, the bombs and cruise missiles only fueled the Serbian terror against civilians. Foreign journalists got a hint of it on the first night. As the bombs fell, gunmen worked the Grand's dingy hallways, beating on flimsy wooden doors with their rifle butts. They herded a Spanish TV crew against a wall and fired a bullet near one of the crew members' heads. By the time the goons reached my room, I was lying in the darkness on my bed, listening to the explosions. They were distant then, and slightly soothing, like an August thunderstorm rolling off in retreat.

I held my breath and lay still. The hammering stopped and a drunken voice shouted. I slipped as quietly as I could to the floor, trying to hide behind the bed. The rifle butt hit the door harder and it sounded ready to splinter. But then I heard the voice receding down the hallway and the battering resumed at someone else's door.

I awoke to anarchy. After a night's bombing, the Serbs were really riled. Masked gunmen were seizing journalists' armored cars, and while I fantasized briefly about mine being full of Serb paramilitaries and stalling out under an A-10 anti-tank jet's strafing run, I remembered the warning about no insurance: replacement value one hundred thousand dollars. I quickly moved it to the hotel's underground lot. When I went to get my soft car, a blood-red Opel rented in Belgrade on the strict condition that I not drive it to Kosovo, I saw CNN's crew being robbed at gunpoint in front of the hotel. I walked a little faster to the side street where I was parked, and saw two more journalists spread-eagled against their car, which was parallel parked just behind mine. Two uniformed interior ministry cops had drawn guns on them. I thought of minding my own business and trying to make a getaway, but instead turned and asked if they needed help.

The cops saw the keys to the Opel in my hand, and immediately realized my car was a better steal, so they ordered me to spread 'em and let the others go.

"Papers!" a cop with a beer gut and a face darkened by a night's unshaven stubble, shouted in my ear.

I unlocked the door and started searching for the registration papers and rental contract, but couldn't find them in the glove compartment. The guns pointing at my back didn't improve my shaky memory. I was sure Zoran had given me the documents before he left, with instructions never to leave them in the car in case it was stolen. But for the life of me, I couldn't remember where I'd put them.

"They must be up in my room," I told the cop from the driver's seat. He motioned for me to give him the keys, and I ran for the hotel, assuming he would give me a break if I hustled.

I was riding the elevator back down when I remembered Zoran had stuffed the documents in the left pocket of my winter coat. When I reached the side street, registration in hand, the car was long gone. I would see it many times in the coming days, usually full of four shaven-headed young men the size of fullbacks in leather jackets, one holding a large Serbian flag outside the passenger window as the car raced through Pristina's streets. A distinctive dent in the front end left no doubt it was my car. At least I'd saved the insurance papers.

By early afternoon, any journalists who hadn't had the good sense, and a vehicle, to get out of Kosovo, were ordered to leave by the government. Foreign journalists were being expelled because they, "by their reporting from the territory of the Republic of Serbia, strengthened the aggressive acts of NATO forces aimed at violent destruction of . . . the territorial integrity of Serbia and Yugoslavia," an edict from Belgrade declared.

The government was trying to get rid of witnesses. I tried to argue with the head of the semi-official media center in the hotel, but he insisted the order was firm. I had ten minutes to pack. I grabbed what I could, stiffed the Grand for a very large hotel bill, and headed for the hard car in the underground lot. I was surprised to see it was still there, but there was no attendant in sight, so I made full use of the armor and smashed through the wooden tollgate.

While I waited for the convoy of journalists to head for the border under police escort, I picked up a straggler, a freelancer from Peru. We reached Skopje, the capital of neighboring Macedonia, in the dark and drove straight into an anti-war protest. People were pelting us with eggs, climbing on the armored car, trying to rip the side mirrors off as I drove around, trying to find a room in a city swamped with foreign journalists, aid workers, spies, and various military types.

After a couple of hours, getting completely lost and battered by protesters, the desk clerk at a small hotel took pity on the Peruvian and me. But he said we could have a room only for one night. The next morning, I was depressed by the thought of trying to find another hotel vacancy just so I could join hundreds of other reporters covering a war they couldn't see. I looked at the eager young Peruvian in the next bed, who wouldn't stop talking about how excited he was about us working together, and I started obsessing about how I could ditch him.

Just then, like a broadcast from heaven, CNN flashed three headlines on the screen. Only the third registered: it said Vuk Draskovic, a mercurial opponent of Milosevic who joined his government as deputy prime minister, had announced all foreign journalists were welcome to return. Draskovic didn't have a lot of authority in a regime that later tried to assassinate him with a swerving dump truck, but his invitation was good enough for me. "I'm going back," I said, jumping out of bed.

"You're what?" the Peruvian asked, looking hurt.

"I'm going back."

"Where?"

"To Kosovo," I replied, stuffing things into my suitcase.

"Are you crazy?"

"Probably."

"You must take me with you."

"No, I mustn't. You're free to keep the room till check-out time. I'll pay the bill on my way out."

The hard car was almost out of gas, and I had no clue which way the border was. I wove through traffic in the groaning hulk, scanning the horizon for some recognizable landmark, and purely by fate I found a gas station on the main road back to the Kosovo crossing. I was the first one there. When I presented my passport, the border police were too stunned to say no.

"Vuk Draskovic says I can come back," I assured them, pointing to my multiple-entry visa.

They scowled and told me to wait. I sat on the curb. If I got turned back to Skopje, I might have to hang myself with the shower curtain of the first hotel room I could find. While the border guards made some calls, I listened to the steady whisper of jet noise as NATO war-planes flew to distant targets.

Suddenly the cops returned with my passport, smiling and showing me the entry stamp, and waving me forward to customs inspection. I'd broken the satellite phone, a portable unit the size of an encyclopedia volume, into several parts, concealing coiled wires in socks, hiding other bits in my shaving kit, under books and wrapped up in clothes. But the customs officials, who were already drunk at mid-morning, were more interested in things they could use anyway.

One held up my Ray Bans. "Take them," I smiled. "A gift from me."

He put them on, beamed at his friends, and then stuck his head back into the hard car. A colleague rummaged and found two Leather-mans. "Yours," I declared.

After looting some batteries, a bag full of film, and a few other items, the border guards let me go with my essentials. The border slammed shut behind me; I'd be the only reporter for a Western news-paper to see the seventy-eight-day war from start to finish.

The cell phone signal dropped fast as I made the winding climb out of the border town of General Jankovic, the lone vehicle heading into the war as a long column of cars crammed full of frightened eth-nic Albanians headed out, trying to escape to Macedonia. If my luck held, I would have time for two brief calls. I made the first to Zoran in Belgrade, to let him know I was back. I wanted him to know where to start looking if I didn't make it to Pristina. After we spoke, there was barely enough of a connection through the Macedonian cell phone service to make one last call. I dialed my apartment in Vienna and prayed that my wife would answer. I was afraid that it would be the last time I'd hear her voice, and I wanted her to understand why I had to go back. "There's no one else left in there who will say what's really going on," I said, knowing she knew me too well to fall for the noble truth-seeker line. "I want to know what happens."

She'd lived with a fitfully recovering war junkie long enough to understand why I really had to be there—that I didn't need to say more.

"Is it safe?" she asked.

"Well . . . Not really," I replied, my heart creeping into my throat.

"Good luck, then."

We both said, "I love you." And the line went dead.

Just as I rounded a curve, I ran into a checkpoint manned by Ser-bian paramilitary fighters. They were stopping the cars of fleeing eth-nic Albanians, demanding they hand over hard currency and other valuables. The Serbs looked just as shocked to see me as I was to see them, waving assault rifles, and yelling at me to stop.

"TV! TV?" he shouted, looking wild-eyed through the bulletproof driver's side window, and into the back, searching for a video camera.

"No TV! No TV!" I hollered back, with a sheepish grin, shoulders shrugged and palms turned to the ceiling, the universal symbol of: "Who, me?"

He waved me on, anxious to get back to robbing ethnic Albanians, away from my prying eyes. The Land Rover made slow progress under all the armor plating, and I had to talk my way through several checkpoints along the route. At the worst one, at a crossroads about halfway to Pristina, a fat commander with a bullet dangling from a gold chain on his bare chest frowned at my passport. "Canada. NATO," he sneered, and several of his men crowded in, nodding eagerly, as if they smelled a roadside execution coming on. It was the first time in my life someone had suggested Canada was dangerous.

"Mila Mulroney. Wife of Canada's prime minister. She's a Serb," I said, leaving out a few other facts—she was born in Sarajevo, we shared the same birthday, and her husband, Brian Mulroney, had been out of office for almost six years. The commander turned to a young soldier with coke-bottle glasses and a few days' growth of beard, apparently the intellectual of the group. He confirmed my story, and there were smiles all around. Permission to proceed.

Within a couple of hours of crossing the border, and after several scares, I was finally standing at the front desk of the Grand, hoping there were no hard feelings that I'd momentarily skipped out on the bill. I still had the room key in my pocket. The nervous desk clerk looked at my passport, up at me, at my stamped entry visa, back up at me, back at the passport, and finally blurted out: "You cannot stay here! Our countries have broken off diplomatic relations!"

"You must be joking," I said.

A younger man came out of an office behind the front desk. I recognized him as a Serbian intelligence officer who had kept a close eye on foreign journalists in the weeks before the NATO air strikes began. He escorted me to my room, saying that higher authorities would decide whether I could stay. He called room service to order two bottles of Coke for me, made me promise several times that I did not have a satellite phone, and left. I sat there waiting for him to come back with the cops and take me away. But he never did.

That night, I pieced the hidden parts of my satellite phone together, adjusted the small dish at the window to get a signal, and then crawled into bed with my laptop to file a story on police in black balaclavas terrorizing the city, unfazed by NATO bombs. I was afraid that the blue glow of the laptop's screen would give me away to anyone looking up from the blacked-out city, so I bent my knees to make a kind of pup tent and pulled the blanket over my head. The boot-up tune was so loud that I cursed Bill Gates and held a pillow over the computer until it was finished. Then I typed commands to send the story, listening to car doors slamming outside, voices in the hallway, wondering if my luck had run out. Story filed, I pulled the satellite phone apart and hid the pieces under the mattress, shoving the largest ones far under the bed. Over the next eleven weeks, I spent so much time lying on the filthy carpet, groping for the phone bits and then shoving them back into the dark, that the crook of my right arm broke out in a ghastly pink rash.

The hotel staff had warned me not to leave the building, or speak English in public, so I acted dumb to survive and carry on reporting. Each morning, I put on my bulky winter coat, carried an empty plastic shopping bag, and joined the lineups outside the few state shops that were open. Speaking English would have gotten me arrested, or worse, so I pointed at the items on store shelves that I wanted to buy. I started out with things that seemed safest, least likely to provoke questions, because they were at eye level or within arm's reach. I especially needed things I wouldn't have to cook later, which restricted my early war diet to bad chocolate, pickles, stale bread, and when I could stomach it, greasy garlic sausage.

Having one hand was my salvation. I think the middle-aged Serbian lady behind the cash register thought I was a disabled war veteran, able only to grunt. It was unheard of for workers at state-run shops to get up and help a customer. They found smiling a severe imposition. But whenever this one overweight babushka of a cashier saw me come in, she would smile like my own grandmother, come out from behind the register and follow me up and down the aisles, placing the items I grunted for and pointed at into my basket. I still feel guilty for violating her kindness, for making her think I was a hero of her wounded nation. I was tempted several times to reciprocate her compassion with honesty, to take the risk and say thank you, but I thought she would probably batter me to the floor with a jar of dills.

I figured the long waits in food lines would bore any security agents tailing me and make it easy to shake them. So once my shopping bag was half full, I set out to see if I could find Emina's house. She had shown me the route by car the day before the bombing began as we rehearsed our evacuation plan, one that included moving her sister's family from a ground floor apartment next to a police checkpoint to what we thought would be a safer place in an older ethnic Albanian neighborhood. On foot, I quickly got lost. So I wandered, mute and carrying a shopping bag, past police roadblocks and ethnic Albanian sentries on the lookout for raiding cops and paramilitaries, all the while avoiding eye contact and trying to will the world to ignore me. But I had food in a bag and numerous people, Serbs and ethnic Albanians, stopped me to ask where I'd bought it. I just shrugged my shoulders, gestured at my open mouth, and walked on.

I finally recognized a metal gate at the lane to Emina's house, and when I found her, we hugged, and shocked relatives brought out food and orange soda for a welcoming party. They were scared, but in a festive mood, after a night of sitting on the roof and watching NATO bombs blow up. "Of course, the children are sometimes afraid of the explosions," Emina said. "But we explain that they are helping us to be free."

I hadn't even finished my orange drink before Emina said it was time to leave. She insisted we go to the home of Bajram Kelmendi, Kosovo's leading human rights lawyer. "The police came to his house last night and murdered Bajram and his two teenaged sons," she said.

"Do you really think it's a good idea for you to go there with me?" I asked, knowing there was no way I could get in and get the story if she didn't.

"We have to," she said, getting up. "Let's go."

As we walked through almost deserted back streets to Kelmendi's house, Emina told me the police still had the place under surveillance. I was sure we were walking into a trap, but Emina was as calm as ever. At Kelmendi's house, his distraught widow, Hekibe, was seated at one end of the living room, and twenty women, mostly elderly and wearing headscarves, sat on chairs and couches against three walls, weeping with her. I sat next to her, afraid that if the police were watching, and had figured out who I was, they would hurt her for talking to a foreigner. I asked Emina to make sure Hekibe knew I was a journalist, and that I would quote her by name. Then I asked if she was sure she wanted to take the risk.

"What more can they do to me?" replied Hekibe, a lawyer and secretary-general of one of Kosovo's main political parties. I felt weak.

The night before, just after 1 a.m., five Serbian police officers in fatigues and armed with AK-47s had called on the sixty-two-year-old Kelmendi. One was holding what looked like a bomb made out of two cylinders taped together. "Open the door!" another shouted at Hekibe, and when she refused, they kicked it down.

The police warned that the bomb was about to explode and gave the family five seconds to leave. Hekibe called the police emergency number and asked them to send someone quickly to defuse the explosives. The person who answered hung up on her.

When the bomb didn't explode, the men stormed into the house and found the Kelmendis' oldest son, Kastriot, eating bread in the kitchen with his wife and their two children, Elena and Sokol, aged six and two. Bajram's teenaged son, Kushtrim, went upstairs to wake his father, who, when he saw what was happening, couldn't move. The police ordered the rest of his family to lie face down on the floor, and pointed the barrels of their rifles at the Kelmendis' heads.

"Bajram was looking at us from the stairs," his widow said. "I thought he was already dead in his heart. I asked him, 'Are you alive?' The police said, 'Keep your head down or we will shoot.'"

Bajram's daughter-in-law, Vjollca, interrupted and told me she had pleaded with the police to spare them. "I said, 'If you know God, and have children, and in the name of your sisters and mothers, please don't do anything.' They told me to shut up or they were going to hit me. They asked me for foreign money, German marks or American dollars. I told them I had none, and they said if they found some they would kill one of my children. Then they asked Bajram, 'Where are your weapons?' He replied: 'I am a lawyer. I don't keep weapons.'"

The police were so sure of getting away with what they were about to do that they didn't bother covering their faces. Hekibe looked straight into their eyes before they left with her husband and Kastriot

206

and Kushtrim. The death squad dumped their corpses at the side of a road. The body of the father lay between his two sons.

"They were executed," Hekibe told me. "Bajram was hit with more bullets. There was blood all over his body. They were angry with Bajram because he was a big fighter for the national cause and our rights."

After the murders, men drove past the Kelmendis' house in Bajram's indigo Opel Vectra as if they wanted to taunt Hekibe with the power of their impunity. As I thanked her for her courage, and expressed my condolences one more time, I wondered whether the men in the Opel had added Emina and me to their target list. At the door, I stuffed my spiral notebook down the back of my pants, hoping that if I got stopped, I might somehow talk my way out of it and keep the notes long enough to get the Kelmendi murder story transmitted to Los Angeles. Emina walked off alone without a word and I headed back toward the Grand, the muscles down my neck and back tensed for what I thought was the inevitable tap on the shoulder.

I reached my room without getting stopped and the notebook was wet from the rivulets of sweat rolling down my back. I stuffed it under the mattress and, exhausted from fear, fell asleep in the middle of the afternoon.

Clanking and hammering in the parking lot beneath my window woke me up. Six Serbs were breaking the locks of the armored Land Rover, changing the slashed tires, and replacing the ignition. I grabbed my camera and ran down the stairs. "What the hell do you think you're doing?" I shouted at them. They gave me a silent *Huh?* look, so I answered the question for them. "You're stealing my car."

"We are not stealing anything," one smirked. "It is being taken in the service of the nation." With that, they brushed me off like a buzzing fly, so I used up the last frames of the only roll of film the customs officers hadn't looted to take pictures of the men stealing my rented armored car.

I wasn't stupid enough to drive around Kosovo in an armored vehicle with TV emblazoned on the sides, so I didn't need it. I was more worried about explaining to the bosses that they'd have to pay the British owner $100,000. As long as the shopping ruse held up, and I could get to Emina, I was still in business. The next day, officials in the Serbian media center let me know that they were taking heat for my Kelmendi story, which they'd downloaded from the Internet. But they let me stay anyhow, and I moved around the countryside by hitching rides with Greek TV crews, Serbian photographers, or journalist Aleksandar Mitic, who shared my Canadian alma mater and reported for Agence FrancePresse in Kosovo. The only restriction was that I couldn't enter "operational areas," which were clearly demarcated by the smoke rising from torched homes, and the streams of terrified people ordered to leave the country. That still left me with a lot of room to roam.

Claims from outside Kosovo, including by various officials in Washington and Brussels, that the Serbs were engaged in a wholesale campaign to drive all ethnic Albanians from Kosovo, and commit genocide, simply were not true. Toward the end of the war, when public support was flagging, Defense Secretary William Cohen claimed that up to one hundred thousand ethnic Albanian men were missing in Kosovo, and might have been murdered. It was a gross exaggeration of the crimes in Kosovo, where more sober assessments by war crimes investigators after the fighting stopped and the propaganda was dialed down concluded that between five and ten thousand ethnic Albanians were killed. NATO itself admitted to killing up to fifteen hundred civilians, while Yugoslav authorities said the actual death toll was several times higher. Many of the Serbian civilians were killed when NATO bombed bridges, marketplaces, or other targets that critics of the war said amounted to a campaign of terror aimed at breaking Serbia's will to fight.

There is no question that the Serbs carried out mass expulsions and murders, which were violations of the laws of war, but KLA rebels and fear of NATO bombs also moved at least some of the 850,000 people who fled their homes. The Serbs' expulsions were more selective than the senseless juggernaut of deportation and destruction portrayed by news media excluded from the war zone. Some of the expulsions I witnessed seemed to follow the logic of forces fighting an insurgency and air attacks at once, not the inexplicable brutality of "ethnic cleansing." Often, the Serbs moved in to deport people after the KLA or NATO attacked, or they cleared out border areas over which they wanted complete control in case NATO ground troops invaded. In Pristina's Sunny Hill neighborhood, where Emina and I had rescued Mala and her five kids, KLA gunmen battled Serbian forces in broad daylight, just six days after the air war began. It was the first time the guerrillas had ever launched a full-scale assault on the provincial capital, and the next day, Yugoslav troops, Serbian police, and paramilitaries moved through several ethnic Albanian neighborhoods, firing AK-47s, breaking into homes, and giving families just a few minutes to leave.

I only realized what was happening when I was in my room late one afternoon, and heard the muffled sound of thousands of shuffling feet, broken intermittently by Serbian shouts and jeers, or a child's cry. I hurried down the stairs, through the lobby, and onto the street, where a stream of some seven thousand ethnic Albanians, eyes locked forward, silent except for whispered words, were walking toward the railway station, where they were loaded into trains for deportation across the Macedonian border. Many held hands. The weakest leaned on each other for support. An elderly man hobbled on crutches near a mother pushing her baby in a stroller. I ran up to a frightened man with a wife and two children who tried to explain in halting English what was happening. "Police came to my house and said, 'Go! Go now! Go to Albania!'" he said as a policeman shouted for the crowd to keep moving.

The man said his family had been expelled from Pristina's Velanija district, where Emina lived. Desperately searching the faces, I begged for hers to be among them. At least then I would know she was alive. I didn't see her again until the war was over, but days after Emina was deported, I bumped into her sister on Pristina's main street, walking with several friends. Hours before the war started, when Emina and I had sat in her sister's living room trying to work out a plan, we thought she would be the most vulnerable because her window looked out on a police checkpoint. Yet throughout the war, she and her family were allowed to stay in Pristina along with thousands more ethnic Albanians, while Emina and her neighbors were forced at gunpoint to leave with thousands of others.

After I filed the story on the expulsions that night, I lay in the darkness, enshrouded by silence, except for the white noise of NATO jets and distant explosions. I felt scared and angry with myself, and wondered what I thought I was doing. What truth was there in this place that was worth dying for, or getting others killed, that didn't get lost in the spin of good versus evil, us against them? Before NATO intervened, I cursed them for taking so long. Now here I was, alone, waiting for the shrieking howl of a warplane coming in for an air strike. At times, the city was so quiet that I could hear a car door slam in the street below and follow footsteps into the lobby, hear them climb the stairs and walk down the hallway. In this darkness, the sound of heavy soles on carpet scared me more than the warplanes.

Getting a story was risky enough. Filing it to Los Angeles often felt just as dangerous. I tried to keep my satellite connection time, from the moment I slipped the satfone parts out from their hiding places to the second they were concealed again, down to a few minutes, in the pitch dark. One night, the connection kept dropping out after a few seconds, and despite several tries, I couldn't get the story transmitted. Giving up and not filing at all just wasn't an option. It would have meant a day's work, and incalculable dangers, were all for nothing. So I gathered the phone and computer under both arms, crouched down, and sneaked to the end of a deserted hallway to try for a better signal through the large window there.

My heart was thumping in my throat, but I got the connection. I stared at the digital leafs of paper lilting from one side of the screen to the other, showing that my email attachment was being uploaded, and it was taking so long I felt as if my life were slipping away with each drifting page. The elevator just down the hallway jerked and whirred to life and I panicked, certain that I'd been spotted from the street. I clicked "Send" just as the elevator doors opened at my floor, and crawled toward my room as footsteps drew closer from the other direction. I managed to softly close the door just as the footsteps came around the corner, and I sat on the floor in the pitch black, panting. It was days later, when it was safe enough to move about the hotel, that I realized a waiter was living next door to me, and the bear of a man with a gentle smile who delivered my watery soup at dinner was the person who had almost scared me to death.

About halfway into the war, after the local government rewired a few lines of the phone system blown up in an early air strike, I could leave the satfone hidden and go down to the hotel's front desk to connect to the Internet. The hotel staff were used to me being around. But I usually didn't linger in the lobby until the middle of the night, to limit the chances of bumping into a drunken paramilitary fighter who wouldn't be so indifferent. One night, I was listening to the long electronic squawk of my laptop's modem straining for a connection when I noticed the two desk clerks in the office behind the front counter leaning intently into the flickering aura of a portable TV set. I assumed it was tuned into a private Serbian channel that had started broadcasting soft porn soon after the bombs began to fall. I had to admire the Serbs' singlemindedness in a state of war.

It wasn't long before I hated the NATO warplanes as much as the Serbs, who, a matter of months earlier, I'd thought could use a good pounding. Now any of us on the ground could end up dead in bombing raids that were routinely killing civilians, so it made no difference who had the strongest claim to right or wrong. The people killing from the safety of great speed and height seemed as cowardly and arrogant as the Serbian murderers they had come to stop.

One afternoon, when I visited Pristina's main hospital to see several children wounded in an air raid, I walked out to the parking lot to find a dozen nurses and doctors in white lab coats, heads tilted back and hands shading their eyes, craning to see a NATO jet high in the sky. At this distance, it was a tiny silverfish darting in and out of the clouds. A flash of sunlight glinted off the canopy and suddenly everyone was pointing at the jet. Just a couple of miles away, a Yugoslav army anti-aircraft rocket roared into the sky, leaving a spiral trail of gray smoke behind. In a split second, the jet was barrel-rolling straight up, trying to outrace the rocket. And like every other spectator in the parking lot, I willed the rocket to catch it, saying silently to myself, "Come on baby, *hit* the damn thing this time." The NATO warplane won the race and escaped. I didn't hang around to watch the rocket site get bombed.

I'd come back thinking that I'd be closer to the truth of what was happening in Kosovo. That, I tried to convince myself, was worth the risk. But mine was a lone voice. The Serbs were quick to restore the TV service in the Grand's media center after NATO bombed Pristina's telecommunications links, so on most days, I was able to go out and see some of the war and get back in time to hear NATO's skewed version of it from the stage in Brussels. I would see civilian casualties of NATO air strikes, and then sit in front of the television to hear NATO insist that evil Serbs had done it, and each time I heard the claims, a question nagged more persistently: If they're doing the right thing, why do they have to lie about it?

Three weeks into an air war that was supposed to be over in a few days, NATO bombed a column of ethnic Albanian refugees in eleven wagons drawn by horses and tractors as they traveled next to a low mountain ridge, along a dirt road from Prizren to the Albanian border city of Kukes. At least twenty died, most blown to pieces or incinerated by the blasts of laser-guided U.S. bombs. Some of the survivors, who emerged shocked from nearby woods, said Serbian police had expelled them from their homes. Others said they wanted to escape the NATO air strikes.

I made it across Kosovo to the scene, next to low mountains near the village of Meja, within an hour of the air strikes. The remnants of wooden carts and farmers' tractors were still smoldering, and a barely conscious woman lying on the road was weakly sucking in her last breaths. The body of a boy, around seven years old, lay nearby. The force of the blasts had flung a middle-aged woman over a barbed-wire fence and wrapped her around a tree. A blond doll hung over the side of a destroyed wagon, and a child's purple boot stood upright in the road below.

About one hundred yards up the road, in the direction the column of refugees was heading, another bomb had blown a truck in half. I couldn't tell for sure whether it was a military vehicle, but it looked like it was parked next to the farmhouse when the bomb hit it. Another blast struck a larger, two-story farmhouse next to where the refugees were killed. When I poked my head in, an elderly man and woman were still moaning for help in the rubble of the destroyed wall and small barn where they had tried to hide. Muharem Alija, fourteen, walked out of the ruins trembling and covered in dust, with a trickle of tears and dried blood on his cheek.

Near the bomb craters I found several heavy aluminum blades, around two feet long, which I'd seen that week in Pristina next to the wreckage of a civilian car that was carrying three police when it was destroyed in a direct hit. One of the fins had Alcoa stamped on it. They were the tail fins of laser-guided bombs, and I knew it would have been impossible for Yugoslav aircraft to carry out repeated strikes in an air-exclusion zone controlled by NATO warplanes.

But in Washington, the Pentagon put out a story, citing the accounts of refugees who had reached Albania, that Yugoslav fighter planes had bombed the refugees, and somehow not been shot down. The U.S. military would have known that was an unlikely feat since NATO's far superior aircraft were flying more than six hundred sorties a day over Serbia, many in the busy air corridor over Kosovo's western border. It later withdrew its claim that Yugoslav bombs killed the refugees. Pentagon officials attributed what had happened to "the fog of war."

In fact, if NATO's spin artists had done a quick check of the alliance's own mission reports, they would have seen that American F-16s had carried out attacks at the precise place where the refugees died that morning. NATO warplanes were still bombing the other side of the ridge as I walked through the scorched pieces of bodies and tractors. The next day, NATO spokesman Jamie Shea finally confirmed the obvious, and claimed an American F-16 pilot thought he was bombing a military convoy from fifteen thousand feet because he wanted to stop Serbs who were setting fire to ethnic Albanian homes. "The pilot attacked what he believed to be military vehicles in a convoy," Shea explained. "He was convinced he had the right target. He dropped his bomb in good faith, as you would expect a trained pilot from a democratic NATO country to do."

Watching Shea on the big screen in the Grand's media center, my mind drifted back to Mogadishu, where I heard American spokesman David Stockwell insisting that Somali women and children, armed or not, were combatants. I wondered why it was so difficult for the military just to say, "We screwed up, we're deeply sorry," instead of trying to mold the truth to fit their fiction of an epic battle of good versus evil.

Not a single one of us thought to ask an obvious question: How could a highly skilled fighter pilot, who said he studied the target area for twenty-five minutes before striking, see military vehicles in his bomb sights instead of slow-moving, horse-drawn carts and farmers' tractors?

A month later, I was standing among the remains of dozens of refugee wagons after a NATO bombing killed at least fifty-three Kosovo Albanians in the village of Korisa. They were in a group of several hundred people who had spent the previous month hiding in the mountain woods, trying to escape Serbian reprisals. They were running out of food, and when they came down from their hiding place, police ordered around 430 to camp out on a dirt lot for the night, while another 200 crammed into a nearby motel. Many of the refugees were asleep on or next to their wooden wagons when American bombs struck the dirt lot and blew them to bits. When I arrived twelve hours later, several tractors and wagons were still in flames. Abandoned mattresses were scattered in covered wagons, and shredded blankets and clothes soaked in blood lay in the dirt beneath them. At least a dozen of the dead were children, one of whose bodies was carbonized by the inferno that swept through the camp. NATO insisted it had bombed a Serbian military "command and control center." I searched for several hours in the twisted ruins of burnt steel and splintered wood and couldn't find anything, not a soldier's helmet, a spent shell casing, a shred of uniform, that would suggest any member of the security forces had been among the refugees when they were bombed.

There were so many refugee corpses in the local morgue that they were stacked on examination tables and laid out on the floor. An infant's body, buttoned up in a terry cloth sleeper, was peppered with shrapnel. On the floor nearby, in a row of corpses, there was a blue body bag spattered with blood. It was labeled with the number four, no bigger than one on the back of a child's baseball sweater. Through the small plastic window, I could see a boy's head, turned a little to the right, mouth slightly open. His lips were pressed against the plastic, and it looked slightly fogged, as if he were still breathing.

I thought of a child space traveler, asleep in suspended animation, waiting to awake in a new world.

14

CHECKMATE

War can only be abolished by war, and in order to
get rid of the gun, it is necessary to take up the gun.
MAO TSE-TUNG

Milosevic waited until the blood was knee-deep and then surrendered, ensuring that thousands of people had died needlessly in the war over Kosovo. NATO troops moved in to take control of the territory, the United States and Britain quietly dropped their opposition to Kosovo's independence, extremists on both sides of the ethnic divide continued to murder, expel civilians, and burn homes, and the story quickly dropped off the front page. Two weeks after NATO's victory, Serbian professors led me down a gray marble staircase to the women's bathroom in the basement of Pristina University's economics department. The bodies of professor Milenko Lekovic, cafeteria worker Jovica Stamenkovic, and guard Miodrag Mladenovic lay on the bathroom floor in pools of congealing blood.

The small hammer that the ethnic Albanian killers had used to cave in at least one of the Serbs' skulls was inches away from the professor's wire-rimmed glasses, which had landed lenses down on the floor. His hands were tied behind his back with a leather shoelace. He was gagged with several strips of packing tape wrapped around his head. The cafeteria worker was slumped in a corner, with a bullet in the left side of his forehead. The guard lay on his side, in a semi-fetal position, his mouth gagged with a burgundy red necktie.

Their executioners had called the night before to redress an imbalance in the education system. Milosevic had purged most of the university's ethnic Albanians in the 1990s, and now that his regime had lost control, they were employing some of the same brutality to even the balance as quickly as possible. It was an easy crime to get away with. Serbian forces withdrew under the dictated peace agreement terms, and when NATO troops moved in, they failed to fill the power vacuum. Like most Serbian targets, the university was unguarded, so the murderers walked right through the front door. While I was taking pictures of the bodies, and scribbling notes, two British soldiers arrived, at least two hours after they were called to the crime scene.

A British army sergeant pointed his assault rifle at the ceiling of the women's bathroom, poked his head through the door, and inquired: "Serbs or Albanians?"

"Serbs," a disgusted faculty member replied from the hallway.

"No problem," the sergeant said.

"No," the Serb shot back. "Problem."

I was fast running out of reasons to remain in what was left of Yugoslavia. The paper found a way out for me in early 2001, when I was sent to New Delhi to run the South Asia bureau. The move was complicated by the fact that our only child, Scott, was just eleven months old, and more vulnerable to India's various contagions. But Sai Hung and I were both looking forward to new adventures. She would have the much harder job of running a home in a city where the power was out for several hours on an average day, shoddy wiring made turning on a light switch potentially life threatening, the tap water was lethal, the mailman and phone lineman were constantly demanding bribes, and once simple tasks such as buying vegetables meant perilous journeys into the fly-infested health hazards that passed as markets in New Delhi. But she was tough and solved the daily crises on the home front so well that I was able to stay on the road for weeks, sometimes months.

The New Delhi bureau had been dark for months. The previous correspondent had defected to the *New York Times* and there weren't any other volunteers to work in what was then a news backwater, including Bangladesh, Sri Lanka, and the Himalayan kingdom of Bhutan. I liked the thought of being someplace off the news radar, where I imagined I could write about something other than killing, death, and hatred. Trouble is, I started the posting with a natural disaster, a massive 7.9 earthquake that killed around twenty thousand people in the Indian state of Gujarat, and it was downhill from there.

That summer, the Taliban took eight Christian aid workers prisoner and put them on trial in Kabul. It's normally the kind of story a reporter instinctively runs to and thinks about later. But I figured the Talibs were far too pious to execute God-fearing foreign aid workers, and thought covering a trial that ended with their deportation would be anti-climactic. On that logic, in the languid weeks of late August, while the 9/11 plotters were in the final stages of preparations for an attack that would shock the world and make South Asia the hottest story for months to come, I was planning another search for Ahmed Shah Massoud in northern Afghanistan. India was a loyal ally of Massoud's Northern Alliance, and along with Iran and Russia, it helped keep Massoud's guerrillas in the fight against the Taliban and Al Qaeda while the rest of the world stood by. So it was a good place to renew the quest.

Massoud had appointed one of his closest friends of twenty-three years, Massood Khalili, ambassador to India, which refused to have diplomatic relations with the Pakistan-backed Taliban regime. Khalili, the patrician son of a famous Afghan poet and a believer in a mystical Islam called Sufism, shared my faith in fate. One day, I sat on a sofa in the ambassador's reception room in his New Delhi compound, among elegant armchairs beneath a large chandelier, and explained how I had chased Massoud across northern Afghanistan five years earlier, and failed to get an interview with him. I described how I had looked through Massoud's library, trying to understand the man by leafing through the books he was forced to abandon to Talibs who read nothing but the Koran.

Khalili smiled wistfully. "You will meet the Commander," he said. "And you will spend as much time with him as you desire. I am sure of that."

I had picked a good time, Khalili assured me. The Taliban were preparing a massive offensive. And Massoud had just summoned Khalili to his base in northern Afghanistan to discuss pressing matters, which he would not discuss over the phone. The ambassador asked him if he could wait a week.

"He said, 'No, no. If you are standing, run. If you are sitting, stand and run,'" Khalili told me.

The ambassador explained that I would have to enter Afghanistan from neighboring Tajikistan, and the fastest way to get a visa would be through Moscow. He suggested I courier my passport to the *Times*'s bureau there and ask colleagues to arrange for the visa. So my passport was stuck somewhere in Moscow on the night of September 8, waiting for the bureaucracy to inch forward, while just across the border Khalili and Massoud sat on the banks of the Amu Darya, known as the Oxus River in the fourth century, when Alexander the Great crossed it with his invading Macedonian forces.

Around midnight on this fateful night, Massoud told his commanders and aides that he wanted to be alone with his old friend. They lay on mattresses on the floor, in the flickering light of a small lantern, staring at the ceiling and reminiscing all the way back to the mujahideen war against the Soviets, when the two first met. One of the treasured books Massoud always carried when forced to leave others behind was a collection of verse by the fourteenth-century Persian poet Hafiz. To Khalili's ears, the fellow Sufi's *ghazals* were so moving that he was certain it was the most beautiful poetry written in any language for seven centuries. It could also be used to predict the future. A curious reader need only rifle the pages and randomly point to one verse, which would reveal his fortune.

"I'll wish," Massoud told Khalili. "You open the book."

The ambassador's finger touched a page, and in the first or second verse of the ghazal, he read out: *"Oh, you two who are sitting tonight together, value this night. Many years will pass: Nights will go, years will come, months will disappear. You two will not have this night again. Value it."*

The men lay silent in the lantern's soft glow for at least ten minutes: "I don't know what he was thinking, or what I was thinking," Khalili later told me. "We were both just quiet."

The next morning, Massoud asked the ambassador to be his translator in an interview with two Arab television journalists who had been waiting some ten days to see him. Khalili had a bad feeling when he heard they were Arabs, and said he'd rather go wash up, but Massoud insisted. When the journalists introduced themselves, one said he didn't work for any particular news agency. "I belong to Islamic centers based in Paris, London—all over the world," he said.

Khalili leaned over and whispered to Massoud, "They are not journalists. They belong to *that*," his euphemism for Al Qaeda.

"Tell me some of your questions, and then I will answer," Massoud told the Arabs. Out of fifteen questions, eight were about Osama bin Laden, queries such as: "Why are you against him? Why did you say he was a killer?"

"OK, start your camera," Massoud said, his chin against his chest, a sign he was in a foul mood.

"What is the situation in Afghanistan?" one of the Arabs asked. Khalili had spoken only half of the first letter of the first word in his translation when the room exploded in a ball of fire and searing black smoke.

"Oh God, save me!" the ambassador screamed. "You have always been with me. In this time of difficulty, save me. Liberate me!" Then he felt a hand grasp his wrist.

"That was the last touch of the Commander," Khalili told me. "In the echo of my prayers, he died."

The blast left Khalili blind in his right eye, deaf in his right ear, and badly burned over much of his body, which was peppered by about one thousand pieces of shrapnel. Three hundred pieces were still in his left leg months later. Just seconds before Massoud led him into the interview, the commander did something that would save his friend's life. Khalili was having trouble getting his passport to slide into his shirt pocket, so Massoud picked it up and slipped it in for him, right over his heart. When Khalili lay barely conscious in a hospital bed, his wife found eight bits of shrapnel embedded in the passport's pages.

Another survivor of the blast, Afghan journalist Fahim Dashtey, was standing just inches from the camera bomb when it exploded, severely burning his arms, legs, and face, and forever changing the way he saw himself in the world. "The important thing was the shock that I got," he told me, struggling to hold back the tears more than three years later in Kabul. "A couple of years before this catastrophe, I read one of the Russian novelists—I can't remember if it was Tolstoy or Dostoyevsky or someone else—but he was saying, 'I am very sad for the people who need a hero.' And I thought: How crazy is this guy? He doesn't know how lovely it is to have a hero, *to be* with a hero. But after this blast, when these sentences came back to my mind, I understood that the guy was right. Now I realize I am one of these people who need a hero—who *lost* a hero."

Months after Massoud's assassination, in the fading grace of the Afghan ambassador's quiet New Delhi residence, Khalili said, "Ten times a day, I ask the question, 'Why did I live?' I haven't found the answer." He winced at the memory of his friend and mentor's murder, and the devastating blow it had dealt to his tortured country. "I don't see the power of death now. I was once scared of death. I'm not saying I'm so brave against death now. I just say, 'OK, fine. Come again.'"

The murder of Massoud was bin Laden's opening gambit in an epoch-making terror attack that the Afghan guerrilla had warned the West was coming. Few bothered to listen. Through decades of war, Massoud had remained a front-line commander who rarely left his men, let alone Afghanistan. But in the spring of 2001, when the Taliban were closing in and the U.S. and other Western governments were tacitly accepting the hard-line Islamists' regime without granting formal recognition, Massoud was persuaded to play politician and make his first trip to Europe to lobby for a harder line against the Taliban and their Pakistani sponsors. In a Paris press conference, Massoud spoke with the calm, clear prescience of a man who knew a terrible truth that the rest of the world did not want to see: "One of the best ways to bring peace and stability in Afghanistan is that the international community must put pressure on Pakistan," Massoud said, adding, "the Americans still do not have any kind of clear and specific policy on the Taliban.

"My message to Mr. Bush is that if he doesn't prevent the Al Qaeda operations in Afghanistan, and if he doesn't help the people of Afghanistan, this problem will not only remain in Afghanistan, but it will spread, especially to the U.S. and to other countries of the world as well."

That was five months before Al Qaeda silenced Massoud forever. Three days after his death, as I was waiting for my passport to make its way back from Moscow by courier, I was walking through my living room when, out of the corner of my eye, I saw cable news video of smoke pouring off the World Trade Center towers in New York.

By the next morning, I had an emergency replacement for my passport and headed to Pakistan, where I immediately started working on a plan to get across the border into Afghanistan. I knew it wouldn't take long for Bush to declare war on the Taliban for sheltering Al Qaeda. I thought my best chance was to hook up with Abdul Haq, a legendary guerrilla fighter who had just returned to Peshawar to plan his own return to Afghanistan as U.S. forces prepared to attack from the air in a belated coalition with Massoud's Northern Alliance fighters.

I met Haq in his Peshawar home the day after his return. Dressed in a white shalwar kameez, he had a regal air, but looked oddly like Rob Reiner, tall and beefy with a sardonic smile. Haq hobbled to his seat, limping on a prosthetic right foot, a stand-in for the one a land mine blast had blown off. It was one of sixteen war wounds he suffered in a lifetime of war that had left him weary of all he knew at forty years old.

Haq became a rebel at sixteen, working underground against the Soviet-backed Communist regime two years before the Soviets invaded in 1979, when he joined the jihad. He chafed at the infighting and restrictions with which faction commanders and foreign handlers tried to restrain him, and in 1987, was the first to bring the war to Kabul's doorstep with a legendary attack on a Russian base near Lake Karga, just outside the capital. Haq led a few of his men through minefields to a spot about a third of a mile from the base's front gate, where they set up three 103-millimeter rocket launchers. They could only carry as many rockets, and had to score at least one direct hit on the small entrance to a sprawling weapons storage bunker. The best marksman in the unit fired two rockets and missed each time. Haq needed a spectacular strike to ignite a new front in the war and seal his reputation as a bold commander. He wasn't about to let a rocket man on an off day blow it.

"I gave him a slap and said, 'If you miss this time, I'll kill you,'" Haq told me. He chuckled at the memory.

The gunner scored a direct hit on his last try, and as the unit fled back through the minefields, fire spread through the ammo dump. It erupted with such force that the blast sucked the air out of Haq's lungs. Hundreds of explosions rocked the capital through the night as the raging fire sent a relentless barrage of rockets and shells raining down. They shattered any pretense of Soviet invulnerability in Afghanistan and made Haq a hero to many Afghans who worried that the mujahideen might never be strong enough to take the cities. He could have demanded more when the war was finally won, but Haq did something rare for a mujahideen commander. He laid down his weapons when the Soviets withdrew in 1989 and Afghanistan disintegrated into civil war. He spent the rest of his life trying to bring various factions together into a stable government.

"The easiest thing in the world is to take a gun and fight," he explained. "To talk, and convince people, is difficult. In war, if you don't like someone, you just shoot him. But in diplomacy, whether you like him or not, you have to smile and talk to him."

Haq shared Massoud's distaste for the dog-and-pony shows that mujahideen commanders had to put on to get foreign funding, or to keep the money and weapons coming when their faction's win–loss stats weren't looking good. I asked him about a trip he had taken to Washington, D.C., with an American TV journalist he'd befriended, who persuaded him to make a pitch for more support to Robert McFarlane, President Ronald Reagan's national security adviser.

"Because of the Russian withdrawal, many people in the U.S. government got big medals, promotions, and early retirement, because they did such a great job," he said, sounding bitter for the first time in our conversation. "But these people who they brought to Afghanistan are causing problems in my country. Now for that they are punishing us. How many of the CIA people were fired? None. Now we are paying the price for that."

I suppose Haq knew that American war planners had already settled on Hamid Karzai, another Pashtun little known to the rest of the world, as the man who would lead Afghanistan when the Taliban were removed. The positive profiles started appearing so suddenly in the American media that it was obvious Karzai was being promoted. Perhaps by visiting McFarlane, Haq wanted to improve his own chances of getting a piece of the post-war action, or perhaps he felt enough of the young warrior surging in his veins that he actually thought he could beat a fait accompli. Then again, maybe he was so determined to go back into Afghanistan because he spotted a long-awaited chance to settle a score.

In 1999, while Haq was in Dubai working on another doomed effort to build a more moderate alternative to the Taliban regime, gunmen burst into his home in Peshawar and murdered his wife and their eleven-year-old son. The U.S. State Department concluded that the Taliban probably sent the assassins. But the Pakistan military's ISI intelligence agency kept the Talibs on a tight leash in Pakistan, so the ISI was also on the list of suspects. It also would have kept a close eye on Haq when he returned to Peshawar after the September 11 attacks, and when he crossed the border into Afghanistan the following month on a mission to rally support for King Zahir Shah's efforts to form a government to replace the Taliban.

The Taliban followed Haq for two days before some two hundred fighters surrounded and captured him near Azra, his home village southeast of Kabul. He called for help on his satellite phone, apparently appealing to American intelligence for a helicopter or two to break the siege. But the rescue never came. Haq was quickly executed in the capital.

When I heard the news, I was in Afghanistan with the Northern Alliance as they fought alongside U.S. Special Forces units heading toward Kabul. Al Qaeda's killing of Massoud was an extraordinarily cunning move that would leave Afghanistan without the powerful, strategic thinker it needed to build a stable democracy from the ruins of more than a quarter-century of war. Removing him before the predictable counterattack that followed September 11 improved Al Qaeda's odds of surviving and regrouping in one of their most crucial breeding grounds. Now bin Laden's Taliban allies had neutralized another threat, a war hero who surely would have threatened the Taliban's resurgence after the war in the Pashtun heartland of eastern and southern Afghanistan. Part of me wished I had stayed in Pakistan long enough to persuade Haq to take me with him across the border, no matter the consequences.

The American strategy in Afghanistan was elegantly simple: small and agile Special Forces units joined up with guerrillas from Massoud's

Northern Alliance, and while the Afghans provided a ground force of sorts, the Americans helped direct laser-guided bombs to their targets. Americans also handled the cash payments, suitcases packed with U.S. dollars, that enticed lower-level Taliban commanders to switch sides. Afghan warriors were usually like willows bending with the breeze. Once they felt the wind turning against them, they quickly tilted to join the fight against men who just hours earlier were their comrades.

Everywhere I went along the front lines, I met Afghan guerrillas who were worn out by years of fighting, but had to keep going because it was the only way to make a living—even if they had to wait months at a time to collect their pay of just $12.50 a month. The first American B-52 bomber flew in north of Kabul in the last week of October, lazily tracing white contrails across the clear blue sky high above us before spilling out a long thin line of bombs that took a few minutes to reach the Taliban positions, where they exploded in a massive string of destruction that made the earth tremble for miles around. The Northern Alliance fighters were impatient for much more. Their idea of good bombing dated back to the Soviet days when low-flying jets would pummel villages until they were nothing but rubble. "About forty Russian jets used to come and bomb us at once," a frustrated guerrilla told me. "This fighting seems funny to us."

The Americans were taking their time to be precise, picking off Taliban tanks, trucks, and bunkers one by one, leaving more than enough of the militia intact to escape and rebuild. The Afghans could see the Taliban's end was near and they wanted the war over fast, which would improve their chances of living long enough to see peace. While we waited in an empty two-story building with some guerrillas for the bombers to arrive on their regular run one afternoon, just 250 yards from the Taliban's front line, the men lay on the floor lingering over a lunch of boiled mutton pieces chopped with an axe. Then they decompressed with a few chillums of rich black Afghan hashish, blow-ing sweet clouds of gray smoke and talking about lives lost fighting wars since they were boys.

Out of fewer than ten men at the post, two had lost legs to land mine explosions while fighting the Russians. One complained that the nut on the knee bolt of his prosthetic leg often came loose when he tried to run, which made combat a unique challenge. The other said he couldn't find a leg that fit, so he walked and fought with the aid of crutches donated by the international Red Cross. He carried his AK-47 slung over his shoulder, and had three banana-shaped clips stuffed in a web belt strapped to his back.

"How do you fight without falling over?" I asked the guerrilla, Abdul Zahir.

He flipped out the stump of his left leg, rested it on one crutch, braced himself with the other crutch, and then used his free right hand to hold his Kalashnikov perfectly level with the ground. Hum-bled, and slightly humiliated, I realized that with a little more effort, I might have made a good one-handed rifleman myself.

Everywhere I went along the front lines, Northern Alliance guer-rillas and their commanders were convinced that most Afghan Talibs wanted to throw in the towel early on during the bombing, but Paki-stani, Chechen, Arab, and other foreign mercenaries were forcing them to keep fighting. I'd heard the same line so many times that I dismissed it as rote propaganda—until I heard the fatigue, bordering on desperation, in the voice of a man who identified himself only as Zilgai. He was a Talib somewhere near the Northern Alliance posi-tions at Wollayet, north of Kabul, where local commander Abdul Wakil regularly taunted him from a field radio in a farmhouse com-mand post. Listening in on their conversation through the electronic crackle and whine, one of the deepest and saddest truths about war occured to me: soldiers sent to kill one another have more in common as human beings than they have differences as enemies.

"Fifty-two, fifty-two," radio operator Mohammed Hakim called out over the mike. "Talib, Talib, Talib."

He had to repeat the invitation to talk several times before Zilgai replied from the Taliban lines. Wakil took the microphone and wasted no time slipping in the knife. Grinning at me, he asked the Talib if he'd heard about a raid by one hundred U.S. Army Rangers and Special Forces on a Taliban camp near Kandahar in the early morning darkness.

"That's none of my business," the Talib's voice snapped back through the static, in a tone that said, Give me a break. "If I tell you I don't know about them, you will laugh."

"I just want to ask you: Is it real or not?" Wakil said, sticking the tip of his tongue out like a teasing child. "You don't understand? You don't know about them?"

"If I say that, you will laugh and say: 'How can you not know? You are a Talib,'" Zilgai replied, sounding more beleaguered than angry. "These are not good words. Just leave it alone."

Wakil was in regular radio contact with at least two former friends who had defected from the Northern Alliance to join the Taliban five years earlier, when the wind had shifted in the Talibs' favor. Their names were Mohammed Amin and Habib Allah, Wakil told me, but over the radio, he asked for them by their call names, Gulab and Almas.

"How do you know Almas?" a miffed Taliban radio operator replied.

"He is from our side," the commander replied. "He used to be a mujahid. When he comes in, tell him we are waiting on this frequency. Is there a person there named Abdulhai Khan? Tell him I say hello."

Another Talib cut in with a high-pitched voice that amused Wakil

230

and his teenage guards, who snickered from the corner where they sat leaning on their AK-47 assault rifles. "Please, let us speak to our soldiers," the Taliban soldier said, curt but civil, the way a teacher might scold a mischievous child. "Why are you calling so many times saying, 'Talib, Talib, Talib?' What do you want from the Taliban?"

"The Talib has become a hen," Wakil said to his men, and they all laughed some more. Then he asked Zilgai how he was holding up under the air strikes.

"American fighters come and bomb us," he replied. "It doesn't affect us. It's none of our business. Leave it alone."

"I just want to make sure other people, villagers, are not being killed. Are they?" Wakil asked, and his eyebrows arched with the tease.

"It is both of our sides' problem," the Taliban commander's voice came back through the distance. "They came and killed villagers, common people. They can't kill us. They can't capture us. They can only kill villagers."

When Wakil had had his fun, and was ready for another diversion from the front-line monotony, the two commanders, sworn enemies, signed off with the same words: "I'm OK. Good-bye."

My base while covering the war against the Taliban was the same compound in the town of Jabal Saraj where I'd gone looking for Massoud some four years earlier. The assassinated commander's home, where I'd flipped through his books trying to conjure up a vision of a great warrior, was now occupied by dozens of journalists, camped out on the floors. We bathed from a bucket in a filthy bathroom where a ruined toilet was overflowing. Several of the reporters had dysentery, and they either refused to go, or just couldn't make it in time, to the pit latrine across the yard.

People were talking about how the war was going to drag on into the New Year, and I was sinking deeper into a depression when I returned to my corner on the floor one afternoon to find a neatly written note on my pillow. It was from my old translator Najib. He had made it out of Kabul, slipping past Taliban lines in a caravan of smugglers, on the hunch that I might finally have kept my promise and come back. It was like finding a long lost brother. Najib assured me it was God's will.

When I saw him, we hugged and neither of us could keep from crying. Najib immediately took on the dangerous task of trying to persuade the Northern Alliance commanders that he was not a Taliban spy and should be permitted to work as my translator. After a few threats, he was allowed to stay. We would finally get to watch the liberation we had fantasized about on long drives, and over glasses of sweet tea, so many times.

Fall was giving way to a bitter winter, and high in the Hindu Kush, the warring sides had a common enemy: a fierce wind that howled from the north, stabbing at the soldiers' skin like an icy knife. Back in the 1960s, the Soviets built the world's highest tunnel to join the Salang Pass to the highway north at 11,034 feet above sea level. As Massoud retreated toward Mazar-i-Sharif in 1997, he ordered his men to set off explosives and seal the tunnel entrance to Taliban tanks and other vehicles. But it was still possible to go through the pitch black, slippery 1.6-mile tunnel on foot, groping for passages through the tangle of wires, steel beams, twisted rebar, and broken concrete. It took almost an hour to reach the front line on the other side, where the Northern Alliance and Taliban fighters spent most of their time in mid-November 2001 huddling around stoves in stone huts, praying that they wouldn't freeze to death.

The following month, just hours before the Taliban abandoned Kabul under heavy bombardment, I was back up in the mountains watching the local Northern Alliance and Taliban commanders rekindle boyhood friendships that they had secretly nurtured through the civil war with letters smuggled across the front. The Taliban's local commander, Mohammed Aman Abed, twenty-four, and Del Aqa, the thirty-six-year-old Northern Alliance deputy commander of the Salang, first met as boys during a visit at a relative's house. The war led them down different paths, and while the old friends did what enemies do and tried to kill each other and their men, their hearts really weren't in it. In the winter of 2000, Abed contacted Aqa with a secret letter to inquire how he might switch sides along with hundreds of his men. More letters were exchanged, followed by coded radio messages, but Abed was still looking for the right moment, and the best terms, to join the other side. When American bombs began to fall after September 11, he lost any doubt that he'd rather not be a Talib.

Many of his men couldn't be trusted not to defect, and the Taliban and their Al Qaeda allies were summarily executing suspected turncoats, so Abed and Aqa agreed over the radio to create a diversion. They fired rocket-propelled grenades for an hour, roughly in the direction of each other's forces, making sure they didn't hit anyone. By 2 a.m. the crossover was complete. Twelve hours later, Abed was on horseback, leading fifty defectors from his original force of six hundred along an icy road toward Kabul, where they would join guerrillas and American Special Forces amassing for the final assault on the city.

"The ones who did not want to surrender did not have time to fight with the others," said Taliban soldier Sher Mohammed, who mimicked the whoosh of the rockets by hissing through the gap in his front teeth. "They ran away."

I was doing my best to keep up with Aqa, jogging to match his long stride and panting to suck in some of the thin mountain air, so I could ask him to explain how such an amicable surrender was possible in the middle of a vicious civil war, which was now playing out with such enormous stakes.

"Don't think us so simple," Aqa said, smiling wryly.

As Najib and I fell back to watch him mount his own steed and ride alongside his old friend like conquering legionnaires toward Kabul, it struck me: with a little foresight in Washington, and enough suitcases full of cash, the Taliban could have been severely wounded months or years earlier, and bin Laden wouldn't have had such an easy time plotting his attacks and training Al Qaeda cadres in Afghanistan. The World Trade Center towers would still be standing, and thousands of people would still be alive, including no doubt, Ahmad Shah Massoud.

15

A BLINDING LIGHT

Until the day of his death, no man can be sure of his courage.
JEAN ANOUILH BECKET

I n the spring of 2003, when false reports of bin Laden's imminent capture in Pakistan set off a buying spree on Wall Street, the clock was ticking down to the U.S.-led invasion of Iraq to topple Saddam Hussein. A *USA Today* reporter's firsthand account of closing in on bin Laden with Pakistani intelligence agents only left me more confused. He later admitted to making it all up. Unsure of which way I should go, toward Pakistan to chase what instinct told me was a bogus story, or toward Iraq, where U.S. forces were about to embark on the most complex mission since Vietnam, I shrugged off nervous editors in Los Angeles and chose northern Iraq.

I was desperately trying to find a way in through neighboring Iran and had been trying for weeks to get an Iranian visa through the usual channels. But my daily barrage of calls, faxes, and emails to various officials in Iran's Ministry of Islamic Guidance and Culture and assorted diplomats was getting me nowhere. With time running out, I flew to Dubai and went to the Iranian consulate on the eve of the Persian New Year, when it would close for a week. I had only a few hours left to get a visa or miss the start of the biggest war in a generation.

While I was futzing around with the bin Laden arrest rumor, several busloads of foreign journalists had gone to the Turkish border, where the government suddenly gave in to pressure and opened a crossing into Iraq for just a few days. Forced to hedge my bets, I'd gambled that the reporters were all going to be stuck there, waiting for refugee stories, looking foolish. Now it looked like I was going to be caught out in left field, stuck in Dubai, the Las Vegas of the Middle East, running up expenses with nothing to write except, perhaps, something about the rich and clueless gambling and sniffing around for Filipina hookers.

Our fixer in Tehran assured me that a semi-official facilitator, who arranged journalists' visas for a fee of a few hundred dollars, had faxed the necessary approval for mine to the Dubai consulate. The people at the visa desk searched their files and found nothing. I dialed the fixer every ten minutes, begging her to do whatever it took to get me into Iran the next day. Iranian officials weren't helping, and the facilitator wasn't answering. The fixer finally reached him on his cell phone, and she said from the background noise, it sounded like he was in a café.

"The consulate is about to close!" I shouted into my cell phone. "They are literally shutting off the lights and getting ready to lock the doors!"

I could hear the fixer saying something in Farsi on another line.

"OK," she came back to me. "He says he'll send another fax, but it's going to cost you more."

"How *much* more?" I asked.

"Three thousand dollars."

"Pay it," I said. "I'll give you cash when I get there."

I ran back into the consulate just as a clerk switched the last light off, and pleaded with the lone person left locking up behind the visa counter to look for a fax, just one more time. After a few minutes, he returned and nodded his head in the direction of the payment counter. It was as if I'd won the lottery. I was on my way. But it turned out I was only hurrying to wait.

The war in Iraq's north unfolded much as the fighting in Afghanistan had. Under the protection of a no-fly zone, enforced for years by American and British jets, two main Kurdish factions were firmly in control of most of the area. Turkey, a NATO ally, refused to let American troops invade northern Iraq across its border, so teams of U.S. Special Forces worked alongside Kurdish peshmerga guerrillas to direct air strikes against Iraqi forces, gradually pounding the Iraqi army into retreat, just as American troops and Northern Alliance fighters had the Taliban. It was a fine military strategy, but with hundreds of journalists embedded with U.S. and British forces fighting spectacular conventional battles in the south, the northern front was pretty thin on news.

Until the fall of Kirkuk and Mosul, the two most important northern cities held by Saddam's forces, mine was a commuter's war. I was based in Erbil, a Kurdish city that at first was largely empty because of fears that Saddam would attack with weapons of mass destruction. Since it turned out he didn't have any to fire, there wasn't much to worry about. Apart from the odd terrorist attack, and stray American bomb, Kurds in areas under peshmerga control knew there was a war on only from the tremors of distant B-52 strikes that gently rattled their doors and windows.

I'd had a feeling it was going to be that way. The *Los Angeles Times* had offered to spend more than ten thousand dollars to fit me out with a chemical-biological weapons suit, a gas mask, and a Kevlar flak jacket with matching helmet. I settled for just the gas mask and the body armor. I couldn't imagine sitting in the back seat of a car, fully protected in my high-tech suit and mask watching my translator and driver expire, choking their last painful breaths in a gas attack. Besides, the evidence that Saddam had any weapons of mass destruction was hardly convincing. And I look silly in a combat helmet. So I packed the jacket and gas mask, but never wore either of them, not even to try them on.

I only had second thoughts twice: the first time was when I was waiting with dozens of other journalists for a news conference, and an explosion on the outskirts of Erbil sent a huge plume of white smoke billowing into the sky. It turned out to be a rather large fake gas attack, but that fact was easily ignored by TV reporters, who needed dramatic images to get on the air at a time when real war was hard to find in northern Iraq. Kurdish officials blamed Saddam's supporters, claiming they were trying to terrorize the public with a fake gas attack. But the blast could just as easily have been set off by someone allied with the United States to keep reminders of non-existent weapons of mass destruction in the news. Later that day, I got to wondering why, if the imminent threat of chemical and biological attack was as real as the Bush administration insisted, it had done nothing to protect hundreds of thousands of Kurds who were likely targets.

While journalists were doing regular drills with their expensive gear, and pumping up the phony threat by filling dead air on TV with their breathless gas attack drills, the Kurds' only hope was a homemade mask invented by the local scientists' union. It consisted of 150 grams of burnt wood crushed to bits the size of coffee grounds and turned into charcoal by baking it in the kitchen oven. The charcoal was wrapped in cotton cloth to form a filter, which was then sewn onto the front of a vinyl hood. Breathing holes were poked through the cloth with a screwdriver. The principal flaw was in getting a good seal against the poisonous air that would be swirling around the wearer's head. The last defense against the deadly vapors was a shoestring, to be pulled tightly around the victim's neck.

Since the war obviously wasn't going to come to me, I went looking for it. And on most days, it was very hard to reach. Front-page play from the north was so rare that I once raced sixty miles against a tight deadline to match an embedded CNN reporter's shameless report of paratroopers in the U.S. Army's 173rd Airborne Brigade landing in deep mud to "secure" an airfield that had been under the control of their Kurdish allies for years. U.S. personnel had been there before, too, to make sure the runway was long enough for transport aircraft to land on once the war was underway.

This was the first war since Vietnam in which the Pentagon allowed journalists to travel with combat units. I'd always been a loner in war zones, and I wanted to keep it that way. I think embedded reporters give up their independence in a kind of Faustian bargain for the better protection they get traveling with heavily armed Western troops, who can escape in armored vehicles or call in massive air power if they get in a bind. I prefer to travel on my own, in a soft-skinned civilian vehicle with a local translator and driver. Of course, the hazards are potentially much higher, especially in an age when journalists in a war zone are seen as fair game. Without so much as a sharp fork to defend myself, I'm easy prey for anyone who wants me. But as long as I get away with it, it is the only kind of reporting that's worth the risks.

On the front line west of Erbil, I chatted in a small, shadowy room with several Iraqi conscripts who were among hundreds of soldiers sneaking into Kurdish territory in wave after wave of mass defections. They described the rapid crumbling of the once-feared Iraqi army's 5th brigade as soldiers turned on officers and ranks split under relentless American bombardment. Listening to their stories, seeing the joy and relief in their weary eyes, it was obvious that Saddam's army wasn't going to put up much of a fight in the north.

In Qurshaqlu, a Kurdish village near another front, shepherds praised the U.S. Air Force for dropping at least a dozen bombs on their houses and livestock, because one of the blasts had done them the favor of seriously wounding Haji Shaban, a man who had shaken Saddam's hand in the mid-1980s. Shaban had lorded it over his neighbors ever since. To his neighbors, seeing him carried away, screaming in pain, was worth the destruction of several houses and the deaths of more than three hundred sheep, whose fly-blown carcasses lay scattered around the village, many with their hooves pointing skyward in a comically macabre tableau of twenty-first-century warfare.

Sulaiman Bapeer, a fifty-two-year-old shepherd, told me at least one bomber began attacking the village at 3 a.m., sending frightened villagers crying and screaming into the darkness. The air strikes continued for the next two hours, until the muezzin in the local mosque made the first call to prayer. Bapeer said about forty Kurdish guerrillas were based in the village and they had an anti-aircraft gun mounted on a roof. When I suggested the bomber's pilot must have seen it and suspected his village was in fact an Iraqi army camp, even though it was several miles from the Iraqis' front lines, Bapeer said he doubted that theory. "During the night, how could he see this anti-aircraft gun?" he asked.

I tried to explain that modern warplanes have sophisticated equipment that allow crews to see in the darkness. Bapeer pondered that thought for a moment and said, with a shepherd's disarming logic: "Then how come they couldn't see the sheep?"

In a much less comical "friendly fire" incident, at least sixteen people were killed when a U.S. Navy jet attacked a convoy carrying some of the allied Kurdish Democratic Party's top commanders as they worked with American Special Forces on a fresh offensive. The April 6 bombing almost killed BBC television correspondent John Simpson, who was wounded by a bomb that exploded ten feet from him. His interpreter was among the dead.

The harder I pushed to get to the real war, the less Kurdish translators and drivers wanted to work with me. I'd been so lucky over the years that I'd taken it for granted I could always find someone willing to risk his life out of some sense of duty to a bigger cause, or for the rush of it. But most of the Kurds I worked with were clearly in it just for the money. Faced with the slightest danger, they quit. I was on my third Kurdish translator in less than a month, and sensing from wary replacement candidates that I had developed an aura of impending death, when a ground offensive by Kurdish guerrillas and American Special Forces to take Mosul, Iraq's second largest city, finally got under way.

Now two weeks into the war, I was paying daily visits to the troops, lounging in the soft spring grass as forward controllers called in air strikes on Iraqi units weakly holding the front line. Following a set pattern in the north, Iraqi forces had suddenly withdrawn from a heavily bombed ridge overlooking the highway to Mosul the night before, and when the Americans and Kurds moved up the road, they headed straight into an ambush. Iraqi soldiers pinned down the intruders with machine guns, rocket-propelled grenades, and mortar bombs in a daylong battle for control of the bridge.

I huddled in a shallow, hilltop foxhole with several journalists, directly across from a Special Forces unit searching for targets through long scopes mounted on tripods. The Iraqis were trying to drive them back by firing 82-millimeter airburst mortar bombs that howled overhead before exploding in mid-air and raining down burning, jagged shrapnel. We were sitting under the open sky, and the mortar rounds were missing us by only a couple of hundred yards, in front and back. The adrenaline rush felt so good, so life affirming after weeks of feeling left out of the war, that I actually enjoyed it at first. But within minutes, it was clear the Iraqi troops were correcting their fire, walking the rounds ever closer, and it was a matter of luck that we managed to crawl out before one of us was killed.

The Americans guided bombs to direct hits on Iraqi tanks, trucks, and other targets that exploded with bright orange flashes, sending huge pillars of black smoke towering into the blue sky. The local peshmerga commander, Sarbast Babiry, thought the bombardment was too light, and as he pored over a grid map with a Special Forces sergeant, he demanded to know why there was a pause in the bombing.

"We're bringing in more planes," the American assured him. "The planes were out of bombs."

"OK, Fort Apache, I have the coordinates for the mortar position," an air controller lying next to us called over the radio. "Advise when ready to copy."

Within seconds, the sky was shrieking with incoming warplanes that unloaded several more bombs. After a few minutes' silence, the Iraqis replied with more mortar bombs and sniper fire that whistled over our heads. In mid-afternoon, the air controllers' radio crackled to life with a status report, including a body count of Iraqi troops killed in action, or KIA. "Egypt Tango, Egypt Tango, this is Talon, over," the air controller said.

"Go ahead, Talon," the radio came back.

"Talon Tango reports four trucks destroyed, fifty [Iraqi] KIA, and one mortar position destroyed. Over," the controller said.

The Iraqis weren't able to inflict any casualties on the Kurds, Americans, or the international press corps that day, although they sure seemed to be trying. I couldn't blame them. The other journalists and I were wandering around their front line like tourists just off the bus, and our gall must have made Iraqi soldiers gung-ho to take out a few reporters. But American technology was so superior that by firing artillery or mortars for any length of time, the Iraqis could be sure of drawing a laser-guided bomb down on their heads.

By the next day, the inevitable collapse of Mosul's defenses was well underway. There were too few U.S. troops to secure the city of some 1.7 million people when Saddam's forces surrendered, so U.S. military commanders left Mosul, a landmark of human civilization for at least eight thousand years, in the hands of marauding Kurdish guerrillas, who supervised the wholesale looting and destruction of large parts of the city.

The Americans and peshmerga may have liberated Mosul, but anarchy ruled it. Nothing was safe. Looters stripped luxury hotels, the university, police stations, people's homes, and Saddam's palace. They plundered and burned the city's branch of the central bank. Children joined adults in ransacking the education directorate building. I saw one boy in front of a giant portrait of Saddam happily tossing reams of students' files, exam papers, and other ministry documents into the air, in this war's answer to the ticker tape parade.

The more practically minded headed for the sprawling base of the Iraqi army's 5th Corps, where they leisurely searched through warehouses for the best available weapons and walked off with assault rifles, rocket-propelled grenade launchers, and assorted ammunition by the armful. Through their own negligence, Pentagon planners had guaranteed that Iraqis would be well armed as they waited for the call to start killing Americans. And just hours after Mosul fell, as I talked to middle-class Iraqis burning with rage at the chaos that greeted their liberation, it was obvious that they had something other than flowers and kisses in mind for foreign troops.

"They even stole from this mosque, the cars and computers of the engineers, all sorts of equipment," said a mechanical engineer, standing outside a large mosque that Saddam had started building in hope of improving his Islamic credentials as his regime collapsed. "We think that America has encouraged people to do that."

From Mosul, it was 130 miles to Saddam's birthplace outside the city of Tikrit, and reluctantly, my fourth Kurdish translator and driver agreed to take me there as the first U.S. Marines advanced on the city from the south. We would be traveling from the north on a four-lane highway, through a vast desert where there wasn't a single soldier, foreign or Iraqi, to be seen. With the U.S. military bearing down from the other direction, we drove the most obvious escape route for the Iraqi army and pro-Saddam paramilitaries. The peshmerga guerrillas manning the last checkpoint on the edge of Mosul didn't want to let us go. Himdad, my translator, turned in the front passenger seat to tell me: "He says it's too dangerous," as if that settled the issue.

"Tell him I know that," I replied. "That's why we're going." It wasn't bravado. I knew what I was getting us into, and taking such a big risk scared, as well as shamed me. But I also had a job to do, and I was eager to get it over with. Security tips from peshmerga safely removed from any danger rubbed me the wrong way. "Now let's not waste any more time, so we can get back before dark," I snapped at Himdad. "If we see trouble, we'll turn back."

He reminded me of that promise several times as we headed farther down the virtually deserted highway. And each time, I told him to keep going. We hadn't even been shot at yet. But the closer we got to Tikrit, the larger that risk loomed. For mile upon mile, Iraqi military bases spread out across the sun blasted sands on the other side of the highway. They were the former strongholds of some of Saddam's most loyal troops, including members of the elite Republican Guard. At Hawa, a dark statue of Saddam stood on the army base's front lawn, his arm raised in salute, near an Arabic sign that declared: "The Republican Guard is the Guardian of the People."

Relentless American bombing had changed that in a hurry. The desert was littered with abandoned military trucks and armored vehicles. We passed an Iraqi bus that was engulfed in flames, apparently from a bomb that had hit minutes earlier, exploding just in front of the vehicle and spraying shrapnel through the tires and windows. Iraqi army sentries who had been dug into a sandbagged bunker outside the Hawa base's front gate had changed out of their uniforms before melting into the population. A soldier's boots lay discarded on the roof, and a green uniform was left on the floor, next to a chair toppled in the doorway.

The hasty retreat of Iraqi forces, and the failure of U.S. troops to fill the void for days, left hundreds of people free to help themselves to vast stockpiles of arms and ammunition. The heavy blasts of U.S. bombs falling closer to Tikrit shook the sand beneath me as I walked up to the fence of an army base to get pictures of Iraqis gleefully carting off guns. They seemed especially happy with small machine guns that would be easy to conceal inside a jacket or knapsack. The looters staggered under the weight of their pilfered weapons as they loaded up car trunks, the beds of pickup trucks—even a bicycle's wire basket— with guns and ammo, before hurrying back to climb the fence and steal some more. Some carried eight machine guns at a go. I took pictures of the ones who were laughing. Then I made a run for the car, hoping no one was itching to test his aim. The driver and translator didn't say a word to me for several hours during the drive back to Erbil.

"That wasn't so bad, was it?" I said as we pulled into the hotel parking lot, exhausted from the stress. There was a cold silence. Himdad quickly glanced at the driver and then, still staring straight ahead at the windshield, replied: "You cannot do this to us again. We quit."

I swore at them for abandoning me in the middle of a hot story, gathered my satfone, cameras, and assorted cables, and for the fourth time, went looking for a new team. It was taking longer each time, and the quality of the candidates was plummeting. I found someone who could speak only basic English, which wasn't enough for the work I was trying to do. He summarized long replies into a few words, and I needed to know every word that was spoken, the flashes of anger, despair, or black humor. But beggars can't be choosers, so I told him we would try a day in Mosul to see how things worked. The news had shifted to Tikrit, and the *Times* had someone there embedded with the Marines, so I thought I could ease into things with the new guy. Until we drove smack into a seething mob in front of the governor's office.

I jumped out of the SUV thinking it was just a peaceful protest by a few thousand people, and stopped at a lamppost to ask bystanders what it was about through the nervous translator, who was having trouble getting the Arabs' anger into English. At the crack of automatic rifle fire, I reflexively ducked and turned to see the mob surging toward the governor's building, which was guarded by U.S. Marines and Special Forces. I pressed the record button on the tape recorder in my shirt pocket and shouted, trying to keep the translator from doing the sensible thing and running away. "Why do they not like U.S. troops?" I asked, and as if on cue, they opened fire on the crowd, with a short machine-gun burst followed by several longer ones.

"Stand back! Let's go," the translator said, in his clearest English of the day.

"Ask him again," I said, grabbing the translator by the shoulder, desperate to get one clean quote before we had to flee. "They're angry at the U.S. troops now. Why?"

"We want democracy! We want peace!" he translated the shouting around us. "We want democracy, not someone who conquers our land. We want a government that is for everyone, not just for Kurds."

"Death to America! Death to Americans!" another man hollered in my face. "Americans are here to steal our oil. They are here to conquer our land. They are here to steal our oil! Death to America!"

"These thieves! Kill them all!" another shouted. "They want to steal our land! They want to steal our oil! Death to Americans!"

Out of the corner of my eye, I saw a boy who looked about eight or nine years old break away from the crowd and run toward the building's front gate. He headed straight for a Marine on the back of a Humvee who was shooting bursts from a .50-caliber machine gun, which can fire more than five hundred bullets, each around an inch wide, in a minute. The weapon pounded as it fired, and I ducked even though the barrel was pointed well away from me. But the boy, who was right in front of it, picked up another rock and gleefully ran up again to hurl it at the Marine gunner. It looked like a scene from the Israeli–Palestinian conflict, but this was supposed to be another day of Iraq's joyous liberation. A child battling heavily armed American soldiers with rocks was such a great picture that I moved up into the main intersection, with a perfect view down a broad street of the battle raging from both sides in front of me.

Minutes earlier, a French TV crew had fled in their SUV under a hail of rocks from protesters smashing the windows and trying to yank the doors open. For a fleeting second, I thought I might follow the French lead and get out. But the same old force took over. I walked into the violence, not away from it. I was getting pictures no one else had, shooting Marines and a defiant boy in the same tight frames.

The firing intensified and split the crowd into smaller groups thrashing about in the chaos. A group rushed past me carrying a man with a deep gash across the top of his oozing scalp. It looked like a bullet had cut a new, bloody part in his hair. One of the men saw I had cameras, raised his hands to form a rectangle, and flicked an index finger as if he were shooting a picture. But they were too close for me to take one with the lens that I had on the only one of two cameras that still had battery power. So I quickly turned the lens to remove it, jammed it between my knees, and reached for the shorter lens to make the switch as the guns continued to hammer and the screaming mob of a few hundred Iraqis roiled in closer, all around me now.

It was like being engulfed by a giant, voracious creature, formed from separate organisms that combined to satisfy a mindless craving for prey. In joining the rampaging group, the people shouting and striking out at me had sacrificed any sense of moral restraint to the mass. Faces pressed in. Children laughed. Men shouted and spat on me. The image of Cleveland's body lying in the Mogadishu dirt flashed through my mind, and I wondered: "Is he coming to take me now?" A hand thrust into my pocket and grabbed my cash. Another snatched the lens from the grip of my trembling knees. Like an animal acting on instinct, I focused all my energy into holding on to the cameras, protecting the picture of the boy battling the Marines.

The cameras were hanging from my shoulders and people clawing at me jerked them in both directions. The straps slipped down my arms, but I twisted my wrists, and managed to tangle the straps up with my jacket before the crowd could consume them. I was swept off my feet by the mob, riding it like white water rapids, stupidly trying to defy the laws of nature and save my cameras instead of my own skin. "American! American!" the crowd was chanting in Arabic.

It didn't matter what my name was, which flag I saluted, or what god I did or did not worship. In this central square in one of human civilization's oldest habitations, notions of rationality and morality had, for the moment, been killed off by primeval animal rage. The mob would do what it did. I had a strange sense of relief, as if the struggle were over.

I've seen enough people killed by mobs to know that when the victim is flat on the ground, the end is probably near. Ever since that October day in Mogadishu, when I heard the voice and pressed the shutter release anyway, I've always thought I'd gladly take my chances with bullets and bombs, but that if a mob ever got hold of me, my time was surely up. It would be, I knew, poetic justice. And so now I tried to be calm, and do what I'd always promised myself I would: Die with dignity. But in the meantime, just try to stay vertical.

A punch knocked my head one way, and a rock bounced off my forehead, starting a trickle of blood. I lost sight of the translator, and caught only quick glimpses of him as the mob pushed forward. When I didn't see him again, I assumed he was being killed, or already dead, somewhere nearby. More rocks hit me. I turned my wrists a half twist and let go of the cameras. They vanished into the mob, as if disappearing under a wave.

Only then did I notice that the rioters had ceased to act as a single organism. About twenty Iraqis had formed an inner circle around me. One grabbed the stump of my left arm and held it up, shouting what I assumed was some kind of appeal to humanity over anarchy, like: "Can't you see? He's a cripple!"

"He's innocent! He's innocent!" another defender bellowed. "Leave him alone!"

And then I was knocked flat, lying on the street, looking up at enraged men trying to break through and get me. At least two of the attackers were brandishing homemade knives. The one I saw most clearly burned its image into my brain. It was a long piece of sharpened metal, broad at the base and filed to a lethal tip, and stuck in a roughly cut plastic handle. The man holding it was stabbing at the air as he tried to pull himself over the locked arms of two men who were pushing back, fighting hard to save me. "Let me through—I want to kill him," he screamed.

The mob had dropped me next to a row of shops, all of which were shuttered except one: a small tea shop that was an essential meeting place for men who wanted to catch up on the latest conspiracy theories and plot their next moves. My defenders dragged me several yards to get closer to the front door, but the attackers smashed the windows. Terrified people inside the shop tried to pull the large corrugated metal shutter down to block the entrance. As they struggled to close it, my defenders yanked it up, and the mob hurled rocks and fists at their backs and heads. Hands of people whose faces I couldn't see pulled me through the two-foot space between the floor and the shutter. It slammed down after me.

Men stinking of sweat and fear pulled me to my feet and kissed me three times on my cheeks, as they would a brother or close friend, and they apologized for what had happened through my Kurdish translator who had been rescued and dragged into the shop, too. The mob was still hammering at the shutter, and the metal rolled like thunder as they tried to rock and tear it from the steel runners. My saviors pushed me to the back of the tea shop and when they saw the back of my shirt soaked in blood, and the cut on my forehead, insisted that they take me to the hospital. I told them not to worry, that I was fine, and I didn't think it was a very good idea to go outside at that point. But a man with an AK-47 assault rifle pushed past us and ran up a spiral staircase to the roof of the shop, where he opened fire to disperse the mob.

One of the men in the tea shop opened his jacket to reveal a 9-mm handgun tucked into the waistband of his pants. He grinned and said something to the translator. "He says he's one of Saddam's police," he told me. "He promises he will protect you."

I thought the odds were much better that he would get me out into the street and either hand me back to the mob or kidnap me to make some money. But I knew my welcome in the tea shop had about run out, so I agreed to leave with him on two conditions: "I don't go anywhere without the translator," I said. "And we all hold hands, you, me, and him, from now until we reach the American soldiers."

And so, we made our move. But we only got as far as the middle of the empty intersection when a Marine leveled his rifle and shouted: "Don't move or I'll fucking shoot you!"

The three of us dropped to our knees, and the Iraqi turned and ran.

"Go back!" the Marine hollered. "Now!"

"I'm a journalist," I shouted. "If you send us back there, they'll kill us." And for the first time, I choked back tears.

The Marine conferred with two of his compatriots and then one told us to take shelter behind a concrete barrier just outside the gate, where mere days earlier, an Iraqi sentry had stood guard for Saddam's governor. When I crawled into the tight space, one of the Marines saw my blood-soaked back. "You're wounded," he said.

"That's right," I replied, trying not to lose it. "Please let us in. There's no way we can survive out here."

He asked for some ID. I handed it through the gate, and within minutes, a military press officer was there to welcome us into the governor's building, now full of young American troops. It was the other side of the battle, but like the Iraqis, they were, in effect, captives in a captured land. They were the front line, badly outnumbered by a mob that wanted to take back the power, and many Iraqis were obviously willing to die trying. At least ten in the crowd of some three thousand had been killed under heavy American fire.

It was afternoon now, and there was no telling what would happen when it got dark. I'd seen the corpses of soldiers like these in Mogadishu, after they ran out of ammunition and couldn't fight back any more. The whole mess stunk of Somalia. U.S. troops were caught in the middle of a local political fight they didn't understand, and which their presence only made worse.

During a brief break in the shooting, we slipped past a line of U.S. troops who had taken up firing positions behind a long table, flipped on its side in one of the governate building's front doorways. The floor was covered in brass-colored cartridge casings, and the air was acrid and hot. I pulled up a chair to watch while they scanned the street, buildings, and park for protesters and snipers, and fired more bursts. Their commander paced back and forth behind them, urging them to hold the line and make good kills.

"I think I got one, sir," said a soldier, as the men on either side of the shooter cheered him on.

"Way not to take any shit, Donora," the commander barked from above.

I realized an open doorway wasn't the best place for me to sit, so I moved into what was once the governor's large reception room. Before long, an Arab tribal leader and pretender to the governor's throne, Misha'an Juburi, swaggered in. Juburi, a corrupt thug who had returned from exile in Syria to claim suzerainty over Mosul, realized I was the only foreigner in civilian clothes, and sat in the chair next to me to rant against U.S. forces, who were the only thing standing between him and a lynch mob. By Juburi's account, the riot began around eleven thirty in the morning when a crowd of a thousand people were listening to a speech by an official from the Patriotic Union of Kurdistan, one of Iraqi Kurdistan's two main factions. The official was standing on the governate building's front steps, guarded by U.S. troops, when others raised a huge American flag on the rooftop.

The Americans denied the claim, but I had my doubts. On previous days, I'd seen several Humvees racing through the city with large American flags flapping in the wind. They didn't appear to be doing anything else but making sure they got the Stars and Stripes in as many Iraqi faces as possible. A Spanish reporter who had also taken refuge in the governor's offices said Iraqis pelted the American troops with chunks of concrete and rocks for some twenty minutes before the troops opened fire to stop the mob from overrunning them.

As Juburi vented, Lieutenant Colonel Robert Waltemeyer, commander of the 10th Special Forces, stormed into the room in full combat gear. Towering above Juburi, the colonel demanded to know what was going on. "Why are these people attacking my building?" Waltemeyer asked.

Juburi, who insisted he was the rightful claimant to the governor's chair because he had taken the building with five hundred of his militiamen before American forces arrived, dismissed Waltemeyer with an officious shrug. "When someone speaks like this, how can people accept it?" he asked me. "I'm the man who took this city, the first one in, and look how he talks to me."

Several hours later, during a lull in the shooting and rock throwing, I spotted our driver cruising the streets nearby, searching for us. He had bolted when rioters smashed a side window and tried to drag him from the car. We got his attention from the front steps of the governate building, and he pulled up to a side gate, which we climbed over to make a quick escape from the city.

Back at the hotel in Erbil, I reached to shake my translator's hand and thank him for sticking it out through a very rough probation. I hadn't been working with him for more than a few hours, not long enough for me to remember his name. White as a sheet, and still shaking, my fifth translator of the war quit.

When I got up to my room, and undressed to wash the dried blood off my face and back, I noticed a two-inch slice through the back of my pants, surrounded by a rust-colored blood stain. I put the toilet lid down and stood up to get a clear view of my butt. There was a gash about an inch wide and an inch deep in the upper part of the left cheek. I realized someone wielding those knives in the mob had stabbed me. I quickly got dressed and took a taxi to the Italian war surgery hospital in Erbil, where the doctor who stitched me up said I was lucky the knife hadn't gone in a few inches to the right, where it could easily have severed my spine.

While I lay on the operating table, nurses lifted an Iraqi man, who had a bad bullet wound in his shoulder, onto the empty table next to mine. He muttered something to the doctor, who turned back to me and laughed. "He says he knows you," the doctor explained, and shook his head in disbelief. I looked closely at the man's face, and our eyes locked on to each other's.

"I think he helped save me," I said. "He took an AK-47 onto the roof and shot at the crowd trying to get me."

The doctor translated and the man weakly nodded, wincing in pain while nurses unwrapped a makeshift bandage stuffed into his wound to staunch the flow of blood.

"He says the Americans shot him," the doctor said, and all I could reply was, "Tell him thank you. And I'm sorry."

The next day, the U.S. military told the *New York Times* for its secondhand story on the riot that Marines had saved me. I bumped into Michael Goldfarb, a reporter for National Public Radio, who was standing in the crowd gathered around the big TV screen that broadcast live war coverage in the hotel lobby. He was getting ready to leave Iraq and wondered if I was interested in hiring his translator, Ahmad Shawkat, a balding, fifty-two-year-old chain-smoker. Ahmad smiled with what seemed like a shy grin. After what I'd been through, I doubted he was built for the trouble we were likely to get into. But then neither was I. And I knew first impressions are frequently wrong in times of war. Bravado often hides cowardice, while the meek prove to be the most courageous. I didn't have much choice anyway. I had already decided to hire Ahmad before he even handed me the business card he had printed on computer paper. "Iraqi journalist, Writer and Translator," it read. "English Arabic and Kurdish." He left out numerous other talents, such as carpenter, lecturer in anatomy, and sage.

Ahmad, a father of eight, had been tortured numerous times in horrific ways in Saddam's prisons for opposing the regime. Ahmad's allegorical short stories were among the evidence used against him. He gave me a copy of one in the car during a late afternoon trip back to Erbil, a story on stapled mimeographed sheets that told of a man with a key unable to unlock his past. I was tired and just skimmed the first few paragraphs. I couldn't make sense of it, and stuck the story in my pocket to read another day. I never did.

Ahmad and Goldfarb had become very close friends while working together, and during the few weeks we were a team, I sensed Ahmad trying to get to know me as more than just another foreign journalist passing through. He invited me to dinner at his home to meet his family, but I told him I was too busy. He dropped hints about his tortured past, and I didn't press him for details. I wanted the safety of distance. It was the same old cop-out: friends can't disappoint, betray, or die on you if you have no friends at all. So most of the time, on long drives to one place or another, Ahmad stared silently out his window, and I out mine.

"Pesh*merchants*," he often said as we drove past the long lines of fellow Kurds moving their loot from Mosul to Erbil. I would laugh, and join him in a few sanctimonious condemnations, and then we would fall silent again.

But the gulf I tried to maintain between us wasn't wide enough to deter Ahmad. Whenever we were in Mosul during our few weeks together, he pointed out historic sites and cultural landmarks and gradually had me see the city he loved as something more than just another godforsaken place where people killed each other. He took me to looted museums and libraries and lingered, talking to old friends, to make sure I felt how they suffered at the destruction.

Ahmad told me the Biblical story of Jonah and how God had told him to travel to ancient Nineveh, close to present-day Mosul, and when Jonah tried to avoid it by sea, he was swallowed by a whale and spit out at Nineveh anyway. Ahmad showed me Christian landmarks, tiptoed past unexploded cluster bombs to guide me to ancient hilltop ruins, took me to the Assyrian palace at Nineveh, walked with me beneath giant stone statues of winged lions and bulls. He insisted that I meet his eccentric friends, bohemian artists and writers who had helped him keep the flame of liberty alive. I saw their defiance as a freedom that bombs and bullets could only defile. We drank tea each day in the courtyard garden of his friend Junayd al-Fakri, whose crumbling two-story mansion overlooking the Tigris was the location for some of the opening scenes in *The Exorcist*. I remembered sitting terrified in the darkness of a movie theater years earlier, looking at this very place, and my skin crawled at the mysterious ways that people's paths cross.

On our first morning together, I asked Ahmad to take me to the governate building. The American troops had beat a tactical, if temporary, retreat from the seat of power, and everything had returned to

256

normal, almost as if nothing had happened. As we crawled through traffic, I spotted the tea shop owner replacing his smashed front window. We stopped and I asked Ahmed to tell him I wanted to pay for the damage. The tea shop owner would have none of it. "You are my brother," he beamed, and clasping his hand around mine, insisted we be his guests. A full, complimentary tray of steaming tea in small glasses arrived and soon after that, we were surrounded by about forty-five Iraqi men, all smoking and jabbering, eager to talk about this new democracy they were being promised.

In the haze and noise of the tea room, a common laborer's opinion counted as much as a noble sheikh's. A man claiming to be a retired army colonel angrily denounced the United States as a colonizer. Others whispered that the colonel was really one of Hussein's Ba'ath Party agents.

"I'm just an ordinary person and you can see, with the [American] soldiers gone, we can all sit and discuss politics peacefully," said Rewat Badran, an unemployed worker. But like many in the room, he wanted to move slowly in these first days of democracy. They knew how fragile freedom is and wanted to be careful not to destroy it. "It's too early for democracy," Badran said. "We're still wounded, we're still bleeding. Things have to return to normal first."

Sheikh Abdul Sattar Wais Ibrahim, a leader of the Sharabi clan, strolled in from the street to join the tea shop debate. He warned that American forces only had a few months to stabilize Iraq before its people would insist the foreign occupiers leave. "We, as Iraqis, didn't call the Americans to come and liberate us," he said. "They came on their own and destroyed everything belonging to the previous regime. Since they are very strong, and able to do so many things, we want them to give us security and keep their promises. We want to live as human beings."

257

When the spring floodwaters of the Tigris subsided, Ahmad took me into his secret world, a row of riverbank cafés where we found one brave owner who had started making small pizza-like lunches, which Ahmad followed with tobacco mixed with molasses that he slowly smoked from a bubbling shisha pipe. We sat there on the riverside patio, staring at the fast-flowing water, talking about what democracy might mean in this troubled land where autocrats had flourished for so many centuries. I stared out at the river. I couldn't imagine a more peaceful place.

Soon it was time for me to leave Iraq, and get back to my regular beat covering the original, and largely forgotten war on terrorism in Afghanistan. Ahmad organized a taxi for the long ride to the Jordanian border. He spent a day planning the trip, carefully selecting a driver he would trust with his own life. I loaded my things in the trunk, got into the back seat, and said goodbye through the half-open window, promising Ahmad I would be back to see him soon, to spend time by the river, and take him up on the offer of a home-cooked meal. He smiled his wry, pained grin, and said he'd look forward to it. But as the window rolled up, I could tell from his eyes that he knew he'd never see me again.

The long drive out took me past places that I barely noticed, with names that didn't register until, over the coming months, they became known the world over as insurgent strongholds, the newspaper datelines of the coming carnage, such as Samarra, Balad, Fallujah, and Ramadi.

Soon after I left Iraq, Ahmad got some funding through the staff of General David Petraeus, the intellectual commander of the 101st Airborne, who had taken a liking to Ahmad when he accompanied me for an interview one day. After I finished questioning Petraeus, the general struck up a conversation with Ahmad. The general was interested in his insight, and ordered one of his aides to make sure Ahmad had a press card granting him full access. Petraeus also invited Ahmad to participate in an advisory council. Ahmad decided it was his duty to represent his Shiite minority within the mainly Sunni Kurdish community. I could see him being seduced by the whiff of power, and it scared me. With the American money, he started a weekly newspaper and an institution to promote democracy. He called his weekly *Bilattijah*—Without Direction—and he used the new platform to criticize all sides, making fresh enemies at a very dangerous time.

Months later, Goldfarb called me at home in New Delhi to ask if I'd heard the news. On October 20, 2003, a man, maybe two, followed Ahmad to the rooftop of his office and murdered him with a single shot into his back. Speculation focused on the usual suspects, Saddam's Baathists and Islamic extremists, but the list of possibilities would have to include anyone Ahmad had offended, and there were many. He was a man determined to speak his mind, whatever the personal risks. In my eyes, that made him more of a democrat than the war leaders who declaimed grand speeches from a safe distance, and cheapened the word *democracy* to a platitude. But Ahmad wasn't innocent, and if fate had ever allowed us to sit beside the Tigris again, I would have told him so. He had taken American government money, which put him in the pay of one side in a vicious war, and whatever truths he wrote were tainted by the charge that he was a collaborator.

Listening to Goldfarb tell me what happened, I cursed the people who had given Ahmad the money, and myself for those moments by the rushing river when I assured Ahmad it was now safe to believe.

16

MAKING ENEMIES

When you're wounded and left on Afghanistan's plains, and the women come out to cut up what remains, jest roll to your rifle and blow out your brains an' go to your Gawd like a soldier.

RUDYARD KIPLING

When the United States turned its attention to Iraq, the Taliban and its Al Qaeda allies won back the momentum in Afghanistan. American and Afghan forces had trounced the Taliban and rooted out bin Laden's bases after the three months of fighting that followed Al Qaeda's September 11 attacks. But U.S. Defense Secretary Donald Rumsfeld's strategy of relying on air strikes to support small Special Forces units fighting alongside ragtag Afghan militia forces left the Taliban and Al Qaeda leadership an easy escape route through the mountains into Pakistan. Since Pakistani authorities were at least negligent, and possibly provided direct support to the militants, the Taliban's mullahs were able to regroup, and recruit and train new fighters in madrassas. Soon after Kabul fell, Mullah Omar vowed to lead the Taliban in a guerrilla war against U.S.-led forces. I remember Afghans laughing at the threat, giddy with their new freedom, when the West's promises seemed so real. But within months, the armed extremists were crossing back into Afghanistan to deliver the classic death by a thousand pinpricks.

In the early months after the Taliban's fall, the country seemed to be making great progress outside the militants' former strongholds in the mainly Pashtun provinces of eastern and southern Afghanistan. Millions of girls were going to school again and commerce was taking off in major cities such as Kabul, where warlords flush with CIA pay-offs and drug money were building million-dollar mansions. In streets where women once feared to tread unless enshrouded by burkas and escorted by a male relative, Chinese hookers were now turning tricks with the aid of new cell phone networks. Compared to the fear and drudgery I'd seen under the Taliban, it looked like the unstoppable march of freedom that was the stuff of Bush speeches.

I finally realized how badly things were going for U.S. forces when I headed to the barren, war-ravaged province of Zabul in the fall of 2003, intending to write a soft feature story on American soldiers training Afghans to fight better so that they could take their country the final mile, and bring an end to generations of war.

I drove on a whim into Taliban country with my fixer, Wesal Zaman, and a letter from General Mohammed Moin Faqir, commander of the Afghan National Army's Central Corps. It was a kind of *laissez passer* instructing any Afghan officials who read it to let us move unharmed and unhindered through their various fiefdoms until our work was complete. The governor in Qalat, the dreary, dust-blown provincial capital, seemed impressed by our letter. Reclining on pillows on the floor of his bedroom, he listened stern-faced to our request to visit an area where Afghan troops were on a mission with U.S. forces. We had something moderately risky in mind.

The governor suggested that the remote village of Dai Chopan would be the perfect place to visit, because an anti-Taliban sweep was underway. In the next breath, he explained it was far too dangerous for us to go there. I assured him that we understood the risks, and that they went with the job, so no one would hold him responsible if we got into trouble. The governor stared at me in deep thought for a few seconds, looked at Wesal, and asked: "Does he believe in God?"

I assumed he was asking whether I was a Muslim, but the translation was literal, and I wanted to be honest. A simple "Yes" would have been faster. "I believe in the possibility of God," I replied. "But I see too much evil, too much suffering in the world, to be certain that God exists."

The governor pondered the answer grimly, as if nothing less than our lives, and his honor, were at stake. "All right," he told Wesal, "I'll give you a guide. But if anyone stops you on the way and asks questions, you must tell them that the foreigner is a Muslim. And no matter what he says, make sure you translate with quotations from the Koran."

An elderly villager needed a ride back to Dai Chopan, so the governor appointed him to lead us there, on a six-hour journey along washboard dirt tracks that twisted and turned through some of the most dangerous territory in Afghanistan. The Taliban claimed to have thirteen hundred fighters in the mountainous region around Dai Chopan. Three hundred of them had attacked and killed eight Afghan soldiers and then fled into the mountains a few days earlier. But there were few vehicles on the road when we traveled down it, and no one stopped us, so the trip went smoothly—until we reached a military checkpoint on the high ground overlooking the village.

Afghan national army soldiers stopped us first. They looked at our letter from their Kabul commander, made a brief radio call, and then cleared us to drive on. No more than twenty yards down the road, American soldiers in a Humvee stopped us. They didn't care that the

Afghans, whom the U.S. military's own propaganda insisted were an independent force in a sovereign, democratic country, had given us permission to proceed. The Americans ordered us to pull back to the Afghan checkpoint and radioed U.S. commanders at Bagram airbase.

Twenty minutes later, as the sun was setting on a vast desert where the Taliban roamed free, an American soldier approached and said a Colonel Rodney Davis, a public affairs officer at Bagram, had denied us permission to enter Dai Chopan. "My orders are to tell you to return to Kabul and speak to Colonel Davis." He pointed off into the menacing void. "It's that way."

I exploded. "It's going to be dark in less than an hour, and it'll take us at least six hours just to reach the highway," I bellowed. "You're a soldier and you're sending unarmed civilians into the desert? You should be ashamed of yourself. We're going to get killed for sure!"

"I hear what you're saying, sir," the soldier replied calmly, trying to stifle a smirk. "But they's my orders."

I pulled out my handheld satellite phone and dialed as many official phone numbers as I could find. But it was a Friday, the Muslim Sabbath, and anyone of any authority at the embassy and other offices was enjoying a day off. I strode up to the U.S. checkpoint and tried reason again, a little more reserved this time. "There's no way I'm taking two Afghans off into the desert in the darkness to get all of us killed," I told the soldier in charge. "We're going to wait right here, and as soon as you turn around and go back to Dai Chopan, we're going to follow you."

"Do what you have to do, sir," he said, more like one human to another now. I got the feeling that he knew how bull-headed, and dangerous, his superiors were.

We didn't get far up the road before we had to take cover from stray bullets, exploding rockets, and mortar bombs. The troops had seized three truckloads of rocket-propelled grenades, mortars, artillery shells, and anti-aircraft rounds from Dai Chopan and set fire to the heap in an empty field. As the ammo cooked off, a barrage was hitting the rocky hills above the village. We joined some Afghan men and boys cowering against a cliff. The mix of terror and astonishment in their eyes seemed to say, "You're a foreigner, one of *them*, so why are you hiding with us? Why don't *you* stop this?" I asked Wesal to explain that we were journalists, civilians who had nothing to do with the military, and were just as scared of getting killed as they were—probably more.

Darkness was approaching, which left us a choice between getting hit by shrapnel or a ricochet, or taking our chances with Talibs roaming the mountains. We waited for a brief lull in the explosions and raced straight to the village administrator's home. The district commissioner was in the middle of a meeting with thirty angry men in turbans and rough cloth cloaks, crammed shoulder-to-shoulder in the flickering light of an oil lamp, having an animated discussion in Pashtu. I didn't want to interrupt, so we waited until the local chief turned to me and explained what the trouble was. He said Afghan militia fighters who were working alongside U.S. troops had gone on a looting and torture spree, and at least one of their victims was lying battered and unconscious in a village house. The militiamen were from Kandahar, and loyal to three warlords whose treatment of local people before the Taliban's rise was so vicious that it helped build popular support for the extremist mullahs' takeover of Afghanistan. The U.S. military was officially paying the warlords' men to act as guides, which struck me as odd since no armed force in the world could match the Americans' satellites, drones, and other technology that map terrain and eyes the enemy in real time. The guides were also well armed—hardly the kind of people to win hearts and minds.

Haji Abdul Karim, a delegate to the *loya jirga*, or traditional council, drafting the country's new constitution, pressed through the crowd of elders to show me several cuts above his left eye and raw welts criss-crossing his back. He said the Kandahari guides had beaten him and stolen $220. I was skeptical. People talked about abuse and various assaults on tribal and religious morals all the time in Afghanistan, but I'd never met anyone who could back up significant allegations with hard proof. It was half a year before the world would see the grotesque pictures of American soldiers abusing Iraqi inmates at Abu Ghraib prison, and like many people, I thought the American military was too disciplined to carry out such flagrant violations of the laws of war, not to mention common sense. I told the meeting that someone would have to take me to the victims and provide proof of their allegations or no one would believe them. Two men were assigned to lead us to their house on the edge of the village.

We piled into our car at dusk, and just as we were about to pass an encampment of American soldiers on the other side of a narrow river, an Afghan soldier ran to stop us. We didn't have permission to drive through the village, he said, and our letter from the commander in Kabul meant nothing to him. I launched into a rant about how he should be ashamed, an Afghan in uniform taking orders from Americans instead of one of his own generals. The tirade was making our guides nervous. They bolted into the darkness. We turned around and went back to the district commissioner's house and quickly fell asleep on his hard dirt floor.

At dawn, we awoke to the grinding noise of military vehicles shifting gears in a rush to leave. The American soldiers and their Afghan

266

allies were pulling out in a convoy that kicked up golden swirls of sunlit dust.

If the Taliban wanted revenge, we were now sitting ducks. We waited to see the back of the last American vehicle and then headed for the house with the beating victims. On the other side of the river, we met a four-wheel-drive Hilux truck, the Taliban's favorite off-road transportation since the years when they dominated Afghanistan, as it headed in from the countryside. A fierce-looking man in a black turban scowled down at me. He was a dead ringer for a Talib, but he let us pass without a word.

In the small courtyard of a mudbrick farmhouse, Doolkhoor, a forty-year-old mother, sat on the bare earth, nursing her broken shoulder. Her right arm was bound tightly to her chest with a strip of cloth. She pulled a blanket over her face so that her husband would not suffer the dishonor of another man seeing his wife's face. One of the Americans' Afghan guides had beaten her with a rifle butt, he told me. Her two adult sons lay in a cramped bedroom with broken bones, deep cuts, and large patches of purple and black bruises covering their bodies.

Nasrullah, twenty-one, was the worst off. He lay on the floor, covered in a rough blanket, softly grunting. I thought he might be faking, so I asked his father, Shamsullah, to show me the injuries. He lifted the blanket, and pulled up his son's shirt so I could see the dark, puffy mass of bruises and welts that covered his back. Nasrullah's buttocks were even more of a mess. I winced just looking at them. One of the Afghan fighters who had beaten Nasrullah had hammered him in the back of his head with a rifle butt, caving in his skull. Two empty plastic intravenous bottles hung from a nail in the wall above the bed. A village health worker had brought them in a feeble attempt to restore essential fluids as his brain hemorrhaged. Several headache tablets spilled out of a small blue plastic bag next to his pillow. There was also a tube of pain-relief gel, bottles of vitamin syrup and antibiotics. My mind flashed to images of the battered corpse of South African anti-apartheid activist Steve Biko, who died after white police tortured him. The nearest doctor was six hours down the dirt track we'd come in on, and Nasrullah's parents were too frightened to ask the American soldiers for medical help.

"Nasrullah hasn't spoken yet," his father said. "He has been unconscious since he was beaten."

His older brother Abdul Rahim, twenty-five, lay a few feet away, his right arm in a knotted cloth sling. His buttocks, hips, and back were covered with large bruises, severe cuts, and lash marks. "There were three guys who were beating me," he said. "One was standing behind me. The two others were standing on my feet. They were kicking me, and the one on my back was beating me with sticks. I was still able to get up, and then I tried to go and see my brother. So they hit me with the butt of a Kalashnikov, and I was unconscious after that. I don't know what happened then."

The militiamen had come looking for hidden guns, which are as common as shovels in rural Pashtun homes, if not more. Being armed didn't necessarily mean you were an insurgent. Men had to defend their families against all sorts of dangers, and anyone who couldn't was a disgrace. Abdul Rahim said he tried to bluff the militiamen at first, but then handed over a pistol and a Kalashnikov assault rifle. They insisted he was hiding more weapons, and when he denied it, they accused him of feeding the Taliban. "Come with us. We will take you to the Americans," they told him.

But as they walked toward the American soldiers' riverside camp, the militiamen suddenly turned and took the brothers to two empty, roofless rooms, about nine feet by six feet, normally used for storing harvested almonds, behind the family orchard. The U.S. soldiers' camp was just a few hundred yards down the hill. The Americans' guides tortured his brother in one room while he waited in the other, Abdul Rahim said. "I heard him shouting, 'Don't hit me, for God's sake, don't beat me—if you have a God.'"

Their twelve-year-old brother, Bakhtullah, found the men unconscious in the storage rooms. A neighbor, who was robbed of a watch, a chicken, and fifty-five dollars in Pakistani rupees, arrived with two other men, wrapped the tortured brothers in blankets, and carried them home.

When I arrived, the dirt floor of the torture chamber was littered with cigarette butts. There were several empty, heavy plastic bags that had contained U.S. military meals ready to eat, or MREs. Just a few hundred yards down the slope, we found the detritus of the American soldiers' camp.

Everyone I spoke to in the village said the Americans were not present during the torture and other abuses, but after spending a night in Dai Chopan's deathly silence, I doubted anyone within several miles could have missed the screams of men suffering prolonged beatings. How could American soldiers just a few hundred yards away have been deaf and blind to what paramilitaries under their command were doing? Milosevic had used a similar dodge in Kosovo by claiming that he couldn't be held responsible for isolated acts carried out by people beyond his control. But international law is clear on the subject: soldiers with command responsibility, who are supposed to know what their troops are doing in a combat zone—especially to non-combatants—can be guilty of war crimes.

When I made it back to Kabul late that afternoon, I immediately contacted Davis, the military public affairs officer who had tried to keep me out of Dai Chopan, to ask for an interview with a senior

American commander to discuss the villagers' allegations and show photographs that I'd taken of the brothers' injuries. I especially wanted to ask why the U.S. military was subcontracting torture and interrogation to militia members loyal to known war criminals. The colonel replied to my request with the standard spin. "The coalition enjoys a great relationship with the Afghan people," Davis wrote in an email. "The coalition is reasonably sure—virtually certain—Afghan militia forces conduct themselves in a professional manner while operating under coalition control and we've had no reports to the contrary."

I spent a few days trying to contact Davis, but he wouldn't take my phone calls, and he soon shut down completely by blocking all my emails, which were automatically returned to sender. The Pentagon later justified Davis's stonewalling by saying I didn't have the proper press credentials.

Hamid Karzai's palace advisers were more sympathetic. The president, who had no control over military operations in his own country, had been pressing U.S. commanders for months to change tactics because they were alienating ordinary Afghans, and sending fresh recruits over to the Taliban side. Of course, Karzai had much better access to the American brass than I did, but he hadn't got much further with them. He immediately ordered his government to investigate the events at Dai Chopan, and paid compensation to villagers whose homes and shops had been looted during the almost three-week offensive. But nothing more came of it, and the story soon faded.

It was in a bazaar, over two years later, right in front of the Americans' main base at Bagram, where I finally found documentary evidence of the lie behind several years of public insistence by the

American military and government that Pakistan was a steadfast ally in the war on terrorism.

Wesal mentioned one day that a friend of his had bought a flash memory drive from an Afghan shopkeeper selling stolen military goods less than two hundred yards from Bagram's main entrance. The Afghans were selling them as cheap, used goods, along with watches, folding cots, knives, sunglasses, and numerous other military items. They claimed to have no idea what was on the flash drives, which were the size of packs of chewing gum and slid into a computer's USB port. The fences working in the bazaar were either unable to read, or were uninterested in, what was on the pilfered drives. Wesal said his friend's flash drive contained secret documents that I should take a look at. We were too busy following the rapid resurgence of the Taliban and their allies, so I told Wesal to remind me some other time. A few months passed, and on a slow day, he brought it up again. The bazaar turned out to be a trove of confidential military files that made my jaw drop.

Some of the digital files provided a peek at what occupies a soldier's mind when he's alone with his laptop, far from home: pictures of kids, wives, and girlfriends, souvenir snapshots of themselves posing in the dusty badlands of Afghanistan, stacks of Pakistani rupee notes and weapons seized from suspected Taliban guerrillas. There were video clips of servicemen pumping iron in the gym, cockpit videos of air strikes against suspected insurgents, and a few close-up profiles of erect penises. Then there were more intriguing shots: Afghan prisoners, including one in a police uniform, leaning against a mudbrick wall, blindfolded by several rounds of tightly wrapped tape, his hands bound behind his back.

But most shocking were the photographs and detailed personal information on Afghans spying for the U.S. military. The files included the spies' names, addresses, birth dates, and similar information about their wives and children, as well as detailed records of meetings with their U.S. military handlers and the intelligence provided. It was a stunning breach of security, one discovered with a forty-dollar payment to a teenager peddling stolen computer parts. In a country where some of the world's most skilled intelligence forces, including spies from Russia, Britain, Iran, China, India, and Pakistan were competing for secrets, I assumed I wasn't the only foreigner who had his hands on Bagram's secrets.

When my story was printed, the military's senior public affairs officers at Bagram suddenly started calling me. The *Times*'s lawyers negotiated with the Justice Department and the Pentagon for the return of the flash drives in exchange for guarantees that neither I, nor Wesal, would be prosecuted. The U.S. Army's criminal investigators would spend months trying to figure out how one of the most important front-line bases in the war on terrorism had sprung so many leaks.

Judging from the addresses, slide show titles, and other details in the documents, the owner of the flash drive that contained some of the most sensitive information was a soldier in the 7th Special Forces Group (Airborne), a U.S. Army unit based at Fort Bragg, North Carolina, which before 2001 normally operated in Central and South America and the Caribbean. One of the computer file folders was full of intelligence reports, marked "Secret," which were part of an operation code-named "Implicit Agile." Also among the digital documents were secret PowerPoint presentations for senior U.S. commanders at Bagram, such as one from August 2004 that highlighted "obstacles to success" along the border and accused Pakistan of making "false and inaccurate reports of border incidents." It also criticized "political and military inertia in Pakistan." Half a year later, the U.S. military was still complaining privately that improvised explosive devices, or IEDs in military jargon, were being smuggled in along numerous known routes from Pakistan, just as they had been for decades. A Special Operations task force map, which showed the militants' main cross-border smuggling routes in early 2005, included a comment from a U.S. military commander who sought some way to make "Pakistani border forces cease assisting cross border insurgent activities."

An intelligence report from late 2004 described how Pakistani authorities had arrested fourteen Taliban members in Quetta that fall. They were moved to a jail in Peshawar, and two months later, they were released after a member of parliament from the pro-Taliban Jamaat-i-Islami party spoke to ISI intelligence officers. The same report confirmed that senior Taliban leaders lived in and around Quetta. The ISI had also arranged medical care for the Taliban's fugitive leader, Mullah Omar, who lost his right eye to shrapnel in the war against the Soviets and has a $10 million U.S. government bounty on his head.

"Pakistani ISI has been providing medical treatment for Mullah Omar's eye," the U.S. military intelligence report said. "Mullah Omar now has received an artificial eye that moves in conjunction with his good eye."

"These Taliban leaders generally change their residence about once a month, but are seen visiting local madrassas in Quetta," it added, and named four intersections in the Pakistani city where the leaders had been seen during regular visits to mosques and madrassas.

Another secret intelligence report, which said the source had reported reliably sixty times in the past, identified a colonel in the Afghan army's 205th Corps who had allegedly received a list of thirty people approved by a former Taliban justice minister, who were to be given defense ministry jobs so that they could launch attacks on the coalition's Kandahar airfield. And in early 2006, the Defense Intelligence Agency warned that five years after the U.S. military toppled the Taliban regime and forced Al Qaeda to flee Afghanistan, six provinces along the Pakistan border were "Al Qaeda strongholds."

"These locations allow Al Qaeda members easy entrance and exit over the Afghanistan/Pakistan border," the report said, adding: "Al Qaeda maintains close ties to the Taliban and has received technical support and training from Pakistani militant groups." It also said "Pakistan's Inter-Services Intelligence Directorate poses a HIGH intelligence threat to U.S. and Coalition forces." Pakistani intelligence agencies were recruiting sources among U.S. troops' Afghan interpreters, collecting information on American counterintelligence operations, and providing "passive support to pro-Pakistan, anti-Coalition militias and the Taliban, to maintain pressure on the U.S.," the report said. At the same time, another secret DIA document concluded "al-Qaida continues to provide operational expertise and to train and equip anti-coalition militants, primarily Taliban" and forces loyal to Gulbuddin Hekmatyar, who received the lion's share of covert American aid during the mujahideen war against the Soviets, only to become one of America's fiercest enemies after the fall of the Taliban. Another DIA document, from early 2006, reported that eighty members of the Iranian military's elite Quds Force were working closely with warlord Ismail Khan in Afghanistan's northwest.

There were warnings, printed in small red letters, on secret military maps that were among the most intriguing documents on the flash drives. The maps were prepared in 2005, and were among digital files belonging to a member of an airborne Special Forces unit. They showed the locations of all Pakistani military units and control posts along the Afghan border, dozens of them, with the number of people stationed at each, their weapons and other details.

"Shall obtain permission at least 15 minutes prior to entering Pakistan airspace," the red-letter alerts declared.

Officially, the U.S. military isn't permitted to cross into Pakistan at all, so it was a tantalizing mystery that Special Forces soldiers highly skilled in airborne assaults would have maps cautioning them to get permission before crossing the border. Musharraf has said repeatedly that he won't allow such violations of his country's sovereignty. But following several air strikes on border villages, Pakistani tribesmen have insisted they came under attack from American helicopters. Both the United States and Pakistan denied it, and without harder evidence, their potentially explosive claims never got traction.

I poked around, trying to find someone to confirm my suspicion that the secret maps at least suggested U.S. Special Forces were prepared to enter Pakistan, with just fifteen minutes' notice to its government or American commanders, if the order came down. I got nowhere. But another document on the flash drives showed that U.S. Army Special Forces were at least discussing covert operations in Pakistan.

In November 2005, a Special Forces officer met in southern Afghanistan with an operative who had crossed the border from Quetta with the aid of a trusted Afghan source, who claimed he could lead U.S. troops to Taliban "high value targets," called "TB HVTs" in military shorthand. The Quetta operative was "willing to take American personnel to the current safesites of TB HVTs in Pakistan particularly Quetta and conduct on the ground reconnaissance/ surveillance on their behalf with the endstate being the capture/kill of selected TB leaders," the secret report said. When the Afghan source warned "that it would be extremely difficult to capture a HVT and move them to Afghanistan even if they were dead," the American officer asked whether his contact in Quetta "could arrange specific direct-action operations in Pakistan on behalf of U.S. Forces."

There is no doubt that the CIA operates in Pakistan's border areas, a fine distinction, perhaps, since CIA operatives include paramilitary agents. But while Musharraf secretly approved operations by U.S. civilians in Pakistan, in cooperation with his own ISI and other security agencies, he publicly insisted that the U.S. military must stop at the Afghan side of the border. Pakistanis in the tribal areas on the Afghan border regularly claimed American forces were launching attacks from inside Afghanistan. In mid-January 2006, a mud brick compound was destroyed in a strike on the remote Pakistani village of Damadola. Bin Laden's deputy, Ayman al-Zawahiri, was the apparent target of the CIA Predator missile, but the attack killed sixteen innocent people. Protests erupted across Pakistan, and days later, Zawahiri taunted the U.S. president, calling him a loser, in a videotape diatribe: "Bush, do you know where I am?" bin Laden's deputy asked. "I am among the Muslim masses, enjoying their care with God's blessings and sharing with them their holy war against you until we defeat you."

The consistent conclusions of the flash drive documents, written over several years, left no doubt that the U.S. military believed, and had ample evidence to support, the Afghan government's view that insurgents with some level of assistance from the ISI had bases inside Pakistan, and were receiving training there. They were killing American, Afghan, Canadian, and other allied forces in an escalating offensive that had spread across at least half the country in the five years since the war against the Taliban and Al Qaeda began. Yet the U.S. military's top commanders continued to insist publicly that Pakistan was a loyal ally.

In 2006, the U.S. handed over military command of most troops in Afghanistan to NATO, leaving the alliance, and Karzai's weak, corrupt government as the fall guys if the experiment in building a stable democracy from the ruins of a failed state continued to collapse. The Taliban and their allies had taken advantage of sparse troop deployments and the West's refusal to force Pakistan to close down all militant camps and round up Taliban leaders, and built a self-sustaining guerrilla network in Afghanistan. By the end of 2006, it had expanded to the provinces surrounding Kabul, and cells of suicide bombers were operating in the capital. That fall, the NATO commander, British Lieutenant General David Richards, warned that if Afghans didn't see significant improvements in their lives within half a year, up to 70 percent would throw their support behind the Taliban.

Given the militants' head start, it was hard to see how Karzai and his foreign backers could make up enough lost ground in six winter months to defeat an insurgency that was steadily gaining support. Throughout the five years that I reported on Afghanistan's troubled transition to democracy, there was one constant. Whenever I asked ordinary Afghans if they thought they'd live long enough to see an end to war, invariably they answered: "When foreigners leave us alone, we will have peace."

17

THE LABYRINTH

"I believe in killing people who try to hurt you. And I can't believe we're being pushed around by these two-bit pricks."
PRESIDENT BILL CLINTON, REACTING TO IMAGES
OF SOMALIS DESECRATING DEAD U.S. SOLDIERS,
AS QUOTED BY AIDE GEORGE STEPHANOPOULOS

When I returned to my beat in South Asia, a central question haunted me: Why were Western leaders, President George W. Bush foremost among them, still heaping praise on Pakistan's President Pervez Musharraf for his help in the war on terrorism when mounting evidence said he was playing a double game, allowing militants who shared some of his strategic goals to operate while moving against others, such as foreign Al Qaeda fighters?

Militant leader Maulana Fazlur Rahman Khalil was one of five Al Qaeda leaders, including bin Laden and his Egyptian deputy Ayman al-Zawahiri, who signed the 1998 fatwa that launched a global "jihad against Jews and Crusaders" by declaring: "The ruling to kill the Americans and their allies—civilians and military—is an individual duty for every Muslim who can do it in any country in which it is possible to do it." Al Qaeda's twin bombings of U.S. embassies in

Kenya and Tanzania came less than six months after the fatwa was issued. The Clinton administration retaliated with cruise missile attacks on Sudan and a network of militant training camps, including Khalil's, near the eastern Afghanistan town of Khost. Washington called them Al Qaeda terrorist bases. As Clinton aides planned the cruise missile strikes, intelligence reports said bin Laden was expected to attend a meeting of several hundred "terrorist leaders" at the camps to plan future attacks.

Following the 9/11 attacks on the United States, teenaged boys with weaker links to terrorism than Khalil were wasting away in cage-like cells in the U.S. prison at Guantanamo Bay while he was free in Pakistan, still rallying the faithful to wage jihad against the United States and its allies.

I knew Khalil's tentacles, and those of his disciples, reached back to the battles in the streets of Somalia that had killed Cleveland. I wondered why Khalil, who as leader of the Al Qaeda affiliate Harkat ul-Mujahedeen had other Americans' blood on his hands and continued to recruit for attacks on the U.S. after 9/11, was not on trial for those and other crimes?

Mubashir Zaidi, a Pakistani investigative reporter whom I worked with, had figured out where Khalil lived. I wanted to go and ask him for an interview, expecting to get some of the answers straight from his lips. When I sought him out, I had no idea that I'd followed his footsteps for a long time before I ever heard his name.

When I went after him in early 2004, I returned to a twisting path that led back at least a decade, to the day in Mogadishu when I signed a letter requesting an interview with another notorious militia commander: Mohammed Farah Aideed, whom U.S. forces were trying to arrest as an alleged mass-murderer. A couple of British reporters came up with the idea and asked me if I wanted in on it. I took the pen and signed straightaway. I admit the letter was on the fawning side, as journalists usually are when trying to persuade unsavory people with oversized egos that it's in their interest to speak to a world that detests them. There was something in the letter about how foreign forces were denigrating Aideed, and how we were his best opportunity to be heard, to set the record straight.

The letter was delivered to the man we thought was most likely to get it to Aideed, the warlord's financier and arms supplier, Osman Ato. It was still in Ato's pocket when American Special Forces rappelled down ropes from Black Hawks into his compound on September 21, 1993—just four days before Somalis shot down their first Black Hawk—and hauled him off to an island prison for four months.

Someone from the State Department in Washington called my editor at the time, Paul Warnick, to ask whether he realized how biased I was, and whether he thought such an obviously flawed journalist should really continue reporting from Somalia. He read the letter over the phone as proof. Editors at my British colleagues' newspapers got similar calls.

Warnick was a gruff, hard-drinking journalist of the old school. He thought the phone call from Foggy Bottom was amusing and told me not to worry about it, assuring me the bureaucrat who called was a humorless asshole. But Warnick wanted to make sure that I understood how the system worked. He knew I was having fun, and that one way or another, I had to learn this was not a game. I admit to being naive back then. I couldn't believe an institution as powerful and with as many major problems on its hands as the U.S. State Department would waste its time with a puny Canadian reporter. It would take me years to learn how little I knew of what was actually going on in Somalia, and just how high the stakes really were.

More than a decade after I was the uninvited houseguest of Raymond Marchand, the mysterious oilman, I read once-secret diplomatic cables and realized why the Somali gunmen who picked me up on my first trip to the city decided Marchand's villa was the best place to drop me off. After the U.S. abandoned its embassy to marauding looters in 1991, the oil company's compound became a sanctuary for American diplomats during their brief trips into Mogadishu. In the diplomatic euphemism, they were visiting to "assess the political and security situations." Conoco, a Houston-based oil giant, rented its Mogadishu compound from Ato, who used some of his profits from trafficking guns and qat, and presumably his tenants' rent, to bankroll Aideed's militia. Ato also ran numerous garages that built and maintained the battlewagons, known as "technicals," that Somali gunmen used to terrorize the city. Some of the same technicals guarded Ato's drug shipments on the long, treacherous drive in from the K-50 airstrip where I landed on a qat flight from Kenya. With no apparent motive for being in their corner of hell, they must have decided I belonged at the Conoco compound.

Conoco was one of four American oil companies that persuaded Siad Barre to grant them drilling rights in almost two-thirds of Somalia during the dying years of his regime. Marchand, Conoco's general manager in Somalia, was the only foreign oil boss to stick around after Siad Barre fell in early 1991. Diplomatic cables declassified in 2005 make it clear that while Marchand was purportedly protecting Conoco's oil interests amid Somalia's anarchy, he was also providing essential assistance to the U.S. government in a strategic country.

American diplomats recommended to Washington as early as October 1991 that Conoco's villa and compound be used to house American staff and provide office space if a temporary U.S. mission opened in Mogadishu, according to a cable obtained by The Somalia Declassification Project, at Illinois' College of DuPage, which has used the Freedom of Information Act to probe the links between the U.S. government and the oil company's interests in Somalia. Conoco was the only U.S. firm that kept an office open throughout 1991 despite mounting chaos in the streets. Marchand finally gave up and left in early 1992, not long after my brief stay in his house, because leaders of the faction that controlled north Mogadishu "accused Conoco of siding with Aideed and financing his war effort," U.S. diplomats reported.

But Marchand continued to visit the Mogadishu compound and offered it, along with Conoco aircraft, to U.S. officials whenever they required transportation and housing in Somalia. Marchand also arranged for American diplomats to avail themselves of the services of his well-placed Somali friends. In June, a cable to Washington praised Ato for being "most helpful in arranging safe passage" for Somalis in a rival faction's territory. It was Ato who got them safely through roadblocks manned by trigger-happy militia fighters, so that they could collect back pay from a visiting American diplomat, according to the cable.

Almost a year after I'd stayed with Marchand, Conoco's man in Mogadishu was preparing to host a much more distinguished guest as the U.S.-led invasion loomed. Bush called career diplomat Robert Oakley out of retirement to be his special envoy to Somalia, tasked to intimidate the warlords and persuade them with any necessary inducements, in the event the sight of American troops and firepower didn't cow them. Oakley was no glad-handing diplomat. True to his middle name, Bigger, he was a lanky Texan with harsh, sunken eyes and pinched lips, who spoke in a deep, no-nonsense monotone. He reminded me of Lurch, the butler from *The Addams Family*. Oakley and a small staff of American officials set up what was officially called the U.S. Liaison Office in the Conoco compound. Oakley immediately seconded Marchand from his oil work and named him as a personal adviser, presumably in matters other than rock structure and drill bits.

At the time, a spokesman for the oil company said Conoco was just being "a good corporate citizen and neighbor" by renting its premises to the U.S. government. But in a secret cable sent from Mogadishu soon after the U.S. landing, Oakley asked Bush to write a letter of appreciation to Conoco president Dino Nicandros, whom Bush no doubt knew as a compatriot among Houston oil barons. Oakley suggested the letter should thank Nicandros "for the tremendous support that Conoco as a corporation and Raymond Marchand as an individual have provided here.

"Raymond's contribution to this effort cannot be overstated," Oakley continued, "as he has provided us essential logistics support as well as valuable insight and connections into the various Somali leadership groups in Mogadishu. It is important both to us and to him that he retain the support of top management for his extraordinary contribution."

As an afterthought, Oakley asked the acting secretary of state to phone Nicandros or Conoco's executive vice president to say thanks for the use of the compound. Almost a year into the U.S. intervention in Somalia, Conoco's in-house magazine printed a letter from Oakley's military aide, U.S. Marine Brigadier General Frank Libutti, who heaped praise on Marchand in a vein similar to what Oakley's cable suggested should come from the White House. "Without Raymond's courageous contributions and selfless service, the operation would have failed," the Marine general wrote. It didn't sound like just any polite thank-you note one might write after bunking at a friend's house. The U.S. military and State Department had relied on an oil company executive to find their way through Somalia's treachery.

When Oakley was still trying to manage the U.S. diplomatic mission in Somalia in early 1993, a diplomat's confidential analysis mentioned the close cooperation with Conoco, and its links to Ato, among the reasons why America was giving itself a bad name. The cable to Washington also pointed down another dark corridor in the labyrinth. It said Al-Ittihad al-Islami, or the Islamic Union Party, was quickly gaining support in Somalia. The group was "spreading like wildfire," a January 1993 cable warned. "A year earlier, the fundamentalists were nowhere to be seen," it said. An unnamed informant, the telex added, "said the fundamentalists were patient: They moved into an area by building cells with local contacts. They were never short of money."

Little known outside the Horn of Africa, Al-Ittihad established links to the growing Al Qaeda network in the early 1990s, when bin Laden was based in Sudan. Al-Ittihad's members there warned on the eve of the U.S. landing in Somalia that American soldiers would suffer "the same experience as they did in Beirut," where a truck bomb killed 241 U.S. troops in 1983. Few noticed, and even fewer took Al-Ittihad seriously. It was only in hindsight, far too late, that the roots of Al Qaeda's war against America were traced back to the parched soil of East Africa. It was in Somalia, a former Al Qaeda member would later testify, that bin Laden said he would "cut off the head of the snake."

At the military's morning and afternoon media feedings in Mogadishu, testy briefers sometimes asked us why we weren't out investigating what they called terrorist groups fronting as Islamic charities.

Since the point usually came up when we were attacking them over one screw-up or another, I always assumed the Islamic terror threat was more sleight of hand from the psy-ops people. U.S. military forces being ground down by drug-crazed street fighters in sarongs and flip-flops didn't play right. The enemy had to be international terrorists. It turns out they were at least partly right. Al-Ittihad, and the shadow of Al Qaeda, were there for me to see, much closer than I knew. It took years, and a chance discovery in Kashmir, before I was finally convinced of Al Qaeda's role in Mogadishu's street wars.

Bin Laden boasted about the Al Qaeda connection to the U.S. retreat from Somalia in his 1996 fatwa, which declared a jihad to expel Americans from Saudi Arabia and the rest of the Gulf region. Among the examples he offered of U.S. military weakness, he cited the 1983 Beirut truck bombing and another in 1996 that struck the Khobar Towers housing complex, killing nineteen American servicemen in the Saudi city of Dhahran.

"But your most disgraceful case was in Somalia where—after vigorous propaganda about the power of the U.S.A. and its post cold war leadership of the new world order—you moved tens of thousands of international forces, including twenty-eight thousand American soldiers into Somalia," bin Laden declared.

"However, when tens of your soldiers were killed in minor battles and one American Pilot was dragged in the streets of Mogadishu you left the area carrying disappointment, humiliation, defeat and your dead with you. Clinton appeared in front of the whole world threatening and promising revenge, but these threats were merely a preparation for withdrawal. You have been disgraced by Allah and you withdrew; the extent of your impotence and weaknesses became very clear."

A 1998 indictment against bin Laden in a New York court included allegations that Al Qaeda took part in the attacks on U.S.

and U.N. forces in Somalia. A key source for that claim was a Sudanese Al Qaeda member turned informant who testified that he learned
how to shoot down helicopters while fighting Soviet troops in Afghanistan, where he met bin Laden.

A decade after American forces withdrew from Somalia, I asked
one of Aideed's lieutenants whether Al-Ittihad, or any foreign advisers, had taught Aideed's militia fighters how to bring down Black
Hawks with RPGs. He denied it and insisted they figured that crucial
skill out for themselves. "The idea to shoot down helicopters with
RPGs came as a result of some 'lucky thinking,'" he said. "Someone
climbed a tree and shot down the first helicopter and it went on from
there."

But the source acknowledged that Al-Ittihad provided other
essential assistance in the war against U.S. and other foreign forces in
Somalia.

"We had not been friends of Al-Ittihad as an organization," he said.
"But when the fighting with the Americans started, they came on
board. We had meetings with some of their officials and they gave us
all the support they could—except that they would not back us publicly because they used to condemn our approach to Somali politics.
But we got what we wanted—technique and roadside bombs. We only
knew how to plant a land mine that detonates when the target travels
over it. But this meant any person or convoy could fall victim.

"Al-Ittihad came up with the technique of planting remote-con-
trolled bombs," he continued. "This worked well for us. They trained
some of our militias on how to use the remote detonators. Also, they
supplied us with plenty of land mines. On one occasion, we almost
ran out of them and we had to go to the house of Al-Ittihad's officials.
We loaded a truck with mines and used them to keep the operation
going."

There is other evidence that Al Qaeda provided, at the very least, material support in the fight against U.S. and U.N. forces in Somalia, through a complex chain of fundraising, propaganda, and training that led back to two U.S. allies: Saudi Arabia and Pakistan. According to the U.S. Treasury, the Somalia office of the Saudi-based charity Al Haramain Islamic Foundation had links with Al Qaeda and Al-Ittihad. Money that was supposed to be funding orphanages and Islamic schools in Somalia instead went to Al-Ittihad militants. When Washington declared the charity a "primary source of terrorist funding" following the September 11 attacks, the man in charge of its operations was Sheikh Saleh al-Sheikh, Minister of Islamic Affairs in the Saudi government, and head of the World Assembly of Muslim Youth. The charity was later linked to terror funding in Southeast Asia, yet, with Saudi government encouragement, it continued to expand its operations in fifty-five countries. Al-Sheikh not only remained in charge, but kept his cabinet post into 2007.

Pakistan, which was supposed to be a front-line U.S. ally in the war on terror, was similarly accommodating toward militant leaders who had aided Somali fighters, whose targets included Pakistani peacekeeping troops in Mogadishu. One of the most powerful and mysterious was Maulana Masood Azhar, a Muslim cleric, journalist, and militant commander with close ties to the ISI and Al Qaeda. I first learned of his role in Somalia when in early 2002 I ended up across a desk from a senior police commander in Indian-controlled Kashmir. I was trying to follow the roots of Al Qaeda back to the early 1990s by looking at the kidnapping of Westerners by Pakistan-based militant groups, among bin Laden's most crucial early allies. The Indian police officer obliged with a photocopy of a lengthy confession that Azhar gave under intense interrogation following his capture in Kashmir in 1994, when the downed Black Hawks were a fading memory for most Americans. Few sensed the gathering storm that the Indians warned was heading west.

As the war against the Soviets in Afghanistan wound down in 1989, Azhar attended a training camp of the Harkat ul-Mujahideen, a group fostered by the ISI to allow young Pakistani men to join the jihad against the Russians. Azhar told his Indian interrogators that he only made it through a week of the forty-day training course in handling a Kalashnikov assault rifle and a machine gun, but he made an important connection with Khalil, the militant group's leader. He assigned Azhar to be chief editor of Harkat's free magazine, which published around one thousand copies a month. They were handed out to prospective jihadis during Friday prayers and at speeches by Islamic extremists. Khalil also sent Azhar abroad to spread the militant word, and in 1991 both men visited the southern African country of Zambia, where they met up with a man in the fruit business who dabbled in radical Islam. The visit raised thousands of dollars for the expanding jihadi cause, but more important, it built a bridge for Islamic militancy between Africa and South Asia.

Azhar then took his fundraising tour to Britain, which at first denied him a visa. A Saudi businessman who was a veteran of the Afghan jihad fixed that problem and Azhar traveled to several British cities where he spoke at mosques and raised more money for jihad. He also solved a travel document problem. After providing a thumbprint and some photographs to a forger, Azhar picked up a fake Portuguese passport, which made it easier for him to move in and out of the countries where he was building up a network of extremist contacts.

As Al-Ittihad stepped up pressure on U.S., Pakistani, and other foreign troops in Somalia in 1993, Azhar traveled to neighboring Kenya to support the militants with money, recruits, and propaganda. The timing was fortunate for Azhar because, under foreign pressure, Pakistan had rounded up some five hundred veterans of the Afghan jihad, fighters from various countries who had made Pakistan their new base. Most of them didn't want to go back to their homelands, claiming they would be persecuted, while others were refused entry by their governments, who didn't want Islamic radicals with weapons training in their own backyards. So, with Azhar's assistance, they moved to Sudan, where bin Laden had set up his new base, and where Al-Ittihad was training fighters for the new jihad in Somalia.

The links between Azhar and Khalil and militant attacks on Americans ran still deeper. When Azhar used his fake Portuguese passport to travel to India in 1994, he was arrested in Kashmir, where Pakistan's ISI was using out-of-work fighters from the Afghan war to start a new jihad against Indian forces in the disputed territory of Jammu and Kashmir. Some of Khalil's militants then kidnapped six Western backpackers in Indian Kashmir and demanded the release of Azhar and four other militants. American John Childs escaped, after which the militants dumped the decapitated head of Norwegian captive Hans Christian Ostrø on a mountain path. Britons Keith Mangan and Paul Wells, American Donald Hutchings, and German Dirk Hasert were never seen again.

In another attempt to spring Azhar from jail, his British-born protégé Ahmed Omar Saeed Sheikh kidnapped three Britons and American tourist Bela J. Nuss in India in 1994. Sheikh ended up in prison himself. He and Azhar finally walked free in 1999 when their supporters hijacked an Indian Airlines flight and ordered it to land in Kandahar, Afghanistan, the Taliban's spiritual capital. The Indian government released Azhar, Sheikh, and a third militant to save the lives of 154 hostages after an eight-day ordeal. The triumphant militants celebrated at a dinner in Kabul with bin Laden.

Ahmad Omar Saeed Sheikh was convicted in the 2002 murder of *Wall Street Journal* reporter Daniel Pearl, who was abducted and executed while probing links between Al Qaeda and the ISI. When Sheikh surrendered to authorities, he went to the only authority figure he trusted: his old handler at the ISI, a retired army brigadier.

Sheikh was sentenced to death for Pearl's murder, but five years after the journalist was beheaded, the convicted mastermind was still alive. Pakistani authorities, who have carried out other executions with dispatch, chose to let Sheikh live, and the Bush administration did not press for justice. As he sat on death row in Pakistan, a U.S. grand jury indicted Sheikh for Pearl's murder and the Nuss kidnapping, but Washington did not insist he be extradited to the United States, where his ISI connections could not protect him from the executioner.

In the summer of 2002, I traveled to the Pakistan town of Dir, in the mountains along the Afghan border, a key transit route for Taliban and allied militants, including Al Qaeda, on their way to and from battles against the U.S. in Afghanistan. There, I met the local commander of the Harkat ul-Mujahideen. He wore brown-tinted, rectangular sunglasses and a small, tightly wrapped black turban, and granted me an audience in his madrassa. Relaxed and sitting cross-legged on the floor, he insisted the militant group was functioning pretty much as usual despite being banned as a terrorist organization by Musharraf's government. The commander said he had made seven crossings into Afghanistan to wage jihad against U.S. and allied forces in the year and a half since the Taliban regime fell. He also said he had met with Taliban commanders in Peshawar, the capital of Pakistan's northwest frontier province in July 2003, when Bush administration officials were heaping praise on Musharraf for his courageous efforts in the war on terror.

"People sitting in government offices can't imagine how many Pakistanis are still operating inside Afghanistan, supporting the Taliban," the militant commander boasted to me.

When our interview was over, he asked through the interpreter if I would mind if he asked a few of his own questions.

"Please do," I encouraged him.

"Why are Americans so evil?" he asked with a playful smirk.

I assured him that if I could only bring some ordinary Americans to chat in this remote front line, he would see they were not much different from himself, people of firm faith in God who sincerely believe they are a force for good in a dangerous world. "Your problem is not with Americans, it's with their government," I said.

The commander pondered for a moment and then replied: "If Americans are such good people, then why do they elect such bad governments?"

"You've got me there," I said, and we laughed. Had we crossed paths a few miles east, in Afghanistan, I'm sure he wouldn't have hesitated to kidnap or kill me but here I was his guest, and he my jocular host.

Azhar and Khalil would seem to be obvious targets for American and European prosecutors. Yet as hundreds of other suspected militants were held without trial at Guantanamo Bay, or sent to secret CIA interrogation centers in other countries, Pakistani militant leaders with known links to Al Qaeda were able to train and recruit more militants, raise funds, and preach jihad. Pakistan's government insisted that it closely monitored Azhar, Khalil, and others to make sure they were not involved in violence or efforts to spread radical Islam. But long after Musharraf announced he would rid his country of extremists and terrorists, Azhar, Khalil, and other militant leaders were still in business.

Early in 2004, Khalil was living in Rawalpindi, a suburb of Pakistan's capital, Islamabad, where Musharraf and many of his military officers also live. Khalil's home was a corner house in Rawalpindi's Khayaban district, next to his Khadijatul Kubra madrassa for girls, just around the corner from his Islamic bookstore, and a short walk from a police checkpost. Four miles away, down a dirt road in front of a sprawling military base, Khalil was still running the headquarters of his Al Hilal Trust, which raised funds for jihad and recruited fighters through a magazine of the same name. While Musharraf told the world that he had closed all militant training camps in his country, Khalil was using his magazine to muster his supporters at an "All Pakistan Training Convention" in his headquarters compound, and urging his followers to fight for a global Islamic state.

"We have to retire the debt of our martyrs," Khalil wrote in the November 2003 issue of his magazine, whose cover showed a giant fist holding a sword, rising from flames in the desert to slash the U.S. flag, presumably a call to arms for the new war in Iraq. "We should promise to sacrifice our life, property and heart for the mission of the people who have sacrificed their lives. This is your moral and religious obligation—to help financially those few people who are sacrificing their lives so that they can concentrate on their battlefront and ultimately defeat non-Muslims."

My fixer Mubashir tracked down Khalil's home address, but we couldn't get to him there. His wife said he had flown out of town for a few days. We wanted to see if some of his top aides might be helpful, so we flagged a taxi to deny any spies a traceable license plate number, and drove to another of his madrassas late one afternoon. A few students were hanging around the front gate when we arrived, and with long rays of sunlight casting shadows against the wall, I thought I saw a good picture. I raised my camera to shoot it, but the boys scattered and hid their faces, so I didn't press the shutter release. We told them why we were there, and sent a message with one requesting to see a madrassa official. He returned a few minutes later and said we should come back the next day, which we did, at almost precisely the same time.

We were immediately surrounded by students, and a man claiming to be the headmaster invited us into a dark side building for tea. It sounded innocent enough, and I had to play by their rules if I had any hope of seeing Khalil, so we followed him. While we were waiting for the tea to arrive, he took out a large ledger, demanded our identification documents, and started recording the details of Mubashir's driver's license and national ID card in his book. Then he turned to me: "Give me your passport," he said sternly.

"It's in my hotel," I said. "Take me there and I'll be glad to show it to you." He made it clear we weren't going anywhere.

"Ask him if he's a cop," I blurted to Mubashir, who was trying to keep things calm and didn't reply. "Mubashir, unless this man is with the police, he has no right to detain me. Let's go," I said, and headed for the door. Before I could make it the few yards to the taxi, my path was blocked by a group of jeering madrassa students. I barged through them and up the dirt road, hoping to reach the military base at the intersection. The students, shouting and shoving, grabbed my arms and tried to push me back. I struggled free and was about to make a run for it when one kicked my feet out from under me.

Mubashir reached me, and tried to persuade me to come back to the compound. I knew from experience that your chances of surviving are much better if you stay out in the open, with lots of witnesses, so I sat on a rock, and tried to stare down the laughing madrassa students. I could see several men on the periphery making hurried cell phone calls, presumably to get instructions from higher authorities. Mubashir told me it was time for me to call a government minister. There was no other way out, he insisted, suggesting I ask Information Minister Sheikh Rashid Ahmed to rescue us.

I thought that was a bad idea. Sheikh Rashid, one of Musharraf's most trusted ministers, was a thug who once boasted that he used his farm just outside Islamabad as a training camp for jihadis fighting in Kashmir. It was a particularly odd thing to brag about, since, as the principal mouthpiece for Musharraf's government, he would know that all the training camps were supposed to be closed. Still, I didn't relish spending the night at the headquarters of Khalil's militia, so I called Rashid and told him our predicament. He was on his way to the airport, but said he would pass by the madrassa to sort things out, and asked me to hand the phone to one of the madrassa officials. Within minutes, they let me go, and as we were driving past the military base, we met Rashid and the convoy of troops guarding him. In a brief chat at the side of the road, Rashid scolded me for going to a madrassa without government permission.

"Surely I don't need a permit to visit a school in a democracy," I replied with a knowing grin. Rashid said people can get hurt in such places. I said my real concern was that the madrassa's headmaster had confiscated Mubashir's identity documents, and asked the minister if he would undertake to have them returned immediately. As his handlers hustled him into a limousine, an aide assured me he would take care of it. That night, we were headline news on state-run television, which took its orders from Rashid's ministry. We were accused of making a phony film to make an innocent school look like a militant training camp. One of the TV report's close-up shots provided viewers with a long look at Mubashir's driver's license and national ID, a not so subtle way of flashing a green light to anyone who might want to go after him. The propaganda campaign went on for a few more days, and the U.S. State Department intervened to make it clear that Rashid should back off.

When I asked Pakistan's then interior minister Faisal Saleh Hayat why Khalil was allowed to blatantly defy the government's ban on his militant group, the minister dismissed him as "a small fish" and insisted he wasn't "doing anything half-significant." Yet in his magazine, sold on newsstands across the country, Khalil was saying much the same thing that he did when he joined bin Laden in his declaration of war on the West. And if his people ever handed Mubashir's documents to the government, it never returned them to him.

More than two years passed before Khalil finally returned our calls. Six men had abducted the militant leader and his driver just outside Islamabad. The men beat them so badly with rifle butts that they blacked out and were dumped, unconscious, in a park. After he came to, Khalil called Mubashir and asked him to visit. Lying in a hospital bed, he was remarkably clear on the details of what had happened when we tried to visit him in 2004. After his thrashing by assailants unknown, Khalil apparently wanted to make amends. "It was just a misunderstanding," he assured Mubashir.

18

FRIENDLY FIRE

A certain degree of neurosis is of inestimable value
as a drive, especially to a psychologist.
Sigmund Freud

O ver time, Staff Sergeant Cleveland's power over me had weak-
ened. His voice had faded, his visits grown less frequent. He
was still there. I had just learned to live with him. Whenever I gave in
to anger or fear, sadness or shame, he was in command again, like the
late December afternoon when I was photographing Afghan soldiers
laughing at the bullet-riddled bodies of Taliban fighters on the side of
a highway. For a fleeting moment, I found myself looking down on
Cleveland's corpse. During an especially long stretch of bad luck,
when I just couldn't catch a break, I decided it was Cleveland's fault,
his *curse*, and begged him to stop punishing me. I flailed about, trying
to find some way to reach a truce. His grip grew stronger whenever I
was among the dead.

On the morning after Christmas 2004, a massive 9.2-magnitude
earthquake struck beneath the sea, off the coast of the Indonesian island
of Sumatra. With the force of more than twenty thousand Hiroshima
atomic bombs, a rupture so mighty that the Earth wobbled on its axis,

the quake cleaved an eight-thousand-mile stretch of the ocean floor, raising portions up to sixty-five feet. Centered off the coast of Sumatra, almost twenty miles below the surface, the seismic shock displaced billions of gallons of seawater and set off a tsunami that raced at the speed of a jet plane across the Indian Ocean. The quake and tsunami would kill more than 229,000 people in at least a dozen countries.

The first wave took a couple of hours to reach southern India's coast. I was strolling in my front garden in New Delhi when an editor on the foreign desk in Los Angeles called to read a brief wire report that only hinted at the devastation in southern India, one thousand miles northeast of the quake's epicenter. There was something like sixty confirmed dead. Less than an average train accident in India, I told the editor, eager to get on with the holiday. Several phone calls later, when the enormity of the disaster was inescapable, I was on a flight to Madras, where a series of powerful waves smashed homes and businesses near the shore, sucking people, their belongings, and even cars out to sea.

Farther south, in the fishing village of Thazanguda, forty-year-old Veerapan Arul lost his mother and sixty-three neighbors to a series of fifteen-foot waves that made a ghastly hiss as they raced toward shore: "They came like possessed beasts to destroy the whole village," the stunned fisherman told me amid the ruins of huts. The southeastern city of Nagappattinam was in the Indian mainland's hardest-hit region, near neighboring Sri Lanka. The tsunami pulverized concrete walls and splintered hundreds of homes. Large, seagoing fishing boats were tossed about like toys and dropped hundreds of yards inland from the harbor where they had been moored. Nature's power unleashed made war look like child's play.

A wave the height of a two-story building snatched Vijay Kumar and his three-year-old son, Rajaraman, and as the boy's father fought to deny the swirling seawater his screaming son, it threw them against a wooden hunk of debris. The blow forced Kumar's arms open, and the horrific sight of his terrified son's face disappearing beneath the froth was seared in his mind. The hardest thing, he told me, was that he would never find a body to bury, and a father's heart would forever be as empty as the ocean is deep.

"What else is there left in life? I have lost my son," he wept. "My God, what did we do wrong to lose him?"

I needed to see Dr. Grinker again. I flew to Johannesburg in early 2005, when I had some time off, and booked two appointments. I felt sick, tormented by the latest mass death, and needed his help with some other unresolved issues. I'd come a long way, from holiday trips to war zones to vacation time recovery in a psychiatrist's office.

Parked in the shade out front, working up the courage to go in, I trembled at the thought of sitting across from a psychiatrist again. I wasn't sure whether I still needed a shrink, or just time and space to find my own answers. I wondered whether the doctor would remember me, and if he did after all these years, would he conclude I was a hapless victim of separation anxiety? Most of all, I was afraid of opening the cellar door on that old ghost. I didn't want to sound like a whiner. I wanted to be rid of it all. I walked from the parking lot to the front door like a lost man.

Dr. Grinker had moved to a smaller office in a street corner medical center, but his desk and other furniture looked just as they had on my last visit ten years earlier. The doctor, smiling like an old friend, greeted me at his door wearing black jeans, black boots, and a black designer T-shirt with *Guess* printed in white letters across the front. I imagined that when our hour was up, he would be heading for a barbecue, a northern suburbs social ritual known as a *braai*. I wondered if I'd picked the right day to ask him to take me back down into the psychic depths.

I tried to hurry him through the clinical pleasantries and his summary of the notes in my file. They reminded me too much of the person I'd been running from for so long. Besides, we had a lot of new ground to cover. Time hadn't healed many of the old wounds. It had opened up many new ones. But the doctor was firmly in control, sitting with his clipboard on a crossed leg, dispassionately asking questions that sent me straight off on a rant about how I felt lost in all the lies.

Dr. Grinker could sympathize. Back in the worst days of apartheid, fresh out of medical school and a year's internship, he was forced into the South African army to do two years' national service in 1982. He landed in the medical corps, living in a barracks with a few hundred physicians, psychiatrists, psychologists, and pharmacists, who were drilled to exhaustion like any recruits in boot camp. Afrikaner officers tried to persuade them of the seriousness of their mission in indoctrination classes.

"They told us there was this threat of our borders being infiltrated by 'the black danger.' In the officers' course, they spoke about sabotage, espionage—all these things. You sometimes wondered if the teachers had any clue what they were teaching. But I think one of the biggest problems was not what was told to you, but what *wasn't* told to you."

For one, they didn't say where the psychiatrist was going on his first deployment when he climbed into the Dakota plane as the only passenger heading north to what South Africa's government euphemistically called "the border." South African troops had invaded Angola in 1975, with CIA assistance. Seven years later, the apartheid regime was still denying it had any soldiers in Angola.

When an engine caught fire on the Dakota, the plane's emergency landing would decide the doctor-soldier's military fate. It put down at an airstrip in the army's Section 10, near the Caprivi Strip of south-west Africa, now Namibia. Angola was on the other side of the narrow finger of land, where SWAPO guerrillas—the same fighters who had sparked my imagination on a poster at university a few years earlier—launched cross-border attacks. This was the dregs of South African army postings. It was desolate territory where conscripts suffered stinging insect bites, isolation, nagging fear, and betrayal. A quick chopper ride, and Dr. Grinker found himself surrounded by a virtual no man's land of thorn bushes, dirt, and minefields, with only a pistol and a Swiss Army knife as weapons.

"We were riding around, looking for the *swart gevaar*—the 'black danger,'" Dr. Grinker said, snickering at the absurdity. The "black danger," the terrorist threat, was nowhere to be seen. "You never, at any stage, saw one person from the local community. It was just thorn trees and the ground was like beach sand.

"If you were killed there, your family would be informed only that you were doing 'border duty.' They wouldn't tell anyone that you were killed in Angola."

I was tensing up just listening to him. Grinker suddenly changed the subject to something more immediate that was troubling him. Bladder cancer had recently killed his eighty-five-year-old father, a veteran of the Second World War, a once fervent Zionist who had returned to South Africa doubting that God existed. As the doctor planned his father's funeral, he had a religious awakening of sorts, and he seemed conflicted between values he'd learned from a father he loved, and a new wonder about the existence of a higher power.

Our hour was almost up, and Dr. Grinker glanced at his notes, to sum up my progress in those ten years. He told me my malaise was "'existential depression,' where a whole lot of the problem is that there just doesn't seem to be much meaning, and much purpose."

With all that was going wrong in the world, anyone who channel-surfed through the video images of bomb blasts, bickering talking heads, and press conferences on cable news qualified for the diagnosis "existential depression." Surely my funk ran a little deeper than that. I told him about the Iraqi mob attack, and he wrote out a prescription for a new antidepressant, Cipralex.

Before I started on it, I wanted to make sure the antidepressant wouldn't be a lethal combination with other pills I was taking. So I told the doctor that I'd been diagnosed months earlier with the same polycystic kidney disease that had killed my father, and I was on hypertension medication. Both of my kidneys were riddled with cysts, but the worse off had swollen to one and a half times its normal size. I had never thought I would die of natural causes, and the dangers of a slowly progressing kidney disease seemed distant enough that I guessed someone would get me long before my kidneys gave out. Just out of curiosity, I had asked a specialist in New Delhi how long I had before the organs packed up.

"It's hard to say with these things," he replied, shuffling papers to get ready for his next patient. "Maybe five years. Ten if you're lucky."

This *was* India, so I wasn't sure if he was giving me a straight answer or lining me up for a transplant, a lucrative business in a country where the poor donate organs for a few hundred dollars, which doctors then parlay into transplants billed for several thousand dollars. Several shabbily dressed young men waiting in the crowded corridor outside looked to me more like potential donors hoping to make a buck than patients at a five-star clinic. But I took the doctor at his word, and now figured Dr. Grinker should know the full prognosis.

With that, the last remnants of Dr. Grinker's clinical shield crumbled. "You know, I wasn't that well since I last saw you," he said. "I actually needed to go in for major surgery, for a liver transplant."

Dr. Grinker learned he needed an urgent transplant not long after Johannesburg's only liver transplant unit started up. His doctors approved him for the waiting list on a Friday night, he went out to dinner with his girlfriend on Saturday night, and on Sunday he got a call from the hospital asking if he had eaten anything that morning because they needed to get him in to the operating theater right away. A young person with the same blood type, and other characteristics that made his liver a perfect match, had just died. Through a series of serendipitous events, Dr. Grinker suddenly had his best chance to live.

"People can wait for months, and sometimes years. I waited a day and a half," he said. "I very much have a sense that, hey, I've been given a second chance and I must now use this wisely and to the best of my ability." He asked why I couldn't look at my near-death experiences in a similar light.

Our final hour was up, and Dr. Grinker led me out the side door to show me the drug store across the street. There was so much left to talk about, but this was it. I struggled to channel a flood of thoughts and emotions into a coherent sentence.

Dr. Grinker said he hoped I would feel better the next time we met. "Go well," he said, and his office door shut.

On my way home, I stopped in London to see my old friend and translator, Harun. When I left Somalia, I confined Harun to a locked space in my mind, and moved on. I didn't write. There was no mail service in Somalia. I didn't phone. Somali entrepreneurs operated call centers in Mogadishu, but I didn't have any of the numbers. And I didn't try to find one. I was happier not knowing what would happen to Harun because I couldn't get over the feeling of guilt I always have after leaving and moving on to the next hellhole.

After the foreign news media lose interest in a war or catastrophe, local fixers and translators are usually struck like Cinderella by the toll of midnight. They watch the journalists, almost family now after all they've been through together, quickly pack up and leave, taking their rolls of dollars, satellite phones, and flak jackets with them. No more wild parties. No more expense account adventures. After their good run, earning more in a week than they normally made in a year, the fixers go back to what they were doing before the world cared: teaching, studying, working in hospitals, driving taxis, fighting for local warlords. If they're lucky, the war economy is replaced by an aid economy and the best get jobs with the U.N., private relief agencies, or as translators for peacekeepers.

But when the last foreign troops pulled out of Somalia in 1995, most of the U.N. and foreign aid agency staff left too, leaving people like Harun with a hard choice: try to find their own escape route or stay and struggle to survive.

True to form, Harun persisted and found me. I got an email from him in the fall of 2002, asking where I was and what I was up to. We finally met three years later, on a frigid January day in 2005, in my small hotel room near London's Victoria Station, overlooking Buckingham Palace Road. I was only there to see Harun and Gutale, who had also taken refuge in London. My hotel was once a grand place that was now part of a chain catering to package tourists willing to pay a tad more for the fantasy that they were living close to royalty. The window was too small, and too far above the floor to offer much of a view. There were large, brown water stains on my ceiling. It was here, in this clash of warm memories of old grandeur and the cold reality of a winter's day in London, that I learned of Harun's long, painful journey.

After our trip to Kismayu in 1994, Harun went to a public call office at the Olympic Hotel, site of the failed raid that ended in the defeat of U.S. forces on October 3 and 4. He was waiting to make his call when a BBC producer phoned from London, fishing for a journalist who could do an interview. The operator put Harun on the line, and he did his first report for the BBC's Somali service. That bit of good fortune was soon followed by three years of death threats. When you speak on the BBC's world service radio in Africa, a lot of people hear, and General Mohammed Saeed Morgan, who had recently seized Kismayu, took exception to Harun's report that the warlord's hold on the strategic port city was less than complete. He was a marked man almost from the start.

It is impossible to report anything significant from Somalia and not offend someone carrying a gun, so Harun's list of enemies quickly grew. Some sent messengers to his house to terrify his wife and mother with warnings that if he didn't stop talking on the BBC, or become a mouthpiece for their faction, he would be killed. Murdering someone in Somalia was very easy. Who was going to do anything about it? There were no police. The best that victims could hope for is that their clans would avenge their deaths. But Harun is from the minority Dir, a scattered clan lacking in the firepower that could have offered him any protection in the turf wars of Mogadishu. He, and his terrified family, were on their own.

In January 1996, Harun returned to Kismayu behind a convoy of ten battlewagons and clan leaders to cover a meeting of the Darod clan, which was trying to forge a united stand against a rival clan whose forces were massing on the city's outskirts, hoping to take back the city they had lost. The unwritten rules of Somalia's clan warfare meant that Harun was safest at night outside the city, and he ventured in only during the daytime to report and file before retreating to the outskirts again. The race back and forth across the front line was the

305

most dangerous. At the clan conference, General Morgan welcomed Harun like an old friend, as if the report that had upset him two years earlier were long forgotten. But soon Harun got word that some of Morgan's men were waiting in ambush on the only road out of Kismayu. The general assured them that he knew which checkpoint Harun and the other visiting journalists were worried about, and that he had already taken care of the matter. He insisted they had nothing to fear.

"As we left, we were attacked in exactly the area Morgan was talking about," Harun told me.

He wasn't hit, but a passenger he had agreed to take from Kismayu's hospital, a man wounded in earlier fighting, was shot again in the ambush. He bled to death in the back seat of Harun's car.

Soon after Harun started reporting for the BBC, a ruthless eight-month street war broke out between the forces of Aideed and his former bagman and arms dealer, Osman Ato. It was some of the worst fighting the already ruined city of Mogadishu had seen, a dirty, fratricidal conflict between members of the same clan. There was never a day when one side or the other didn't complain about what Harun was saying on the radio.

"Sometimes I would agree with them," Harun admitted. "Because in a war, sometimes what you report cannot be entirely true."

Aideed had Harun detained in the Olympic Hotel for a month on some alleged infraction. To escape more punishment, Harun spent five months in self-exile in Nairobi, Kenya. Even if he tempered his reporting a little, that wouldn't be good enough to save his life because the news wasn't all that got Harun in trouble. Two-bit militia commanders knew he had money, so they constantly came by his house, demanding cash for qat, fifty dollars here, one hundred dollars there.

He could get killed just for refusing to buy guys with guns enough bundles of the leaves to satisfy their need to get buzzed for the night.

When fighters at one checkpoint refused to accept two bundles of qat as the toll, the gunmen opened fire. As Harun's car sped off in a hail of gunfire, one of his two bodyguards put a bullet in a militiaman's foot. He later limped up to another journalist's house, saying he wanted Harun to pay the medical and rehab costs. Harun gave him one hundred dollars, in installments.

"We became friends later—good friends," Harun said, and we both laughed nervously, just as we had after numerous near misses in Somalia.

In April 1995, Harun took his wife, Shukri, to the K-50 airstrip outside Mogadishu to fly her out of the country for good. One of Aideed's colonels thought Harun was trying to escape.

"I'm not leaving," he told the colonel. "Only my wife is going."

"We want you anyway," the colonel replied, and ordered his men to arrest Harun and take him back to an interrogation center in Mogadishu, right in front of the Sahafi Hotel. He was grilled for six hours by Saed Qiiq, deputy head of Aideed's criminal investigation division, who sat behind a desk with a thick file of clippings of news reports by Harun and other journalists in front of him. One criticized Aideed for having no political agenda, just an ambitious drive to control the country.

"You must change your way of reporting," Qiiq ordered. "There are lots of people sending reports from this country and it's not all true. You *must* change the way you report. *And* we want you to work with us."

"How can I work with you?" Harun asked.

"There are a lot of foreigners coming to this country. Spies who are working against us," Qiiq told him. "You go to all sides in Mogadishu.

You've got access. We want you to report to us on whoever comes and goes."

Harun refused, saying Aideed's people wouldn't be happy if he spied for their enemies, so he couldn't do it for them either. Qiiq released him without torture or other abuse, but he left Harun with this thought: "There are a lot of nicer people, more than you are. One day there will be a Somali government and there will be accountability. We know all that you have written. We know you are against us. But we just want a fair deal."

In October 1997, Harun decided it was finally time to get out after one of his bodyguards was killed. He paid a Somali people smuggler $2,500 for false documents. He flew to Dubai and then on to Milan, where Italian authorities detained him for two nights before deporting him back to Somalia.

Five months later, Harun tried again. He had quit the BBC, but the network still helped him get a visa to fly to London, and supported his application for asylum when he got there. He is now a proud British citizen. Yet he is still struggling.

For three years as a stringer for the AP and BBC in Somalia, he averaged between $1,000 and $1,500 a month, a very good living by Somali standards. In London, he was just another refugee in a big, indifferent city. He couldn't get full-time work with the BBC, so he was freelancing, a virtually stateless person waiting for British officials to agree that he was a bona fide refugee who deserved asylum, not another economic migrant who should be deported to a homeland where he would surely be killed.

"I stayed home," he said. "I would not go out. If I went out, I would immediately run back. I was scared of people. It was just a mental thing. I thought people might be talking about me, gossiping about me. I had never heard of depression.

"In Somalia, if you said you were depressed, they'd tell you, 'You're crazy. Read two verses of the Koran and you'll be fine.'"

And finally Harun was laughing loud again, and it was like old times, when we were careening around the streets of Mogadishu, safeties off, knowing we could be shot at any moment. It was all terribly frightening and funny at once.

At night, Harun couldn't sleep. Whenever the fear creeped back, his whole body itched. The more he scratched, the more it itched, and all the while, everyone told him there was nothing physically wrong with him. "I thought—this is what I saw—that my whole body was completely dry and dusty. I would say to my wife, 'Look at this dust!' But then my wife would touch me, and she'd say, 'No, there's nothing wrong with you. You're completely fine.' And I'd tell her, '*How* can I be fine? Look at all this dust coming off my body!' I thought it was coming from my stomach, and I told my doctor that I wanted an operation."

"Why would we operate on you?" the family doctor asked.

"Please, there must be *something* in here," Harun begged.

He asked the doctor to at least check his tonsils. From September 1999 until early 2000, Harun visited his family doctor twice a week, complaining of back problems, skin cancer, and numerous other ailments. His doctor sent him home with various painkillers and other prescriptions.

"Then one day I went to him and I said, 'I'm stinking. I think I'm decaying.' He said to me, 'I think you're depressed.' And he sent me to a psychiatrist."

Listening to him, I shivered. We were from starkly different worlds, yet we'd survived some of the worst horrors together, and suffered the same psychic injuries, and we had both wished we were dead. And so I admitted a secret that I always thought would die with me. I told him how much I had wanted to be killed on our 1994 trip to Kismayu, about the furious escape from Khareen, and how I was sorry for risking his life trying to lose mine.

Harun didn't look surprised, or angry, which surprised me. He knew the feeling.

"Almost every day when I was working for the BBC in Mogadishu, someone would phone and they would say that I was going to be killed. It became so normal for me that I didn't care in the end. I was that desperate—I didn't care whether I got killed or not."

I asked whether he kept doing it because the money was good, and even with all that I knew about reporters and war, I expected Harun to say something noble about the truth, or his nation, or his God.

"Really, money wasn't the biggest motivation," he said. "It was fame, mostly. The way you are treated. Not by the warlords and these people. But by everybody else. Because they know you are famous. That's all. They don't care about the truth."

His shoulders squared, and he took a deep breath. I could see he was feeling a bit of the adrenaline rush again. "They know you work for the BBC, high-profile radio. Everybody listens. You are *Harun*. They treat you like a god. They stand up for you when you enter the room, and then you are embarrassed. They respect you. And the most beautiful women come to you. You are invited by every famous person. You get every story first hand because you work for the BBC. So I became addicted and I enjoyed it—except for the harsh side of it."

I understood the buzz he was describing. The work gives you a name and so you are nothing without the work. Yet you want to die because of it.

What Harun told me next was startling. I had long known that before we met he was a journalism student during the regime of U.S.-

backed dictator Siad Barre, but Harun's time in journalism school sent him down a much more dangerous path than mine.

Siad Barre had built an ersatz Soviet-style dictatorship based on his understanding of scientific socialism. In the late 1970s, when the Soviets decided they preferred neighboring Ethiopia as a client state in the strategic Horn of Africa, and armed it heavily to turn back a Somali invasion, Siad Barre became a staunch U.S. ally. In return, U.S. forces got access to Berbera port on the Gulf of Aden, and its communication facility, on a main shipping route for oil from the Persian Gulf. For his support, Siad Barre was rewarded with U.S.-made weapons to defend his brutal regime and threaten his neighbors.

At first, Muslim extremists were among the few people willing to risk opposing Siad Barre, and they went recruiting on college campuses. Harun joined up, along with many of Lafole University's students and professors. I didn't know it during all the times we risked attack by Muslim radicals, but in 1990 Siad Barre's police had arrested Harun as a member of the Islamic militant group Al-Ittihad.

Thinking his biggest reward would come after death, he attended one of the militants' mosques each night, where a Saudi-trained extremist taught that only his harsh version of Islam was true to the Koran, and that it could not be separated from politics. Harun was one of six Al-Ittihad members in the journalism school and spent hours recruiting other students in secret meetings on campus. Starting at dawn each morning, he attended a training camp to learn self-defense and how to dismantle, clean, and shoot an assault rifle.

"I joined Al-Ittihad not because I wanted to, but because I was manipulated through religion," Harun told me. "The reason I never mentioned it to you, honestly, is that I never took them seriously. I just didn't want to go to hell."

When warlords were violently carving up Mogadishu into fiefdoms, and it was too dangerous to reach the Al-Ittihad training camp, Harun quit in the summer of 1991, just as Osama bin Laden and his lieutenants were maneuvering Al-Ittihad to their arsenal in the emerging jihad against the West. He started working as a reporter instead. Names like bin Laden and Al-Ittihad meant little or nothing to me then. So it probably wouldn't have made any difference if I'd known. He was risking his life each time he went out on the street with me. That was all that mattered.

19

EXORCISM

To save your world you asked this man to die:
Would this man, could he see you now, ask why?
W. H. AUDEN, "EPITAPH FOR AN UNKNOWN SOLDIER"

T he Pentagon didn't want the public to know the corpse's name. For years, it left the identity of the dead American soldier in my photograph a mystery, tormenting the relatives of five Americans originally reported missing in action who were among the eighteen who died in Mogadishu that day. The fallen soldiers' families were left to suffer the anguish of guessing whether their loved one was the man whose brutalized body was seen by millions of people around the world. Several thought the soldier was their relative, and lived with that anguish even though they were wrong. Setting the record straight would only cause pain for the families, Navy Commander Joe Gradisher, a Pentagon spokesperson, told the Associated Press. His logic struck me as especially twisted, even for the Pentagon spin operation, when I read the AP report in the *Star* just five days before Christmas 1993. "They were American soldiers," Gradisher told the AP. "That in itself is jarring enough. You don't need an individual's name to express horror at the treatment of the bodies."

So AP reporter Arlene Levinson set out to answer the question herself. She contacted the relatives of each of the five soldiers to see if they recognized anything in my photograph of the barbaric mob dragging the defiled American soldier's nearly naked body through Mogadishu's streets. I wanted to weep as I read their responses.

After my picture moved on the AP wire, Willi Frank, the grieving widow of Chief Warrant Officer Raymond Frank, forty-five, of Clarksville, Tennessee, was glued to CNN, searching for a back surgery scar on the corpse that would confirm it was her husband, a Black Hawk copilot. "I picked out the one that I hoped was him because it looked like it had been the least mistreated," she said.

Popeye Field had a terrible feeling that the dead soldier was his son, Sergeant Thomas Field, twenty-five, of Lisbon, Maine. "I can tell my son's face, and his arms," he told Levinson. "My two sons and myself was all looking. Right now, I couldn't tell you for sure."

Relatives of Sergeant 1st Class Randall Shughart, thirty-five, of Newville, Pennsylvania, and Master Sergeant Gary Gordon, thirty-three, of Lincoln, Maine, refused to speculate.

Nada Morford cried when she spoke to Levinson in her Arizona trailer home. She told of going to the local library, poring over pictures, searching for any hint of her son. She thought she saw something born of her flesh and blood in the pixels, but couldn't be sure. "My son had black eyebrows and eyelashes," she said through her tears, Levinson reported. "He—the dead soldier—had light hair, black eyebrows. But the legs and feet resembled David's late father. I would hate to say this is positively my son, and have it be somebody else's."

Sadly, her hunch turned out to be right. But it was a long time before I knew that. The voice that still haunted me stayed anonymous for some six years, until I read Mark Bowden's *Black Hawk Down*, which identified the dead soldier as Morford's son, Staff Sergeant

William Cleveland, thirty-four, the maintenance crew chief on chopper Super Six-Four. I've heard it said that to exorcise a ghost you are best to utter its name. Once I could attach Cleveland's to the voice in my mind, I wanted to know more about who he was. As I learned about his life, I realized why he had haunted me for so long. In the battered face of his corpse, I saw my own.

The parallel lines of our lives emerged as I read the many tributes to Cleveland in newspapers and on the Internet. We were born in the same year, just six months apart, in 1959. We were fathered by military men, separated from them, and then drawn to war ourselves. Our smiles share a similar, mischievous smirk. Being good at our work wasn't enough for either of us. We had to be the best, no matter what line that took us across. And no matter how different we might have been, soldier and reporter, the fire of war had fused us together.

I know now that it was selfish, but over time I realized I needed forgiveness from Cleveland's family. I wanted to explain why I had no choice that day. I had played that morning over millions of times in my head, and I thought that in the embrace of his mother, both Cleveland and I could be set free. I would knock on the door of Morford's trailer home, and when she answered, tell her in a few words why I had come. I imagined she would be startled, then angry, but would welcome me into her home anyway. As scared as I was, I figured she would want to talk as much as I did. We would sit together, two strangers joined by a soldier's sacrifice, and cry.

The temperature was climbing past one hundred degrees Fahrenheit when I landed in Phoenix in early summer. The desert wind sucked my mouth dry in minutes, and the sun squeezed on my temples like a vise. I rented a car and drove to Peoria, on the outer fringes of Phoenix,

315

where urban sprawl crashes up against a cruel desert. I turned off just before the road would have taken me to Sun City, and past that to Surprise, and took a room on the second floor of the Ramada, overlooking the parking lot, across from a shopping mall. I sat on one of two queen beds, took the phone book from the bedside table drawer, and flipped through it, scanning the *m*'s for the name Morford. There was only one phone number and address that matched, so I went to sleep, hoping to wake up with a final answer to my dilemma: Call first or just knock on the door?

The next morning, I still wasn't sure, so I went for a walk through the mall to think some more. On the sidewalk outside, two U.S. Army recruiters in green fatigues had stopped to chat with a cop in a dark blue uniform. Things were going badly in Iraq, and the pressure was on to find volunteers willing to put their lives on the line. As I passed by, I heard one of the soldiers writing down the cop's contact details for follow-up. I wasn't sure it made sense for the military to be poaching police from American streets to fight a failing and increasingly unpopular war, but I wasn't about to stop and start a sidewalk debate. I got some breakfast, went back to the car, and headed for the trailer park where Cleveland's mom lived.

I had hoped it would be somewhere quiet, where I could speak softly at her door. But it was on a busy five-lane road lined with strip malls, gas stations, a drive-through drug store, and several gated mobile home parks with posh-sounding names like "Polynesian Village," "Casa del Sol Resort West," and "Villa Vista Estates." I pulled up to the entrance to Morford's park and quickly scrolled through the intercom's digital list to find her name. I buzzed, panicking because I knew I'd have only a matter of seconds to persuade her to open the gate.

No one answered. So I drove around for ten minutes and came

back, timing my return perfectly to drive through the open gate as another car left. I felt like a stalker, but I was doing what a reporter is trained to do: if the front door slams in your face, go to the back and knock again. I had to see where Morford lived, and figure out if I could get close enough to look into her eyes and ask her to see me as a human being, instead of some faceless journalist who had violated the honor and dignity of her son and the people he loved.

I drove around the estate, past crisply fluttering U.S. flags on tall poles, the spa and heated fifty-foot swimming pool, the nine-hole pitch-and-putt green and shuffleboard courts, before I finally found Morford's home. It was a pale blue-and-white trailer with a small patio guarded by a fat-cheeked cherub blowing a trumpet, and a few other lawn ornaments scattered among overgrown bushes. I waited a few seconds for a sign that someone was home, but didn't see any movement.

Then I drove back to my hotel and dialed Morford's phone number. I got her answering machine and listened to the brief instructions to leave a message, painting a mental picture of the woman behind the voice. I hung up without saying a word. Hours later, I tried again, and again the machine answered.

"Hello, ma'am," I said, trying to sound unthreatening. "I'm a reporter. This is very difficult to say over the phone, but I'm the photographer who took the pictures of your son on that terrible day in Somalia in 1993. I've wanted for years to meet you, and speak to you about what happened that day, and to try to learn about who your son was. I'm hoping you'll be willing to give me some time over the next few days. I know this is difficult for you, but I really do want to meet you and try to help you understand what happened then." As I repeated my room and phone number at the Ramada, I knew it was too late to correct a terrible mistake.

317

That night, when I returned to my room after dinner, the phone rang. I stared at it for a few seconds, as much afraid of hearing Morford say "Yes" as I was of her saying "No." But when I finally answered, it was far worse than both. "This is William David Cleveland's brother," the voice said. "Can I ask you not to call my mother any more? You just threw her into a real bad relapse."

I sputtered, desperately searching for the right words: "I'm really sorry . . . I was hoping to see her . . . and bring it up gently. I . . . I couldn't get through that electronic gate . . . "

Her son's voice shifted from coldly polite to angry. "I would rather you not try to see her or try to contact her any more. *Please.*"

"It's been ten years that I've been living with this, sir. I'm not looking for your sympathy. But I . . . I really feel bad for what I did. And I want to try to explain what happened that day and why . . . "

"You mean when you took the pictures of him being dragged along the street?" he interrupted, temper flaring.

"I'm begging you," I said. "If you'll give me five minutes of your time, I hope you'll understand it better."

"Sir, you're in the press and it's your job to report what's going on," he said. "I don't hold you personally responsible for anything. I don't feel ill will towards you in any way for taking those pictures. If it wasn't you, somebody else would have. That's what your job is. Just like *his* job was to be there. He was doing what he loved to do. He wouldn't have changed anything if he could have."

I knew he was trying to be kind, but he was excusing a journalist. I wanted to be understood, exonerated, as a person. And I needed to hear it from the woman I'd hurt most in the world, his mother. I was starting to lose it as I thought of her, sitting somewhere alone, in tears. "I only know him from that moment, sir, and for my own conscience and mental health, I'm really trying to find out who he was."

"Well, he was kind of a weird kid that didn't match in with any-body. He lived his own, little strange way. But he always did what he wanted to do and that was protect others."

I felt the staff sergeant's specter draw closer. His brother told me Cleveland was flying in a chopper over Washington State's Mount St. Helens when the volcano erupted in 1980 with the force of twenty-seven thousand Hiroshima atom bombs, flattening everything—trees, animals, and buildings—for 230 square miles. He'd given the family pictures. I thought that tidbit from his brother was a breakthrough, and tried to turn the conversation back to war. I asked about the fam-ily history of soldiers in every generation since the Civil War. His back got up again.

I struggled to reach out again, my voice breaking: "I haven't been able to resolve this on my own for ten years now, and I'm just think-ing that if I could understand what my place was in time, and what his was, that maybe I can bury a few things."

Cleveland's brother eased up and gave me a little more. He told me his father was serving as an engine mechanic on an aircraft carrier when David, which was what his family called him, was born. But he quickly tired of the next questions. He wouldn't help me find either of his brother's two wives, any of his four children from his two mar-riages, or any other relatives. He was turning on me again.

I begged him to give me just five minutes to explain myself.

"I have no interest in knowing who you are. You're nothing to me. You're not the one who was dragging him through the streets. You're not the one who shot him down."

I told him how the military had denied that dead American sol-diers' bodies were abused merely eight days before the same thing happened to his brother. That seemed to make a difference. Cleve-land's brother, a military engine mechanic who was turned down for service in Somalia when he volunteered, said he understood why I had no choice but to take the picture as proof. "I would have no problem seeing myself in his shoes, and if it was me, I would have wanted the picture taken," he said.

I said he'd taken a heavy weight off my shoulders, and then I told him I'd heard his brother's voice telling me not to take the picture.

"I just wish I could've shaken his hand someplace and known him," I said, fighting back the tears. "We were not at counter-purposes. I know those guys cared for people there and were trying to do the right thing. And we were trying to do the right thing in our own way."

The smoke was clearing on a battle of words, but Cleveland's brother wanted to stop talking. He said it was time for him to go pick up his son. Just as he was about to hang up, I realized I didn't know his name and blurted out that last question.

"It's Ray," he said, and the words were a fist to my gut.

"That's . . . that's my father's name," I said, and there was silence. "Sir, please apologize to your mom . . . and I'm *really* sorry."

I dropped the receiver onto the cradle and felt for the presence of the ghost, strained to hear his triumphant laughter. There was only the rattling of the air conditioner and the pulsing of blood in my temples. My face was burning. The tips of my ears and cheeks were on fire but my arms were frozen, and I was cold to the core of my bones. I felt selfish and wanted to just disappear, but I was trapped in myself, crushed and alone. It was as if I were back in the Sahafi Hotel again. I lay down on the bed and sobbed like a frightened child, awash in the same ocean of sorrow and shame that I had collapsed into after taking the picture of Cleveland's corpse.

The ghost may have gone silent, but true to the voice's word, Cleveland would not let go of me.

The next morning, I went to the local library to see what more I could learn about Cleveland from old newspapers. Cranking through reel after reel of microfilm, I stopped at a piece written by E. J. Montini, a columnist for the *Arizona Republic* who visited Morford in her trailer home soon after her son was buried, with a twenty-one-gun salute, at Fort Campbell, Kentucky. His family refused to let TV cameras or photographers attend.

Just over a week later, Morford sat next to a table, covered with an American flag folded into a tight triangle and medals including the Bronze Star and Purple Heart, and opened her family photo album for Montini. She showed him pictures of Cleveland as a baby, then playing with other children, and as a seventeen-year-old boy in the slightly baggy uniform of the Reserve Officers' Training Corps. "That's the way I'd like people to see him," she told the columnist.

Cleveland's mother also explained that she had heard the news of her son's death from her sister, who heard a local TV report that an Arizona soldier had died in Somalia. She called a local station and a staffer read a wire report confirming her son's death. She hadn't got a call from the Army because it had contacted Cleveland's stepmother. His second wife was listed as next of kin after his father died, leaving Cleveland's mother adrift. When she finally got a letter from the Army, it spelled her last name wrong.

The story turned to an inside page, and the microfilm frames blurred as I quickly turned the crank to find out more. Then I learned of the war that had raged in the heart of Staff Sergeant William David Cleveland, one that his grief-stricken mother was still fighting.

David was seven years old when his mother and father, William David Cleveland Sr., split up. She moved with her four children to Arizona, and David saw little of his father as a child. David's first marriage also fell apart. When the army sent him to school, his second wife and their two kids moved into Morford's cramped trailer home and soon there was a lot of bickering. Her son's wife and kids moved out.

"There were hard feelings," Morford told Montini. "I was having severe back problems at the time and was taking a lot of medication. It's almost like a dream to me. After that, though, there was a long time when it was like we didn't exist. There was no contact at all. That's a very hard thing to live with. Especially now."

Relatives told her that David had planned to surprise her with a Christmas visit. And now she would never see him again, or hear his voice, in anger or joy.

"You can't let the ones you love drift apart because you never know if you'll have a chance to get back together," she said. "And if you don't, you'll never forgive yourself. What I have now of David is my memories."

I knew then why my call had hurt her so much. I packed my notebooks into my knapsack and left the library feeling guilty and defeated in the struggle to escape her son's shadow. That afternoon, as my flight took off from Phoenix and banked over the Sonora desert, a dun-colored wasteland dotted with prickly cacti, Joshua trees, and rolling tumbleweed, the scene reminded me of faraway places where I'd watched American men and women wage war with foreign enemies in Somalia, Afghanistan, and Iraq.

I wondered whether the harsh land where Staff Sergeant Cleveland died ever reminded him of the place he was born.

20

WAR IN PEACE

Between him who in battle has conquered thousands upon
thousands of men and him who has conquered himself
it is the latter who is the greater conqueror.

THE BUDDHA

Arizona threw me for a hard fall. Betrayed by my own fantasy of redemption, I sought solace in work, which pulled me back to the unforgiving deserts, and relentless bloodletting, of Afghanistan. In early 2006, the snows hadn't begun to melt in the high passes of the Hindu Kush, and the Taliban and its Al Qaeda allies were already well on their way to making it the bloodiest year since the United States removed the mullahs from power. A hefty cut of the thriving heroin trade, and support from clandestine bases in Pakistan, had allowed the insurgents to expand their attacks from the Pashtun heartland in the south and east to regions of the north and west. The U.S. military, bogged down and bleeding in Iraq, eagerly handed over command of operations in Afghanistan to NATO, leaving allies such as Canada and Britain mired in the mess that thinly deployed American forces had left behind.

Democracy and development, the two forces potent enough to

finally free Afghans from more than a generation of war, faltered as U.S.-led allies tried to battle their way to peace. Afghans had defied militants' threats and elected their governments, but real freedom, not the ersatz stuff of platitudes rolling off Western politicians' lips, would elude them as long as they could not have justice. Yet somehow, that had fallen low on the list of priorities in the multi-billion-dollar reconstruction effort. Without anything close to the number of foreign troops needed to provide a firm foundation for a stable democracy, Karzai and his Western backers tried to co-opt warlords big and small by giving them institutional power in the government and security forces, especially over the police. Drug traffickers held some of the highest offices in the land, even in the counter-narcotics units trained by Western experts to catch the narco lords.

I spent several days with my friend and interpreter Wesal hanging out in the dirt parking lot of Kabul's central courts complex, eavesdropping on lawyers shamelessly haggling with officials on cell phones over bribes to free clients from jail or settle land disputes. Most Afghans who had come looking for justice couldn't afford the ante to get into the game, so they squatted on the edges of the parking lot, keeping a lonely vigil in the swirling dust, waiting months on end for a judge to hear them. Few held out much hope that they could ever defend their legal rights as equals in such a cesspool. There was nothing else for them to do but try. The more I looked at their faces, impassive visages of the vanquished, the more furious I got.

"If I were them," I said to Wesal, "I'd be up in the mountains with the Talibs."

In the shadows of one corridor, half a dozen women enshrouded in burkas sat with their children on the grimy, frigid floor, waiting for their turn to be humiliated in front of a family court judge for having a broken marriage, or suffering domestic abuse. Most of the judges were conservative mullahs and Islamic scholars with little sympathy for a wronged woman's pain, unless, of course, she had the baksheesh to stimulate their compassion. A tea bearer offered to move anyone to the front of the line for cash, and one of the women shouted through the thick mesh of her veil: "Shame on you, you old man! You're demanding a bribe. I'll go tell the judge."

In another hallway, a man evicted from his house because he couldn't outbid his rival for the court's favor screamed in anger: "I want to kill the judge. He is my enemy. What else do I have? I had a house and that was it." Another judge, sitting at a splintering desk in a small office with no heat or power, admitted to us that he took at least $100 a month in bribes, no doubt low-balling his take. After thirty years in the justice system, his salary was only $140 a month, and corruption was the only way to support his family, the judge insisted. "There is no justice for the judges themselves," he groused.

A warlord seized Kabul pharmacist Nader Naderi's three-room house when he fled the civil war in 1992. When legions of foreign troops, aid workers and business people descended on the capital a decade later, the house thief was able to charge $10,000 a year in rent for a building that was virtually worthless before the Taliban regime collapsed. Naderi put his faith in the new democracy and went to court to get his house back. He was trapped in the legal labyrinth for years. "One day when I was sitting with the judges and some other people, one of them was complaining that his washing machine wasn't working," Naderi recalled. "Then another guy sitting there told me, 'He is talking to you.'" Naderi delivered a new washing machine to Abdul Wakil Amini, a prosecutor involved in his case, the next day. "Later, when some monitors came from the court, the police station, and other departments to see my house and to gather all my documents, the same guy asked for a refrigerator," Naderi said. "So I bought a fridge for him."

But corrupt officials just kept milking Naderi, so he stood in silent protest outside the justice minister's office. Each day, when the justice minister arrived for work, Naderi greeted him with, "Good morning, sir." At the end of each day, Naderi was still standing there and bid the minister farewell with "Good afternoon, sir." On the tenth day, the minister stopped and asked him, "Do you work here?" Naderi explained his problem, the justice minister granted him an audience to hear the details, and then issued a written order to the court to give Naderi his house back.

"The next day, when I went to the court with his letter, the guy there told me: 'Give me $4,000, because you have direct orders. For others, it costs a lot more,'" Naderi said. After paying a total of $11,000 in bribes over several years, Naderi finally reclaimed what was his in the first place. Like thousands of Afghans squeezed by the same corrupt system, he was so bitter that he wanted to leave his homeland again. "You can never have democracy if you can buy justice," he said.

That autumn, I took a trip north through the Salang Tunnel. Almost five years earlier, in the final days of Taliban rule, I'd crawled, tripped, and groped my way through the destroyed tunnel's darkness, slicing and bruising myself on the tangle of rusting rebar and broken concrete, to watch dozens of war-weary Talibs come over to the winning side in time for the final assault on Kabul. In a few short years, foreign aid had repaired the tunnel and highway, restoring the backbone between Afghanistan's north and south that Massoud's forces destroyed to cover their retreat from the Taliban. But above the clouds swirling around the Hindu Kush, the tunnel was still a death trap in howling winds and blinding snow. Storms were blowing early and fierce through the high peaks. We made the trip up without trouble, fishtailing past cars and trucks stuck in the snow and ice. On the way back, after removing the chains from our tires, my driver, Zyarat Gul, was in a hurry to make the final leg down to Kabul and skidded on black ice in the tunnel. The car slammed into the concrete curb so hard that the front axel snapped.

Zyarat was elected to go search for help. While Wesal and I tried to stay warm in the disabled car, several police and Afghan army vehicles raced past, not even slowing to take a closer look at who might be freezing to death inside. But several Afghan travelers stopped their cars to ask if they could help, and a few gave us apples and nuts to get us through the night. Zyarat made his way through the blizzard to a public works outpost a mile down the mountain. It was approaching midnight, and the few workers huddling around a small wood stove weren't eager to go out into the snow and deathly cold.

"Is anyone hurt?" one asked when Zyarat said he needed help.

"No," he replied.

"Are there any women?"

"No."

"Are you stuck in the middle of the road?"

"No."

"Then go back to your car and come back in the morning."

It was a lesson in the cardinal rule of the Afghan road, and the new society it was supposed to bring together: Get in the way, and you get action; fall by the wayside, and you just have to wait.

The next morning, Zyarat found a truck driver farther down the Salang Pass willing to haul us and our car, barely squeezed into the small pickup's bed, to Kabul.

"It's a good thing the cops didn't stop," he shouted over the noise of the engine, which was straining under the weight of our car on the way down the mountain. "They would have stolen all of your money!"

In early December, we drove east to the Afghan border, where well-armed Taliban fighters were stepping up cross-border attacks on Afghan police posts after Musharraf agreed to pull back his security forces from areas dominated by pro-Taliban Pashtun chieftains. A group of one hundred militants had attacked an Afghan border post at Lizha, which lay at the mouth of a narrow valley, where a dirt road used by smugglers, guerrillas, and other cross-border traffic led to Pakistan, just a few miles away. The attackers fired at least twenty-seven rocket-propelled grenades during the almost four-hour assault. The twenty-five Afghan border police had only four RPGs and their assault rifles to defend the base, but managed to kill five militants as they crawled and fired along the camp's perimeter. The others retreated down the valley on foot, got back into their waiting vehicles, and then drove past Pakistani border troops to their safe haven.

The Afghan police made repeated but fruitless calls to U.S. forces for air strikes. At least one aircraft flew over the area, the U.S. military spokesman told me later. It couldn't find a target and left. Other Afghan posts had suffered similar attacks as the border conflict heated up, but this was the third one on the Lizha camp in as many months. With each one, the guerrillas were getting closer to their apparent goal, overrunning the post and killing or capturing its defenders. The Afghan police manning it were left to beg for the proper weapons to fight a determined enemy.

We drove to see the shot-up outpost and to interview the poorly armed and demoralized Afghan unit trying to hold the line in a region thick with Taliban, Al Qaeda, and allied fighters. First we had to spend the night in the closest city, Khost, once bin Laden's fiefdom under Taliban rule. His supporters were making a comeback in the area. I shared a room with Wesal and woke him up sometime after midnight, repeatedly shouting in my sleep, "Fuck, we're all going to die!" and gasping for breath, as if choking on smoke. The next morning, I didn't remember whatever terror had come in the darkness. I only woke up with a sense of dread, feeling exhausted for reasons I couldn't understand.

When I was a teenager learning how to ski, I was warned repeatedly that most injuries occur during the last run of the day. That lesson later morphed into a war zone superstition: the most dangerous time is when you're preparing to—even just idly dreaming about—get out and go home. So I feared the worst when, just days before I was due to end my almost six-year tour in South Asia and take a new posting in Jakarta, we set out on a 1,373-mile journey along the Ring Road, which passes through some of Afghanistan's most treacherous terrain to connect its main cities. Canadian troops had only recently finished fighting the biggest land battle in NATO's history to secure a portion of the Ring Road west of Kandahar, in southern Afghanistan. It wasn't long before the suicide bombers were back. The road, which ranged from smooth new pavement to shifting desert sands, was a favorite Taliban killing ground.

Just a few hours into the week-long Ring Road journey, Wesal and I came across a unit of Afghan soldiers standing over the corpses of three Taliban guerrillas. The dead Talibs were lying on the side of the two-lane highway from Kabul to Kandahar, built with a $237-million gift from U.S. taxpayers. Four Taliban fighters on two motorbikes had tried to ambush a civilian truck carrying supplies to a military base, a common tactic on the rebuilt road. Normally, they get away with it and melt back into the population. This time, a pickup truck carrying half a dozen Afghan National Army troops happened by just

329

in time to kill three of the attackers. The fourth escaped. It was dusk when we arrived, around half an hour after the battle had ended.

I got close for a picture and noticed straightaway that the dead men didn't have the untamed look of young, illiterate Talibs I'd seen along the same road a decade earlier. These men had short beards that would have had trouble passing the former regime's fist test. They had the look of men more sophisticated than I was used to seeing in the Taliban. The corpse next to my feet, a young man whose shalwar kameez tunic had been pulled off, had a bullethole in his shoulder. His baggy pants were soaked in blood, but my eyes went straight to his shoes, black ones with grey socks, like any man in town might wear—not the black high tops that Taliban fighters had favored in the past. His knees were bent, as if he might jump up at any moment. The bullethole in his neck left no doubt that this Talib's war was over.

The next day, we reached Lashkar Gah, capital of Helmand province, the world's largest producer of opium for heroin and a stronghold of the Taliban and a few hundred Al Qaeda fighters, many of them recruits from the Middle East. On a previous trip, we had bunked at a U.S.-funded development agency's unguarded compound in the city. The Afghans who ran it were experts at working the insurgent network, explaining the benefits of their projects and meeting any other concerns, to ensure that they were left off the target list. They were perplexed, and saddened, that other NGOs and the foreign military weren't negotiating the same way. Without negotiation, there could be no development, the Afghans told us, and without development, the drug lords and insurgents would never be defeated.

I knew I was tempting fate too much by not letting Zyarat drive as fast as he could through Helmand, but I wanted to chat with the aid agency's head cook, Khudai Nazar. At sixty-four, he was old enough to remember what is possible with peace, and still young enough to believe he might live to see it again.

Back in the 1960s, when American workers and their families lived peacefully in Helmand while working on large infrastructure projects, including a power plant and irrigation canals, Nazar was a twelve-year-old houseboy for Rose and Don Wonderly, of Portland, Oregon. The glowing reference letter they wrote on returning to the United States is wrapped in an opaque plastic sandwich bag with the rest of Nazar's yellowing collection of letters and old photographs, which he pressed into my hands, with an almost desperate smile that challenged me to believe in a different world.

In one snapshot, Nazar is standing on the Wonderly's lush lawn, an oasis in the Helmand desert, surrounded by a white picket fence. Nazar is proudly showing off his new bicycle, a gift from Rose. "The first time I met with her, I didn't understand English," he told me with an American accent. "American people always like children, and they didn't have any, so she said, Come every day to my house and I'm gonna teach you English." By the time the Soviets invaded in 1979, Nazar had worked for a string of American families as a houseboy and cook. Like others, JoAnn and Ronald Thompson of Sacramento, California, praised his bread baking skills. Jack and Maxine Smith loved his pastries and good humor. Their time in Afghanistan was cut short by the Soviet invasion, and as she packed to flee, Maxine urged Nazar to take his wife and their ten children and join the exodus of Afghan refugees fleeing to Pakistan.

"She said, 'Just send me a message and I'll have a house waiting for you—everything,'" Nazar said wistfully. But he stayed and struggled to keep his family alive as endless war destroyed his country. I asked him why he stayed in a place so many others had abandoned, whether love for his country had anything to do with his choice. He laughed and then stared at the creases criss-crossing his hands: "If you pluck a bird's feathers out, how can it fly?" he asked. "If you don't have money or anything, then how can you move your whole family?" As we got up to leave, eager not to give anyone plotting an ambush or kidnapping too much time to organize, Nazar repeated how much he hoped some of his long lost American friends might try to reach him, maybe even risk a visit. Three hours after we wished him well and left Lashkar Gah, a suicide bomber walked into the well-guarded compound of the provincial governor and blew himself up in the parking lot, killing eight people.

Like the voice of a nagging conscience, a book Dr. Grinker had recommended I read had followed me around South Asia for months in the bottom of my battered suitcase. I didn't open Frankl's *Man's Search for Meaning*, not even to riffle the pages and skim for a hint of its voice, until something told me, in my last days in Afghanistan, that it was time. Frankl, a Viennese psychiatrist, spent three years in Auschwitz, Dachau, and other concentration camps: the Nazis' prisoner No. 119,104. Most of that time, he was a slave laborer, forced to dig and lay tracks for railway lines. Frankl and his sister were the only members of his family to survive the death camps. What I found much more intriguing was his take on human nature and neuroses. Freud saw humans as beings driven by the will to pleasure; Nietzsche's view that we are motivated by the will to power inspired Austrian psychologist Alfred Adler. To Frankl, "Striving to find a meaning in one's life is the primary motivational force in man." Sitting in a dingy hotel room no bigger than a cell, in the damp draft of a Kabul winter, I was captivated by a brief passage in which Frankl recalled how he and other prisoners drew strength from imagining their wives, who were either dead or imprisoned in other camps, yet smiling still in the men's minds.

"A thought transfixed me: for the first time in my life I saw the truth as it is set into song by so many poets, proclaimed as the final wisdom by so many thinkers," Frankl wrote. "The truth—that love is the ultimate and the highest goal to which man can aspire. Then I grasped the meaning of the greatest secret that human poetry and human thought and belief have to impart: *The salvation of man is through and in love.*"

I had heard a similar message when I met Mother Teresa in 1996 at her Calcutta headquarters, a spartan building on a bustling side street, known simply as Mother's House. I wanted to talk to her about the estimated 100,000 street children, who were often beaten, raped and forced to work for next to nothing. Mother Teresa was almost eighty-six, and recovering from a fall that broke her collarbone the previous month. She'd also suffered through a string of bad press, including criticisms that her care for the sick and dying was substandard, and that she was too cozy with dictators, corrupt politicians, and other shady characters. By the time I showed up on her doorstep, she didn't have much of a stomach for reporters. The sisters who screened Mother Teresa's throng of visitors tried to persuade me to come back another time. But they didn't kick me out, so I waited in a chair by the door on the first floor as foreign businessmen in suits, Catholic priests and nuns, and backpackers offering to volunteer in the dying room for the destitute, were ushered up the stairs to Mother Teresa's private area on the second floor. After a long wait, a dour-faced sister told me I could come up just for a minute. I could see she was timing me on her watch.

Mother Teresa was in too much pain to sit down, so I asked her questions as she shuffled about the concrete floor on gnarled bare feet. I asked her if, with all her sacrifice, Calcutta's poor had made much progress.

"It is better now because many more people are concerned," she said, her voice weak and hoarse. "Many women and children are continually helping because they are involved in wholehearted service to the poorest of the poor. It's beautiful. The whole world is concerned now."

They struck me as empty words, the sort that made me disgusted with modern religion. I was searching for something else, something that would point the way forward. I asked whose fault it was that so many people were still suffering.

"I don't blame anybody," Mother Teresa said. "I just pray and do what I can. Blaming does not solve the problem."

"But will there ever be a day when everyone has a home?" I asked.

"Of course," she said, and then seemed to hedge. "It depends on you and me and Him. So we pray, yes? That's why we need to pray."

I tried again to get past religion to reality and asked her how, in a world of abundance, so many people still didn't have enough to eat.

"They need our love more than food," she said. I thought she sounded cruel.

My minute was up, and Mother Teresa excused herself as she hobbled over to a hall cupboard, and then back.

"This is a prayer card," she said, handing me a small slip of paper with a black-and-white picture of herself beside the advice "Love Prayer," a message from the Knights of Columbus.

"And this is my business card." It was printed with a verse that began, "The fruit of SILENCE is Prayer" and concluded: "The fruit of SERVICE is Peace."

Then she reached high to touch my forehead in blessing, turned to walk back to her room, and disappeared through sheer white curtains beneath a small sign that declared: "Private." The sister hustled me down the stairs and out the front door.

I stood in the street, swallowed up by the noise and swirling filth of a city where people enter the world and depart it by way of the gutter each day, and wondered what Mother Teresa was talking about. I still have my doubts about her God, but I've slowly come to realize that she was right about love.

The fundamental question for us all is as timeless as the primal urge to wage war itself: What evil do we commit against ourselves as we fight to defeat others? War does not conquer evil. They embrace each other. If we're fortunate, we may manage to wrestle war to our advantage. But it cannot be a triumph. It is always an admission of failure, an acceptance that we cannot do any better. The most we can hope for from war is that we gain something in a Faustian bargain: Its odious barbarity gives us the strength to defeat our enemies, and all the while, it slowly sucks the humanity from our souls.

Others have sought a better way than war, and rather than surrender to the primal urge for revenge sought to disarm it with forgiveness. It happened in South Africa, which managed to avoid a civil war that many thought inevitable, by placing the need for reconciliation above the desire for punishment. State torturers, death squad assassins, and terrorists gave detailed admissions of their crimes in public hearings, and then they asked for forgiveness. Scenes of weeping perpetrators embracing their victims' relatives helped heal a nation that is now a beacon of reconciliation in the world. Smaller victories are being won every day by a movement called restorative justice, which recognizes that crimes are not just committed against individuals, but whole communities, and that offenders harm themselves as well as their victims. When victims agree, mediators have brought them together with perpetrators in jail so that they can better understand the crime, and one another. Some who have gone through the sessions speak of an almost miraculous transformation from visceral hatred to emancipating love.

I longed for something similar when I tried to speak with Cleveland's mother. I thought that by telling her what happened the day her son died, and asking her forgiveness for what I'd done to give his defilers a world stage, we could both find peace.

A NOTE ON QUOTES

As a journalist, I've learned the hard way not to trust people's memories, especially my own. I'm also a stickler about quoting precisely what people say, so that the reader is like a juror listening from the witness box.

In places where I rely on interpreters, I have them type out transcripts of taped interviews to ensure anything that I put between quotation marks is exactly what came out of the person's mouth. In most cases, the quotes in this book are taken from tape recordings or transcripts to ensure their accuracy. In the minority of instances when those weren't available, I went back to one or more people who were either part of the conversation, or witnessed it, and quoted the words as they recalled them.

RELATED READING

Puzzling out the reality of a chaotic life, I turned to a few books to fill in some of the blanks.

Michael J. Durant's *In the Company of Heroes* provided a soldier's view from Black Hawk Super Six-Four, which the former chief warrant officer was piloting when it was shot down over Mogadishu on October 3, 1993. Mark Bowden's classic *Black Hawk Down* filled out the picture of the street battle that I watched unfold from a rooftop of the Sahafi Hotel.

Joseph LeDoux's *Synaptic Self: How Our Brains Become Who We Are* is an engaging look into the inner workings of the human brain as it determines who each of us is.

The official war diaries of the Third Field Ambulance, Canadian Expeditionary Force, the 1st Battalion Black Watch, and the 1/7 Royal Warwicks provided details of the battles that my grandfather and father, like so many fellow veterans of the two world wars, were reluctant to tell. Wilfred Smith's *Code Word CANLOAN* was essential

339

to understanding how my father came to command British soldiers in Europe.

Dian Fossey's *Gorillas in the Mist* brought life to the deserted ruins of the Karisoke Research Center that she founded, while Jane Goodall's *The Chimpanzees of Gombe* shone light on the darker side of our closest primate cousins as they waged war to defend and seize territory near the shores of Lake Tanganyika.

Finally, the declassified diplomatic cables obtained by the Somalia Declassification Project at Illinois' College of DuPage were illuminating.

INDEX

Sutherland, R.D., 53
SWAPO, 73, 301

T

Taliban
  in Afghanistan
    Christian aid workers' trial by,
      219
    decrees of, 161–63
    formation of, 159
    gains of, after start of Second
      Gulf War, 261–62
    Massoud and, 167–68, 219,
      223–24
    Omar and, 261
    American policy and war on,
      223–24, 226–34, 261–62,
      275
    bin Laden and, 234
    Bush and, 224
    Haq and, 227
    Watson (Paul) and, 262–70,
      328–29
Taliban "high value targets" (TB
  HVTs), 275
Tamil Tigers, 158
Task Force Ranger, 16
TB HVTs, 275
Thaliodomide birth defects, 59–60
Thompson, JoAnn, 331
Thompson, Ronald, 331
Tikrit (Iraq), 244–46
Time magazine, 44
Tocqueville, Alexis de, 192
Toronto (Canada), 61
Toronto Star. See Watson, Paul
Treasure Trail Nursery School,
  60–61
Tsunami in Asia (2004), 298–99
Tudjman, Franjo, 181–82
Turkey, 237
Tutsis, 105, 107, 118

U

UCK. *See* KLA
UNITA (National Union for the Total
  Independence of Angola),
  81–82, 84
United Nations and Somalia, 9–10,
  13–16
U.S. Army, 4
U.S. Army Rangers, 16, 230
USA Today, 235
U.S. embassies' bombings by Al Qaeda,
  279–80
U.S. Justice Department, 272
U.S. military, 10, 254, 285. *See also*
  Pentagon; *specific forces*
U.S. Navy SEAL frogmen, 8
U.S. Special Forces units, 227, 230,
  237, 241, 246, 253
U.S. State Department, 107, 226, 285
Ut, Nick, 180

V

Vancouver (British Columbia), 56, 58
Vancouver Sun internship, 73–75
Vietnam, 5, 7, 9, 73, 185
Voltaire, 179
Vucina (The Wolf), 188–89

W

Wahabi theology, 158–59
Wakil, Abdul, 229–31
Waltenmeyer, Robert, 253
War. *See also specific areas of conflict*
  embedded reporters in, 239
  evil and, 335
  guerrilla, 184–85
  icon photographers of, 180
  natural selection and, 113
  reconciliation versus, in South
    Africa, 335–36
  sticking around, 101